ReVision

A JOURNAL OF CONSCIOUSNESS AND TRANSFORMATION

CONTENTS

Places of Hope
Karen Jaenke and Jürgen Werner Kremer, Editors

1 Editor's Introduction: Places of Hope
  Karen Jaenke & Jürgen Werner Kremer

6 Dear 2020
  Leny Mendoza Strobel

7 The Lone Monk
  Kimmy Johnson

8 Coming-to-Presence at My Place of Hope
  Jürgen Werner Kremer

32 Impermanence
  R.L. Boyer

34 Loving Life
  Karen Jaenke

48 Revitalising Hope Through the Power of Story
  Paul Callaghan

52 blessing
  jim perkinson

53 Hope Summons: Meditations on An-Other-World Seeing
  S. Lily Mendoza

62 Fear, Hope, Love in Covid Times
  Glenn Aparicio Parry

66 When the Ancestors Call, How Do We Answer? Princess Bari, a Heroine's Journey
  Helena Soholm

72 Strumming the Strings of Hope
  Michael Gray

75 gift
  jim perkinson

76 Archiving Hope
  Leny Mendoza Strobel

80 Ecomorphic Eudaimonia: Three Principles Toward a World-Worth-Hoping-For
  Pascal Layman

92 Contemplating Hope
  Fariba Bogzaran

98 The Day the Horses Rode By:
  Reflections on the Redemptive Potential of Black Practices of Overcoming
  Isoke Femi

Cover art "Squaring the Circle" by Fariba Bogzaran

Summer/Fall 2020 • Volume 33 • Numbers 3 & 4

What Is ReVision?

Revisioning, as the name ReVision hints, has been central to the publication's forty year historical trajectory. As our understanding of the leading edge of transformative and consciousness-changing thinking has developed, so has the focus of our mission.

From its origins in humanistic and transpersonal psychologies, ReVision has shifted toward a framework of transdisciplinary, decolonial, and indigenous paradigms. From its origins as an academic journal it has shifted toward a publication which includes art, poetry, story, and articles that translate topics for a broader audience.

With a commitment to the future of humanity and all our relations, ReVision is dedicated to the exploration of issues that assert and value the transmotional and interconnected sovereignty of people before any institutions. Sovereignty and self-determination as foundations of peace require our human imagination as part of a sustainable world of stories and cultural practices in a particular place or ecology.

ReVision welcomes submissions from a wide range of disciplines using a broad spectrum of formats to deepen the process of inquiry, dialogue, and engaged participatory knowing and conversation.

Photo by Fariba Bogzaran © 2020

Volume 33, Numbers 3 & 4
(ISBN 978-1-7362314-1-8)

ReVision (ISSN 0275-6935) is published by
The Society of Indigenous and Ancestral Wisdom and Healing.

Copyright © 2021 ReVision Publishing.
Copyright retained by author when noted.
The views expressed are not necessarily those of ReVision or its editors.

ReVision provides opportunities for publishing divergent opinions, ideas, or judgments.

Manuscript Submissions

We welcome manuscript submissions.
Manuscript guidelines can be found on our webpage:
revisionpublishing.org/manuscript-submission.

POSTMASTER: Send address changes to
ReVision Publishing,
P.O. Box 1855,
Sebastopol, CA 95473

Subscriptions

To become a subscriber, mail a check to above address
or go to revisionpublishing.org/subscribe

Annual Subscriptions

Online subscription: by donation (dana).
Your donation supports the online edition of ReVision and is greatly appreciated.
Domestic print & online subscription: $36.
International print & online subscription: $72.
Institutional print & online subscription: $98.
Institutional international print & online subscription: $170.

You may access the online version at any time.
For print editions, please allow six weeks
for delivery of first issue.

Editorial Board

Editor
Jürgen Werner Kremer, PhD
Santa Rosa Junior College, Santa Rosa, CA

Associate Editor
Karen Jaenke, PhD
National University, East Bay Campus, CA

Editorial and Production Management Team

Cristina Kaplan, MA
Poetry Editor

Gary Newman
Design and Production

Samuel A. Malkemus, PhD
Book Review Editor

Consulting Editors

John Adams, PhD
Saybrook University, San Francisco, CA

Matthew C. Bronson, PhD
O'Reilly Scool of Technology, UC Davis, Davis, CA

Allan Combs, PhD
California Institute of Integral Studies, San Francisco, CA

Apela Colorado, PhD
Worldwide Indigenous Science Network

Jorge Ferrer, PhD
California Institute of Integral Studies, San Francisco, CA

Mary Gomes, PhD
Sonoma State University, Rohnert Park, CA

Stanislav Grof, MD
California Institute of Integral Studies, San Francisco, CA

Stanley Krippner, PhD
Saybrook University, San Francisco, CA

Joan Marler, MA
California Institute of Integral Studies, San Francisco, CA

Alfonso Montuori, PhD
California Institute of Integral Studies, San Francisco, CA

Glenn Aparicio Parry, PhD
Circle for Original Thinking, Albuquerque, NM

Joseph Prabhu, PhD
California State University Los Angeles, CA

Donald Rothberg, PhD
Spirit Rock Meditation Center, Woodacre, CA

Meredith Sabini, MA
The Dream Institute of Northern California, Berkeley, CA

Elenita Strobel, EdD
Sonoma State University, Rohnert Park, CA

With profound gratitude, ReVision would like to acknowledge the generous support of Lucid Art Foundation for helping make the full-color version of this issue possible. ReVison is also grateful for the ongoing support received from the Worldwide Indigenous Science Network

ReVision Abstracts
Vol. 33 No. 3/4 • Summer/Fall 2020

Callaghan, P. Revitalising Hope through the Power of Story. *ReVision*, *33*(3&4), 48-52. doi:10.4298/REVN.33.3.4.48-52

The Old People say. 'When we leave this world behind, all we leave behind is our story … so make it the best story possible.' Right now, many people throughout the world aren't living a good story and the evidence suggests the world itself is not living a good story. This article discusses the importance of story, the importance of caring for our place and how understanding and embracing Aboriginal culture through an understanding of the 'Lore' can give us hope that it isn't too late to revitalise and renew this planet and all things on it.

Femi, I. The Day the Horses Rode By: Reflections on the Redemptive Potential of Black Practices of Overcoming. *ReVision*, *33*(3&4), 98-103. doi:10.4298/REVN.33.3.4.98-103

This article explores the story of an event that occurred in the spring of 2019 in Montgomery, Alabama to illustrate the transformative power of African diasporic ways of overcoming. A small parade of all white people, accompanied by horses donned in Klan-reminiscent regalia, passes on the street just outside the room where about 100 intercultural participants have gathered to close out their 3-day pilgrimage to the lynching memorial and the civil rights museum. The spectacle evokes a strong disturbance in the group field, threatening chaos and fragmentation. When black practices of overcoming—including spontaneity, immediacy, expressivity, and reliance upon spiritual power—allows for a redemptive experience in the face of racialized terror.

Gray, M., Strumming the Strings of Hope. *ReVision*, *33*(3&4), 72-74. doi:10.4298/REVN.33.3.4.72-74

Hope is too important to sacrifice on the altar of things we can already identify. When we let the past dictate and define our hopes, then we pull the blinds down on the very source that might restore kindness and heal the damage that our past misunderstandings have inflicted on all living beings. That source of healing is found in the future. But the future cannot be corralled by our expectations like cattle into a feedlot. Hope is only at home in the future, but the future can never arrive. It is an infinite realm of possibility without limit. And if a kinder world is to be restored for all the separated families and if the terrible losses suffered by so many are to be redeemed and to inform our actions--if our world is to begin healing from all the floods and fires, from the isolation and polarization that mark human life on this planet--then we must stop imposing the old solutions which have just perpetuated our problems. We must care again for the most helpless among us, if hope is to nest again in our own hearts.

Jaenke, K., Loving Life. *ReVision*, *33*(3&4), 13-23. doi:10.4298/REVN.33.3.4.34-37

When manmade structures fail, we can return to their deeper source and ground, the intelligent design imbued within the living systems of nature, which form the backbone of our universe. The intelligence of nature, with its 13 billion-year creative evolutionary history, is illuminated by living systems theory, which offers a guide for aligning our personal and collective lives with the principles of balance and vitality that are also the hallmark of indigenous cultures. Living systems theory can be applied to human subjectivity by attending to the feedback loops provided in the processes of affect regulation, dreaming, and the energy circuits of the subtle body. Doing so leads to a grounded hope, rooted in balance, wellbeing, vitality, and intrinsically-gratifying flow states.

Kremer, J.W., Coming-to-Presence at My Place of Hope. *ReVision*, *33*(3&4), 34-47. doi:10.4298/REVN.33.3.4.8-32

Places of hope are located in decolonial and Indigenous spaces outside of the discourse of modernity/coloniality and postmodernity. The ancient Old Norse image of the tree, the well, three women, and three men is discussed as revolutionary flash of memory for the future; as phenomenon emerging from the intra-action of mind and matter; and as integrative state of consciousness overcoming the disappearance of ritual and ceremony in Eurocentered traditions. The principle of hope entails confrontations with personal and collective shadow material as well as intentional choice. Places of hope defined in a decolonial context of ritual performance reframe education and overcome nostalgic notions of the past. The embodiment of flashes of memory facilitates coming-to-presence in specific places with gratitude.

Mendoza, S.L., Hope Summons: Meditations on An-Other-World Seeing. *ReVision*, *33*(3&4), 53-61. doi:10.4298/REVN.33.3.4.53-61

The essay keys off Vera de Chalambert's piece, "Kali Takes America: I'm with Her" (in the aftermath of Trump's 2016 election) and Leonard Cohen's album, "You Want It Darker," both of which name the times we live in as auguring, in mythic speech, a necessary descent to the Underworld as an initiatory rite to seeing–and being ready then, to act–clearly. Through a retrospective look at her time with the Indigenous peoples of her home country, the author argues for tutelage to those who, at this point in time, might be aptly called "Modernity's only remaining Other." Doing so disrupts the dominant narrative's foreclosures around the emergency's claim to inevitability and opens up new/old possibilities for a different kind of hope.

Parry, G.A., Fear, Hope, Love in Covid Times. *ReVision*, *33*(3&4), 62-65. doi:10.4298/REVN.33.3.4.62-65

A pandemic is a time of both fear and hope. We hope that the pandemic will end soon; we fear that we or our loved ones will become ill or die. Our hope and fear have a reciprocal relationship. Our hope is our fear unmasked—and our fear is our hope unmasked. What is called for, as counterintuitive as it may be, is to accept what is as a blessing. The acceptance of what is leads to unconditional love..

Pascal, L., Ecomorphic Eudaimonia: Three Principles Toward a World-Worth-Hoping-For. *ReVision*, *33*(3&4), 80-91. doi:10.4298/REVN.33.3.4.80-91

This personal essay endeavors to capture and communicate unique features of the way in which the author remains hopeful about the future of human civilization and the simultaneous thriving of the biosphere. It is framed around three interlocking principles which are (1) his general philosophical attitude toward hope (2) an ethic concerning the relationship between human systems and nature that can be extended toward an open-vision of an improved world (3) a notion of the kinds of attitudes, practices and personalities that may be needed in order to enact such a path. The tone of the piece is meant to be playful, intriguing, serious and imaginative at the same time.

Soholm, H., When the Ancestors Call, How Do We Answer? Princess Bari, a Heroine's Journey. *ReVision*, *33*(3&4), 66-71. doi:10.4298/REVN.33.3.4.66-71

The 2020 pandemic lockdown offered a unique opportunity for us to listen to the call of our ancestors and realign to our personal and collective purpose on the planet. However, living in technologically advanced societies like ours without much guidance from the elders have made it difficult to know how one can listen for the ancestors' call and move forward in living one's soul purpose. Through the retelling of a Korean folktale of Princess Bari, an abandoned princess, we attempt to ignite the indigenous wisdom of our ancestors to find inspiration for how we can initiate into a new vision that honors our ancient past and wisdom as well as shift towards a sustainable life of healing and connection. The tale of Princess Bari is a story about the patron goddess of shamans or Mudang in Korea, most of whom are women. This heroine's journey will be used as an anchor to discuss current issues and challenges in our society and assist in creating meaningful changes in our collective consciousness.

Strobel, L.M., Archiving Hope. *ReVision*, *33*(3&4), 76-79. doi:10.4298/REVN.33.3.4.76-79

In this essay about Hope, I am reflecting on the function of Archiving and the memories that the Mind selectively chooses to shape one's Awareness—both of which are, in turn, shaped by historical narratives. For decolonizing and re-indigenizing settlers on Turtle Island, the dominant narratives of History are often subverted by much older memories that, although not archived (in the Western definition), continue to speak in many voices and stories. In this meditation, the parts of the Self that have not and cannot be archived hint at something else that offers Hope. In this tacit way of telling, there is an invitation to the reader to try a path where one might encounter the parts of one's self that have not been tracked, archived, and therefore, illegible.

Editors' Introduction

Places of Hope

Karen Jaenke and Jürgen Werner Kremer

We did not set out as experts on hope. Rather, we were called to this topic by the unravelling events and dismal atmosphere of 2020. A startling array of upheavals during 2020--a spreading global pandemic; policy brutality, intensified racial tensions and social unrest; the rise in autocratic leaders worldwide; the undermining of confidence in the American democratic process of elections; the dangerous erosion of commonly-shared truth and standards of truth; the spread of disinformation and cries of fake news; the emergence of militant extremist groups and polarized polis; and the ongoing, escalating threat of ecological collapse—together contribute to a pervasive atmosphere of uncertainty, depression, and even despair about the future.

In response to the many cracks appearing in the edifice of modern civilization, we felt a call to consider the question: from whence springs the deeper sources of hope, that can counter these overwhelming collective challenges, which seem to invite gloom? We decided to gather perspectives on hope from an array of visionary thinkers. "Places of Hope" seeks to offer grounded perspectives on hope, exploring lenses that extend beyond the onslaught of dismal news, discerning in the cracks hidden sources of promise and hope. We ask: what other interpretive frameworks might be applied to this cluster of disturbing events? How does one find hope when a surround-sound of media reporting offers no other future than a return to the status quo?

Photo by Fariba Bogzaran © 2020

The limited perspective of media reporting on these events, the repeated mantra wishing to leave 2020 behind and return to "normal", is explored in Leny Strobel's Editorial "Dear 2020". She writes a letter addressed to the year 2020, questioning the unexamined assumptions and attitudes widely circulating during 2020.

In other authors' responses, certain themes and lessons became apparent.

Michael Gray's article, "Strumming the Strings of Hope", opens with the question: "What are the images of hope that flit and dance through our psyches?" —hinting that hope draws upon the capacities of imagination, as the future is always open, uncertain, and indeterminate, never graspable. Gray finds that a collectively-shared hope rests in the restoration of "a kinder and gentler life" for all who live in some version of misery.

Meanwhile, those who are empowered to "access hope in their own hearts... [are encouraged to create] conditions that inspire hope in others," employing our personal losses as "a window into the pain that afflicts so many all around us."

Gray's own hope is nurtured by the beauty of our planet, a circle of friendship, and ancient traditions that fathom "the nature of what it means to be born a human being." The Buddhist tradition provides the image of a bird with two wings, one of wisdom and one of compassion, suggesting balance between mind and heart.

Yet the very sources of hope which sustained Gray did not work for his son, occupying a different generation and set of life of circumstances. Unable to discern hope in the same things that sustained his father, he succumbed to the ultimate act of despair. This poignant tragedy underscores how "the basis for hope is radically situational and deeply personal." Hope must rise afresh in each person's unique life circumstances, while also encompassing each person's cumulative set of life experiences – admittedly vast and varied. Ultimately, hope entails a unique psycho-spiritual process, to be discovered and nurtured afresh in each human heart.

Gray's article also points implicitly to the underlying role of worldview and spiritual practice as the deeper ground of hope, a recurring theme appearing across several authors. Some worldviews are more adequate than others as the soil from which hope can spring. Similarly, commitment to a spiritual practice can provide a personal methodology for dealing with the vicissitudes of life.

Two authors garner hope from the example of a single, highly evolved human being, leading a life anchored in spiritual discipline and devotion. When confronted by a vivid dream of an ashen landscape of total destruction—an image of our worst collective nightmare—Kimmy Johnson subsequently discovers hope through the example of a lone monk, walking with absolute equanimity through this barren landscape. This inspiring image of the power of the human spirit suggests that a spiritual practice focused on cultivating equanimity can empower one to accept the most devastating scenarios and keep walking steadily forward.

Similarly, Glenn Parry distills hope from the example of an indigenous elder who, despite enduring the historical trauma of a deadly 300-mile known as "The Long Walk," was the "kindest and sweetest soul I ever met, a man of great love, wisdom and patience." Ever thankful for the gift of life, Navajo Grandfather Leon Secatero offered daily "prayers...to the ancestors,

thanking them for everything that has happened to bring him (us) to this moment in time." This powerful prayer teaches "how to accept all of life experience, without exception," as a blessing.

In his own wisdom, Parry finds that "hope and fear are reciprocal." If "we are either hoping for a better situation or fearing that things will get worse, [i]n both cases, the present is somehow unacceptable. The way to break this impasse is to accept what is happening right now as it is—as a blessing. Accept our hopes and fears as they are...All our experience is grist for the mill, something to learn from and grow."

Parry also urges us towards "A love that is based in acceptance, not circumstance, is unconditional. With this form of love for life, all things are capable of being transformed, including our fears and hopes. Unconditional love for life itself is the greatest transformative force." Parry finds that love—the unseen force that binds things together-- "is an original energy in nature." "Love is what we need when the universe feels hopelessly complicated, chaotic and random."

Karen Jaenke's article "Loving Life" strikes a similar chord, while drawing upon living systems theory to showcase an integrative worldview and scientifically-based template for aligning one's personal life with the life force energy of the universe, allowing our entire lives to become an expression of love for life. But first, she confronts the human shadow—the human propensity for unleashing ecological destruction, extending throughout our species history, across 70,000 years. Regarding the manmade ecological crisis as humanity's most mind-boggling challenge and deterrent to hope, she looks to living systems theory and the intelligent design of nature as providing an alternative to humanity's appalling ecological track record.

She applies living systems theory (and its ancient predecessor indigenous science), personally, adopting it as a transformative personal practice, leading to wellbeing, balance and hope. Engaging intentionally with the internal feedback loops of affect regulation, dreams, and the energy circuits of the subtle body, we learn to hear and heed the communicative messages of our own mind-body system as a facet of nature, thus bringing self-as-living-system into balance and attunement with other living systems. These practices bestow a grounded hope, based in the deep structures of the universe, as well as the blessing of living in flow with life.

Layman Pascal similarly regards the ecological crisis as the most all-encompassing challenge to a hopeful future for humanity. In the personal essay "Ecomorphic Eudaimonia," he shares three principles that serve as a container for his own sense of hope. His first principle entails "*leaning into a voluntary hopefulness.* This does not mean to ignore doubt, worry and real limitations but rather to acknowledge, enfold and gesture beyond them as a free choice." Secondly, he looks to "the principle of *ecomorphism,*" or "the possibility of a more benevolent creative participation between culture and nature." He envisions an all-encompassing collaboration between natural systems and human systems, with the latter embodying "the former in multiple domains and formats. That means that a world worth hoping for is neither a biosphere devoid of human thriving nor a human civilization blind to the facts and needs of the environment and other types of beings… the deep recognition of the interdependence and mutual identity of culture and nature must inform our minds, hearts, actions, tools and social procedures if we are to steer ourselves toward worthwhile futures."

Lastly, under the rubric of a new shamanism, he sketches "the type of human being that may be required in order to cultivate and populate… a 'better world' that does not fall prey to the dystopian results of most utopian attempts." Pascal deems that shamanic spirituality is particularly favorable at this moment in history, for several reasons. First, it is deeply ecological in its appreciation of "the patterns and responsibilities that emerge from an experiential understanding of the interdependence of human beings and the rest of the biosphere." Secondly, it is embodied and health-oriented, causing "minds and societies to serve the holistic intelligence of the living ecosystems of our bodies." Third, it facilitates "more profound encounters with non-human intelligences." And finally, it possesses "a genius for flow-states… in which we feel more naturalness and growth in ourselves" as well as encouragement to participate "in new social customs that move us toward a world worth hoping for."

A recurrent and noteworthy theme in these articles concerns the role of one's fundamental worldview in engendering a hopeful attitude—or not. Across the arc of life, especially the adulthood years, each of us is faced with the task of fashioning a worldview to make sense of and integrate the succession of personal and collective experiences accumulating through the decades. The adequacy of worldviews might even be judged by whether they spawn a capacity to generate and sustain hope in the face of the onslaught of life.

To generate and sustain hope, it seems that a worldview must be expansive and facile enough to encompass all our personal experiences, plus those that we vicariously witness in others, while offering a framework for addressing the collective challenges of the current zeitgeist. In other words, worldviews that generate hope must grow from the soil of the past, addresses the challenges posed by the present, and aerate the open-ended unknowns of the future. Optimally, a well-fashioned worldview is sufficiently complex and nuanced to meet the totality of human experiences, while tipping the scales towards hope rather than cynicism and despair.

In the search for an encompassing worldview, several authors—most notably Jurgen Kremer, Karen Jaenke, Lily Mendoza, Paul Callaghan, Fariba Bozgaran, and Layman Pascal—grapple intellectually to articulate the larger metastory of "the greater whole" and its hidden dynamics from which a grounded hope can be fashioned. All authors in this volume also turn to the power of a spiritual tradition or spiritual framework for generating an all-encompassing, hopeful outlook. Additionally, when life events challenge one's hope, an accompanying spiritual practice can offer ballast and buoyancy for the waning spirit.

In "Hope Summons: Meditations on An-Other-World Seeing", Lily Mendoza narrates her journey of overturning the conventional worldview of continual progress to conquer the world—in favor of one that nurtures and aligns with the sensitivities of her own soul. She comes to reject the "prize-winning story" of civilizational triumph, that champions "modern conve-

nience, surplus production, and mesmerizing technological wonders" yet is ever stalked by the shadow of a "constant state of emergency (the sense of there never being enough—of time, resources, energy, material wealth, etc.) that has come to define the modern condition."

Her transformative awakening came during a graduate course on "The Image of the Filipino in Art," a watershed moment in which "I was smitten. I fell in love, awestruck not only by the beauty of Indigenous design, but by the ritual subtlety and cosmological complexity of the worlds that gave rise to such brilliant artistic creations….Walking out of every class session, heaves of emotion and copious tears would overwhelm me, flooding me with homecoming relief after what had seemed like an interminable exile from my own Indigenous soul—the consequence of years of unrelenting psychic disconfirmation through colonial tutelage growing up."

Through three vignettes that narrate her visits among those who still live and carry memory of life outside "the roiling emergency," we glimpse her gradual deepening into the alternative story, with an underlying message: "Things don't have to be this way." The Earth peoples, the rememberers, "remain remarkably grounded in the summons of that alternative world that they and their ancestors before them have sought to keep alive through generations." "Whatever tinge of hope I have, whatever possibility of a different future I can imagine…I owe to their witness."

Mendoza questions whether a grounded hope can ever exist in exile from the Indigenous soul, a theme taken up by Paul Callaghan in his article, "Revitalising Hope through the Power of Story." Callahan pays homage to the bedrock of a life-affirming worldview as found in the lore of Aboriginal culture, which he defines as "*a body of knowledge, stories or traditions that is passed down from members of a culture usually by word of mouth*." Yet "the Aboriginal meaning of the word *Lore* is more accurately and respectfully captured in the Aboriginal word *Ngurrampaa,* which can be translated in English to mean **my responsibility to care for my place and all things in my place above all things**. "The knowledge of how to uphold the *Ngurrampaa*, the *Lore* was provided through story in its various forms including dance, song, art and narrative."

Aboriginal Lore leads to "expansive thought that upholds the sacred responsibility to **care for our place and all things in our place,"** in contrast to the "narrow, one dimensional thinking focused on limited timelines and economic growth." The reductive thinking of the dominant culture has resulted in "a world where the social determinants of a healthy earth are…severely undermined, leading to the symptomatology" that we see today—global warming, widespread species extinction, destructive weather events, pandemics, inequities in wealth with widespread suffering across the human family. Yet "in the Aboriginal way of thinking, all things have spirit … all things are born … all things die … and all things are connected."

So for Callaghan, "The *Lore* is the incubator of love and hope. The *Lore* is the gateway to the path of wellbeing. If we forget the *Lore* or fail to acknowledge and uphold the universal truths it contains, our soil becomes barren. In barren soil we stagnate individually … we stagnate as a community … we stagnate globally. By ignoring the wisdom handed to us by those who have come before us, we create a desert where life withers and eventually dies."

Similarly, Helena Soholm turns to the themes of personal and collective ancestral healing and the guiding wisdom of ancient story as sources of hope. "The messages of the ancestors urge us to build a world that honors the interconnectedness of life and to create sustainable structures and policies."

In the Korean myth of Princess Bari, poor fate and grim life circumstances (of total familial rejection) are transformed into a heroine's journey to the underworld, where she finds her life purpose and a healing medicine for the original rejecting family situation. "After years of toil and suffering, she completes her mission of saving her parents, returning as a powerful healer. For this accomplishment and dedication, she receives a sacred title, becomes the first *Mudang* or shaman, and is worshiped as the patron goddess of shamans. Princess Bari also tackles the social justice issues of gender and power within a highly patriarchal society.

Soholm finds that the tale of Bari has special meaning in our current situation, "where the princess steps into her power to serve in the most meaningful and compassionate way. By healing from one's personal trauma of abandonment and helping those who have caused her pain, Bari demonstrates the ultimate love of a true healer. Her life story illustrates the beauty of a healing arc which begins with the focus on the individual but ends in addressing the needs of the group", thereby giving us "a blueprint for how we can answer the call of our ancestors in a time of uncertainty and crisis." Within cultures where healing and connection to self are not prioritized, consciously working towards self-healing becomes an act of political and social resistance.

Moreover, Soholm finds that the arrival of Covid-19 brings the hidden opportunity to take an inward journey, with the potential for overcoming the distraction, disconnection and dissociation that characterize much of modern life. "The damage caused by the pandemic will leave a lasting scar, but the death of outdated patterns will force us to face a novel and unknown world. Physical lockdown and restrictions on our movement offered a unique opportunity for all of us to travel inwards and sit with ourselves. The external limitations

also offered an opportunity to work on healing and renew our vision for a better future… where kindness and compassion are priorities."

Two authors, Isoke Femi and Fariba Bogzaran, turn to the power of action, through ritual and art respectively, as a means to transform dire circumstances—the weight of cultural oppression and mass death from Covid. Isoke Femi looks to the African-derived practices and ritual technologies that serve as a source of cultural resilience, or "gettin' ovah" in the African slave diaspora. "Overcoming in this context refers to the repeated act of resisting soul loss, or loss of vitality and authenticity." For "African Americans in the U.S., soul loss would be the inevitable result of collective scapegoating over the course of several centuries had it not been for the overcoming practices of African-derived spirituality, finely tuned over the centuries." Through these "practices—of music, spoken word, embodied grace and authenticity—heart as well as soul qualities are preserved and refined," serving as an antidote to "nearly unrelenting projections of inferiority" and the impact of post traumatic slave syndrome.

Under the influence of these applied *getting over* practices, the creative genius of the enslaved and their descendants becomes the collective repository of powers for surviving and thriving that defy depression and despair. Femi shares a contemporary instance in which "a racially, culturally and socioeconomically mixed group of folks find themselves in a situation where the need for practices of overcoming arises." This story "demonstrates the intercultural potentialities of these modes of experiencing."

Fariba Bogzaran's visionary artistic expression provides the enveloping imagery for this issue as well as her exploration of hope in Covid times. In her article "Contemplating Hope", Bogzaran first questions, in Buddhist fashion, the very construct of hope as an escape from facing the present moment. The cover image, "Squaring the Circle", made from the very masks that became a ubiquitous symbol of a deadly virus permeating everyday shared reality, offers an alchemical image for the transformation of crisis into an ordering, unified wholeness. Her article "describes and depicts in imagery her unfolding artistic and shamanic process of incorporating masks and gloves into artworks revealing aspects of the global pandemic. One piece even goes to the precipice of "The Last Breath." A final series of artworks offer images of the portal of light into which souls succumbing to COVID pass.

Leny Mendoza Strobel grapples with the issue of hope from the perspective of archiving, the creation of both cultural and personal archives. Bayo Akomolafe's question "What about yourself cannot be tracked?" is the challenging starting point of her inquiry. Strobel looks critically at the importance of personal history, "the importance of keeping records of the milestones that crown our lives". By contrast, she asserts the importance of what is "illegible about myself, what hasn't been tracked and archived." What we find then is an abundance of "imprints in our hearts, psyche, and our soul", the quality that is powerfully captured in her ancestral Filipino concept of "*kapwa*—the Self-is-in-the-Other". It is this quality of presence that matters more than any archive. The colonial history of the Philippines, despite its assault on Filipino Indigenous cultures, has not managed to destroy her illegible, untracked, and unarchived subterranean self. Strobel challenges the reader: "What about yourself cannot be tracked, is illegible, and cannot be archived?"

Modernity and its notion of "civilization" looks at oral traditions and cultures lacking sacred texts as retrograde and primitive. Yet, as the Talaandig tribal chief Datu Vic Saway points out: "We do have sacred texts—we have the Mountain, Forest, Rivers, Sun, Stars, Moon, Animals—we have the biggest sacred text of Nature!" This reminds us to activate our natural intelligence "to read the Wind …to read the Sky". Strobel describes her process of turning inward, "the gift of the virus, the California fires, the craziness of politics, and the climate crisis." She now lingers with acute settler awareness "among the non-human beings". Part of this dwelling in place is the inner work of decolonization and the quiet work of creating ceremonies of apology and forgiveness for the genocidal history in Northern California, thus addressing "the erasure of native genocide as the "first sin" at the foundation of the U.S."

Where then is hope? Strobel asserts that it can only be found outside and beyond the categories that modernity trades in. It will arise from *something else* that "is the not-yet-visible but palpable, an ineffable movement towards righting the wrongs of the past, seeking reparations and repair. … Hope will always be that *something else.*"

Jürgen Werner Kremer, in his piece "Coming-to-Presence at My Place of Hope," feels compelled to look beyond the standard frameworks of psychology and neoliberal socio-cultural interpretations, because they "have lost their explanatory and guiding power." He explores the possibilities of hope by an indigenous name for those (post)moderns who have lost connections with their indigenous roots. He urges that

"'the West' needs to find answers to the central questions of our times in the radical otherness that indigeneity represents." Kremer contrasts Western interpretations of hope as an abstract notion projected into the future of linear time with hope as part of indigenous presence, a quality of hope that is "embedded and interwoven into a life centered in the ritual embodiment of spiritual beliefs and nurturing conversations with the natural world around."

Kremer has pursued a path of recovery of an indigenous mind process in personal and scholarly inquiries. The prevailing understandings of Western psychology and cultural assumptions about time for him presented a road block to conceptualizing such recovery successfully beyond subjective imaginings. His central ancestral cultural image of the tree by the well, together with three female and three male presences, leads into an inquiry of its viability for today and our future. Rock carvings and other culturally relevant images from his Northern European background constitute the palimpsest of the article (which includes a photo of one of his ancestors); they are the grounding rock bed of Kremer's explorations. What emerges in the article has communal origins based in place and his individual pursuit ultimately needs to return to contexts of communal nurturing conversations with all relations (including animals, plants, rocks, and more). At the root of indigenous presence is visionary sovereignty, an intimate and creative engagement with place, nature, narrative imagination, and ceremonial practices. The recovery of such presence, Kremer argues, requires the composting of hopelessness and shadow material.

Using the work of Walter Benjamin, Karen Barad, and Judith Butler, Kremer develops an understanding of time where quantum field theories and indigenous science understandings illuminate each other and become twins in emancipatory moves. Both perspectives can help us understand our embeddedness in the world and how flashes of memory can bring "the past into the present so that it may become what it might have been." "Remembrance creates wholeness and the possibility of a different world." This discussion has profound implications for psychological theories and beyond.

Kremer ends his contribution with a Hawaiian story relating remembrance to initiation. We need to confront painful memories and bring light into cultural shadow material which, ultimately, means "to confront death for the sake of our present evolutionary challenge". He questions whether we (post)moderns are willing "to commit to the creation of livable communities in which we manifest our obligations and responsibilities to our fellow humans and other-and-more than humans"? The conscious confrontation with death forces the choice between life and self-destruction. He asserts that "the twins Indigenous science and quantum field theory can help us correct pathological thinking as the smooth linearity of time progressing is exploded by flashes of remembrance constellating a depth of presence and obligation to life largely forgotten by non-indigenous people". Hope emerges from staring in the face of death and the possibility of choice in the face of darkness.

All photos by Fariba Bogzaran © 2020

Dear 2020

*This seed is /buried deep /for /sprouting deceptively-perfumed blooms
/where nobody /expects: //if you are /not cruel, /if
//you strive to /do well/by //your fellow Kapwa, /if you /still
//believe in ethics, /I am /here, //grizzled, snow-haired, unafraid.
/"Happy New /Year!" ***

Dear 2020: Many would rather erase you from memory. As for me, who long ago, claimed to Not be a Time being, calendars (especially Gregorian) do not mean much except as reminders of human-centric concepts that have dominated the Anthropocene.

Dear 2020: Even before the pandemic, I had already settled into a semi-solitary, silent, and small way of Being. I made a promise that I would migrate inward and go deeper to get to know my Heart. My mind is in my heart—though this hasn't always been true.

Dear 2020: I apologize for what I call the 'tyranny of Hope'. There are so many in this culture who go overboard on positive thinking and being bright-sided as a way to convince themselves that Hope is a substitute for faith in Unknowing; a substitute for Grief.

Dear 2020: In some villages in India, the virus is a Devi and Corona Mai. People make offerings to the goddess of contagion and pray for protection. In the U.S., the virus is the enemy and we are at war. What is the difference? What and who is cruel?

Dear 2020: What are the seeds buried deep and now sprouting deceptively-perfumed blossoms? Two thousand and twenty years doesn't make for depth. Try 10,000. Try 14 Billion years.

Dear 2020: In this culture, people are Hopeful for things to return to "normal;" I guess they mean returning to the habits that may have caused the virus to emerge in the first place. So many people do not believe in foretelling. Cassandra is always weeping.

Dear 2020: I wish the news media would stop talking about ...2020 and its "disruptions." As if disruptions haven't always been with us. Just a simple turn of our perception towards the global south will tell us that these disruptions have finally arrived on our doorsteps.

Dear 2020: HOPE, for a word-dreamer, is an invitation to turn to non-human voices. To fall into reverie and see how we might live differently if we could hear the voices of the creek around the bend; the lichen on the wooden redwood fence; the fungi on the floor of the redwood forest.

—Leny Mendoza Strobel

*from "HOPE: First 2021 Poem," by Eileen R. Tabios (https://mosstrill.wordpress.com/2021/01/05/eileen-r-tabios-7/)

The Lone Monk

I dream of a landscape of bones – the bones of the ancestors of all the Earth's creatures scattered across the land under a dark sky. White bones against a black and grey landscape. Life has receded back into the depths, leaving only the rocky skeleton of the Earth's creatures. I am alone, a witness to what was and what has come to pass.

I wake from the dream staggered by grief. I am aware that my kind has brought on this devastation – I stand in the wreckage of human greed. The Earth is showing me what is happening to her and where it will lead. Yet even amidst this devastation, I feel the gentle presence of the Earth, a presence that rises soft and steady as a heartbeat beneath my feet.

Some dreams come from a greater knowing, a vastness that extends far beyond the boundaries of a human life. This dream of the Earth's body came to me from that greater knowing – it came and tore at my soul. When given these dreams, these visions of what is ahead or what has happened long ago in the beginning, we are overwhelmed by their power and mystery. They burst through the layers of ego and self-concern, immersing us in the vast expanse of being.

Sometime after this dream, an image came to me of a solitary monk walking across the same devastated landscape. In his right hand he carries a small bell that rings as he walks. The monk moves with ease and equanimity, his stride steady, sure. He seems untroubled by this place, as much a part of it as the whitened bones, the charred earth beneath his feet. He simply is. The landscape is. No resistance...

I can still see the devastation, the suffering of those struggling to survive, of animals hunted to extinction, the scourge of once mighty forests burnt to ash. Yet somehow the image of the lone monk carries the seed of hope I am seeking. He is a beacon, embodying the kind of human response, the kind of human consciousness, both possible and necessary in the face of overwhelming destruction. The seed of hope lies at the center, the center at the heart of the dream from the beginning. I sense, I know, if only for an instant, the immensity, the endless worlds of possibilities that lie at the heart of creation.

The center fades as rapidly as it appeared, and I am left once again at the edge of the world we are destroying. However, in these glimpses through the keyhole of the dream, my seeing is altered, transformed…now I know in the atoms of my being that emanate from the beginning, that this is not the end but another of endless unfolding of All that Is.

Wisdom keepers who offer guidance at this critical juncture of life on planet Earth speak of the universe we inhabit, and of the numberless universes now being discovered by physicists, multiverse universes long known in Hindu cosmology.

Our challenge is, like the monk, to hold All That Is in our consciousness, to commit to the supreme balancing act, a profound acceptance. That power of creation, there from the beginning of the dream of creation and still present, manifests in and through me and you and the galaxies scattered across the vastness of infinity.

—*Kimmy Johnson, Ph.D.*
Indian Valley, Novato, CA
January 2021

Coming-to-Presence at My Place of Hope

Jürgen Werner Kremer

Adik hangs out on the right side of Rosedale Valley Road for a different reason than Ninaatig. Adik thinks it's the only spot where hope lives, and they take out their voice recorder and record the sound of hope. It sounds like green leaves, attached to branches, moving in the wind. (Leanne Betasamosake Simpson, 2020, p. 100)

Hope, in its most profound and indigenous sense, is rooted in presence in place. Once this quality of presence has been disrupted, then hope can arise again from composting the darkness created by the disruption. This darkness is then what grounds hope, gives it body, makes it palpable and enables a return to presence in place. As such, I begin with a brief accounting of the current darkness of the modern world, the spectacle of its illusions and pathologies. I then suggest how this darkness might be composted and how the veils of deception might be lifted through personal and communal practices of remembrance and indigenous imagination. Using my own journey as an illustration, I describe what might be called a material, psychological, and spiritual practice of hope.

I

The end of neoliberal hope.

When the French theatre genius and wild man Antonin Artaud visited the Tarahumara (Rarámuri) Indigenous people of Northern Mexico in 1936 he reported that on occasion the Natives would visit the cities to observe urban life. "They go there, as they say, to see *how the people are who have deceived themselves*" (Artaud, 1983, p. 80; italics in original). Jung (1959), not mincing his words, called the contemporary Western world psychotic. Along these lines, I join many others who regard modernity as destructive dissociative veil that is in a pathological runaway or addictive process, which enforces the denial of the realities of continuous processes, complexities, entanglements, and potentialities. The result is a fundamentally (in its conception) monolithic view of history and the human and natural sciences. *Homo sapiens* has evolved through a series of evolutionary challenges. These challenges led to changes resulting in shared intentionalities and cultures (Tomasello, 2014). (Post)modernity's shared veil of deception constitutes our presentday evolutionary challenge. This challenge can be usefully framed as initiatory opportunity.

One kind of hope—I will term it the neoliberal hope—has been repeated and propagated by so many anchored in Euro-centered worlds, namely: globalizing western-style capitalism and liberal democracy create a better world. This notion was of course misguided from its inception. Consider for example the origin story (and continuing story) of Western modernity's reliance on racism, colonialism, slavery, genocide, heteropatriarchy, and ecocide, i.e., traumatic cuts, separations, and dissociations. Periodic beneficial shifts and advances in the West (e.g., in the areas of health, longevity, suffrage, legal protections) are of course welcome, but are often insecure or fleeting or the cause of new problems. Such events are used by those promoting neoliberal hope to propagate the overall illusion. For example, the fall of the Berlin Wall inspired Fukuyama's phantom vision (1992) of "the end of history," a notion he has amended several times since, but which perseveres (2018, p. xii) despite overwhelming contrary evidence.

Jürgen Werner Kremer, Ph.D. is tenured faculty at the Santa Rosa Junior College. He is the editor of ReVision, the president of the Society of Indigenous and Ancestral Wisdom and Healing, and a consultant with the Worldwide Indigenous Science Network and the UN University for Peace. His teaching and writing is centrally dedicated to the affirmation and remembrance of indigenous mind for the sake of humanity's future.

Žižek (2008) identifies the notion of "the end of history" as "the dominant ethos today ... liberal-democratic capitalism is accepted as the finally found formula of the best possible society, all that one can do is render it more just, tolerant, and so forth" (p. 421). However, at the current historical juncture neoliberal concepts and frameworks have lost their explanatory and guiding power as developments outside the Eurocentric horizon supersede what neoliberalism can grasp; they interrupt what was propagated as a coherent trajectory of progress, with a shared intentionality and cognitive map. "Anglo-American self-deceptions, which always exacted a high death toll abroad, from the Irish famine to Iraq, have become mass-murderous at home; a blusteringly casual attitude to the pandemic has resulted in tens of thousands of premature deaths in Britain and the United States" (Mishra, 2020, p. 13).

Today, the chimera of neoliberal hope has been fully unmasked by the mounting crises of inequality, racism, global environmental and climate collapse, combined with our inadequate will and capacity to address these crises—a lack of clear intentionality in the face of abundantly available knowledge. To this list can be added the breakdown of communities; the loss of ritual and ceremony; the commercialization of attention, emotions, values, and identities; and the unsolved disappearance of thousands of Native American women and girls (and reprehensible treatment of native communities generally). Among the appalling inequities highlighted by the Covid-19 pandemic is the de facto continuation of our colonial, classist, and racist history.

In recent decades neoliberal hope has greatly relied on the powers of the digital world to enrich human life, and the potential benefits of non-conscious artificial cognitive processes, without yet fully acknowledging the destructive outcomes. As just one example, social media-driven propaganda, disinformation, and civic polarization were not a common part of futuristic thinking, yet they are now a signature of our time: "In a hearing today (April 30, 2021, JWK) before a subcommittee of the House Armed Services Committee charged with investigating technology and information warfare, cyber policy and national security expert Dr. Herb Lin of the Hoover Institution told lawmakers that in the modern era we are not formally at war, but we are not at peace either: 'Information warfare threat to the United States is different from past threats, and it has the potential to destroy reason and reality as a basis for societal discourse, replacing them with rage and fantasy. Perpetual civil war, political extremism, waged in the information sphere and egged on by our adversaries is every bit as much of an existential threat to American civilization and democracy as any military threat imaginable'" (Cox Richardson, 2021).

In this darkening panorama, already incomplete and defective cognitive maps get seduced into a deepening dysfunction that profoundly affects "self," "other," and the very future of contemporary societies and species. How to lift this illusionary veil of neoliberal hope, and reclaim a sense of grounded hope?

Part of the answer lies in social action. The Me Too, Black Lives Matter, and the Dakota Access Pipeline movements have lifted the ideological veils of "progress" to expose "the (white) man behind the curtain," namely the vapid assertions of post-coloniality and post-raciality.

In the U.S., one of the two political parties no longer makes any secret of its racism and anti-democratic quest for a dictatorship of a white Christian minority that is kleptocratic, theocratic, and oligarchic in nature. They have mobilized a reactionary movement to achieve that goal. Mainstream pundits now freely acknowledge that the U.S. may be facing the end of the "Grand Experiment" of American democracy, and the rest of the western world watches with apprehension. In this way both progressive and reactionary social movements help clarify the bankruptcy of neoliberal hope, and the need for a new worldview and the recovery of what Western "civilizations" may have unwisely discarded. Ongoing denial and oppression and the resultant crises are now triggering flashes of deeper remembrance and highlighting the fragility of what seemed an inevitable movement forward.

Ultimately, of course, enduring change means not merely personal change, but also communal (socio-cultural) and structural change. Amnesiacs and magical thinkers are today squarely confronted with the choice of doubling down on their self-deceptions and reliance on a neoliberal hope, or to become present to what is happening and nourish a new kind of hope by remembering a human potential for presence on earth that has largely been forgotten.

II

Lifting the veil of denial

At the beginning of the novel *Homeland Elegies* Ayad Akhtar (2020) acknowledges his past denials:

> I wouldn't see it until our private lives had consumed the public

space, then been codified, foreclosed, and put up for auction; until the devices that enslave our minds had filled us with the toxic flotsam of a culture no longer worthy of the name; until the bright pliancy of human sentience—attention itself—had become the world's most prized commodity, the very movements of our minds transformed into streams of unceasing revenue for someone, somewhere. I wouldn't see it clearly until the American Self had fully mastered the plunder, idealized and legislated the splitting of spoils, and brought to near completion the wholesale pillage not only of the so-called colony ... but also of the very world itself. (p. XVII)

Akhtar describes the tearing of the veil of ideological deceptive assumptions of neo-liberalism and the ever more apparent contradictions and failures of late capitalism that indicate changing currents in the spirit of our time. Jung (1959, originally published 1951) labeled the thought process of the spirit of modern times fundamentally as psychotic: "Where rationalistic materialism holds sway, states tend to develop less into prisons than into lunatic asylums" (p. 181, para 282). This is what the Tarahumaras were curious to observe when visiting the cities. The urban exploitation they observed, the exploitation of labor, has now moved, as Akhtar notes, into our inner worlds: *attention is the world's most prized commodity.*

During the unfolding history of racism and racist science the *use* of the Eurocentered brain has become straightjacketed by onto-epistemological and ethical assumptions consciously and unconsciously extolling the virtues of white supremacy and human exceptionalism. These assumptions render invisible what is outside of linear time, outside of the largely dissociative practice of modern mainstream science separating experience from conceptualization; these cuts and separations disturb the balance between different parts of our brain, right and left hemisphere, older and younger parts of the brain. "To be conscious (i.e., to be in modern consciousness) was to be separated from and utterly untainted by anything but itself. ... Solipsism is intrinsic to its style of reflection" (Hillman, 1985, p. 53).

Hillman poses the challenge to "see through," to see past the conceptual constraints into a different sense of presence. Yet, "modern consciousness as white consciousness cannot get there, and what it finds is always dead" (p. 54). Contained in Hillman's notion of "seeing through" (1975) is a yearning to bring to life thoughts and images to connect with aliveness, with experience. "Simply to participate in events or to suffer them strongly, or to accumulate a variety of them, does not differentiate or deepen one's psychic capacity into what is often called a wise or an old soul ... There must be a vision of what is happening, deep ideas to create experience. Otherwise we have had the events without experiencing them, and the experience of what happened comes only later when we gain an idea of it—when it can be envisioned by an archetypal idea" (Hillman, 1975, p. 54).

Hillman locates his psychology in the realm of postmodernity, i.e., "white consciousness [is] forced into the postmodern psyche, into an animistic recognition of shades everywhere even in the brightest day and closest love ... the white immune system no longer reliable" (Hillman, 1985, p. 55). Thus the practitioners of this worldview stand at land's end of modern consciousness, the place where the figments created by the performative mental and material prison of post/modern thinking and practices are forced to confront its abusive illusions. The failures of current neoliberal and other Western assumptions to comprehend the world become all too apparent when looking at the U.S. or Europe from the perspectives of non-Eurocentric cultures and other continents (Mignolo, 2011; Mishra, 2020; Apffel-Marglin with PRATEC, 1998). From India or the Middle East or Asian countries, our contemporary hopes and challenges look quite different. And they certainly do from the perspective of Indigenous cultures.

This is where Hillman's "Notes on White Supremacy" ultimately take us all who are implicated in White supremacy to one degree or another: the logical terminus of his psychological philosophy is the remembrance of an indigenous sense of presence in the world. Indigenous traditions represent decolonial worlds that persist despite the onslaughts of modernity/coloniality, despite their inevitable entanglements with modernity/coloniality. Here (post)moderns can find the continuing presence of performative practices that irrupt as the revenge of the suppressed and persecuted into contemporary conceptual worlds that barely can acknowledge Indigenous existence and fail to perceive much that is central to Indigenous worlds.

Baudrillard (1993, pp. 137-138) notes Indigenous peoples, their knowledge practices, have the power "to destabilize Western rule ... Whites have been mysteriously made aware of the disarray of their own culture … This reversal is a worldwide phenomenon … *Everything* we once thought … left behind forever by the ineluctable march of universal progress, is not dead at all, but on the contrary likely to return … and to reach the very heart of our ultra-sophisticated but ultra-vulnerable systems, which it

> **"The West" needs to find answers to the central questions of our times in the radical otherness that indigeneity represents.**

will easily convulse from within without mounting a frontal attack. Such is the destiny of radical otherness." What has been behind the veil now makes a disruptive appearance. Indigenous embodied maps present a central challenge to the disintegrating constructs of modernity/coloniality. It is not only the history of the oppressed that flashes up thus, but the denial of indigenous origins of *all* peoples that enabled modernity's subsequent varieties of oppression.

How can "the West" not only move its understanding beyond the confines of neoliberalism and the colonial educational systems and academic conventions of the West, but also develop or remember practices that create contrapuntal balancing presences in the face of run-away crises and fixes that resemble the hustles of addicts? How to address the evolutionary challenges made visible in the social media monetization of our attention or Black Lives Matter, Me Too or Dakota Access Pipeline, and other movements? It is increasingly apparent that "the West" needs to find answers to the central questions of our times in the radical otherness that indigeneity represents.

III

Radical otherness

The dis-illusionment process from neoliberal hope to an awakening recognition of shadows, darkness, losses, and forgetting is a powerful opportunity for an initiatory journey. It allows us (post)moderns to step outside the prevailing paradigm and into a process of radical presence that has the potential gift of generating deeply grounded hope.

Hillman had the good intuitive and analytical sense to reach for a sense of presence where "thinking is trying to think the unthinkable" in its connections to experience. Thinking the unthinkable means lifting the veils in acts of remembering and coming-to-presence. As Cixous (1993, p. 38) states succinctly: "thinking the thinkable is not worth the effort." Thinking the thinkable reinforces dissociations from presence, memory, and history. Reaching for radical otherness in thought and presence, thinking the unthinkable, means that the value of a thought measures itself by its distance from the continuity of the known and from the *prevailing paradigm* of modernity/coloniality (paraphrasing Adorno, 1980, p. 90).

The objective value of a thought decreases the closer it cleaves to the dissociative performative requirements of post/modernity. As long as it approaches the pre-given standard, the more its antithetical function vanishes. And its value increases as we (post)moderns find the courage to put our lives, identities, and

> **Stepping outside the prevailing paradigm is an initiatory move.**

normative assumptions on the line. Its cause is founded not only in its value to its direct opposite, in the antithesis to the deceptive veils of modernity/coloniality. It's most important values can be found in embodied thought *stepping outside of the prevailing paradigm, stepping outside the dynamics of oppositions and antagonism as defined by the prevailing paradigm, stepping outside of what the prevailing consensus deems "legitimate." We instead enter into intimate connections with experience, confrontations with the unconscious, and remembrances of personal and collective (hi)stories and entanglements, with the intimacy of place and its history.*

This Artaud-esque act of leaving the given normalcy means standing outside the circles of habitual thought, even standing *outside* the circle of critical responses to habitual thought. This is because the circumference of this circle is, in final analysis, defined not by the critical response, but what the critique responds to—namely the habitual thought patterns of modernity/coloniality. The dynamics of statement and critique, of thesis and anti-thesis, perpetuates a stranglehold that constrains the movements of sovereign visionary presences. Abandoning the circle of the dialects defined by post/modernity means keeping the door to visionary sovereignty open [1].

Instead of measuring our knowing using the tools imposed as purportedly universal givens by the forces of modernity (and deconstructed in postmodernity in moves structured by modern discourse), we are challenged to step outside this paradigm where the intricacies of being and knowing— "beingknowing," one might say—come to presence. We develop practices within an entirely different onto-epistemology and ethics. Rather than representing and controlling we are performing or embodying. We are engaged in the work of coming-to-presence. Stepping outside the prevailing paradigm is an initiatory move.

Performative acts help make us (post)moderns present through inquiries that break Newtonian representational molds. These include chant, invocation, evocation—the ritualization of memory and experience. Reaching outside the circle defined by the constraints of post/modernity, reaching into the well of memory invites flashes of remembrance and presence, a performative practice of mind and matter intra-acting as different parts of our brain synchronize in a mind process outside of the circumference of the prevailing paradigm, defined by the dynamics of modernity/coloniality, post/modernity, and the neoliberal understandings and practices of late capitalism.

This un/settling and unsettled place is outside of the process of decolonization or postmodernity, outside the process of the critical opposition; instead it is a space of decolonial performances refusing the reach of modernity/coloniality (Mignolo & Walsh, 2018). Apffel-Marglin (2011) discusses rituals as the performance of livable common worlds. "What is common is that the world comes into being through intra-actions that typically take the form of rituals, those carefully orchestrated intra-actions meant to bring about a livable world are challenged to move from one world into another, from one way of performing self and other into a different sense of coming-to-presence.

IV

Hope by different names

By all accounts the English word 'hope' is of comparatively recent origin, reaching back to the early 13th century

> In the worlds of Indigenous presence, hope is embedded and interwoven into a life centered in the ritual embodiment of spiritual beliefs and nurturing conversations with the natural world around.

… These non-anthropocentric collective actions endeavor to bring about not just any common world, but a livable common world."

Importantly, in this process "neither nature, nor time/space, nor "Man" are given, but rather are made, nurtured, and woven in intra-actions, the very modernist separation between facts and values, between theory and praxis, vanish" (pp. 162-163). This is a place of cultural and ceremonial practice where (post)modernity/coloniality does not matter, where presence is naturally other with little care for the developments in metropolitan centers and the cult of capitalism.

This remembrance and assertion of decolonial worlds hails the possibility of the end of the Anthropocene, the geologic epoch of significant human impact on our planet and the rise of a posthumanist world in which human exceptionalism has been abandoned. It recognizes the necessity and possibility for egalitarian knowledge exchanges among peoples. It is the place where the addictive and traumatic spirit of our times can reach for transformation. These are contemporary places, memories, and images that un/settle through flashes of remembrance and presence that irrupt into time, mind, and reality as defined by modernity/coloniality. They can re/make the future and they can also re/make the past as the veils are lifted. They bear generative seeds for responses as we (post)moderns and arising from Saxon and Low German (with somewhat unclear origins beyond that). My interpretation of this etymology is that with the rise of linearity, progress, Christianity (monotheism), and, eventually, modernity/coloniality, hope emerged as separate abstract concept distinct from non-linear understandings of time, separate from the complex patterns of responsibilities and mutuality in cause and effect intra-actions that are part of a ritualized conversation with the world. It may well be that the Western abstract concept of hope and the arising of linear future perspectives of progress go hand in hand. Hope only appears in

> The remembrance and assertion of decolonial worlds hails the possibility of the end of the Anthropocene.

the Western world, it seems, as separate perspective once ongoing (ritual) practices affirming and manifesting hope and balance are disrupted.

Ernst Bloch's magisterial *Das Prinzip Hoffnung (The Principle of Hope,* 1954-1959), written 1938 to 1947 during the darkness of World War Two while in exile in the U.S., was originally entitled *Dreams of a Better Life.* Hope is what enables utopian thinking and Bloch regards his version of utopian thinking as connecting to real possibilities rather than chimeras. Bloch understands hope as basic life-affirming drive. Our daydreams reach into the future of a better life, they help humanity move from the not-yet-conscious to the conscious hopeful pursuit of actualizing human possibilities. Bloch's analysis is based in Freudian drive theory and Marxist analysis, but it also connects with spiritual traditions, such as Taoism. Utopian thinking about work, art, technology, architecture, and religion is important for the completion of the human project, the transformation of what creates insecurity or discriminates against other humans. Work then serves to satisfy basic needs rather than the maximization of profit. Hope, according to Bloch, is central to our daily existence and possibilities of a better future.[2]

Lear (2006) defines radical hope as "directed toward a future goodness that transcends the current ability to understand what it is. Radical hope anticipates a good for which those who have the hope as yet lack the appropriate concepts with which to understand it" (p. 103). His discussion is focused on Crow culture and its destruction by violent settler colonialism, but the concept of radical hope is relevant for anybody infected by the Wetiko disease (Forbes, 2008), the Eurocentered virus of progress, the viral story that began gathering strength in the Renaissance (Mignolo, 1995), and is captured in Silko's (1977) witchery story. Lear's interpretations are based in a Western understanding of hope, and it is tempting to transpose his notion of radical hope from the times of Crow colonization to our contemporary challenges. As current concepts and cultural and economic practices prove incapable of resolving the crises in our face and in our bodies, we (post)moderns seem to have the choice of engaging with a process of radical hope whose "aim is to establish what we might legitimately hope at a time when the sense of purpose and meaning that has been bequeathed to us by our culture has collapsed" (p.

104). But we may need to go one step further and look for radical hope by an indigenous name.

The qualitative shift from an Indigenous mind process and the ceremonial life of the Crow culture into a world of cultural threats and destruction governed by an alien mindset, changes hope from what it once was into what it is now forced to be. The understanding of hope shifts. In the worlds of Indigenous presence, hope is embedded and interwoven into a life centered in the ritual embodiment of spiritual beliefs and nurturing conversations with the natural world around.

Here hope is not important as abstract concept that yearns into the future of linear time by way of looking beyond the line-up of historical events. Instead, hope is rooted in a sense of presence that is concretely entangled, neither linear nor cyclical; that reaches into the past and into the future; that is part of a rich present, a thick pattern of entanglements.[3]

Taking radical hope out of the paradigm of linearity transforms it into hope for a sense of cultural practice and presence that the Crow were ripped out of by colonial forces. Stepping outside of the circle of modernity/coloniality means engaging with radical hope by an indigenous name and aiming for a sense of subjectivity and socio-cultural practice that does not exist in modernity/coloniality; it only appears in memories flashing up and spaces resisting the reach of Eurocentered influences. In a sense this means relinquishing hope in the abstract sense of the word, revisioning radical hope, and re-embedding hope into nurturing conversations.

This labor of memory is not on behalf of retro-romantic images, but aims to release knowing and being practices, i.e., biopsychosocial capacities that are obscured by the relentless forces of neoliberal democracies and their capitalisms. The confrontation with these forces has been back breaking and spirit breaking, quite different from a nostalgic neoshamanic trundle intoxicated by rootless optimism. Radical hope inevitably includes the confrontation with shadow material. Hope requires experiences of hopelessness. Neither the images documenting Paul Gauguin's escape from European civilization nor Henri Rousseau romantic "primitivism," while certainly beautifully illustrating the deep dissatisfaction and disillusionment with modern developments, are adequate to evoke the decolonial spaces discussed here; their romanticism omits the challenges and obstacles in the performance of livable common worlds. Radical hope can find its manifestations through the flashes of remembrance of our connections with nature and ancestries, and it is these memories that enable our futures. And they enable inquiries and systemic knowing predominantly prohibited by academic conventions.

Places like this continue to exist in parallel to the violent forces the West continues to perpetrate. Not that these assertions of visionary sovereignty have ever been possible in any pure sense since the beginnings of coloniality/modernity, yet their remarkable qualitative difference has been noted as disturbing and thus continues to be marked by ongoing colonial violence (whether in the form of economic, educational, missionary, gender, or other violence). And such assertions of visionary sovereignty also exist and flash up in (post)modernity as memories of places where rituals and the performance of livable common worlds have been disrupted or seemingly destroyed by the march of progress. The remembrance of embodied practices of presence grounded in intimacy of place allows for the arising of hope by an indigenous name, a sense of radical aliveness originating from the indigenous inheritance all peoples carry.

V

Indigenous roots

Native Elders have frequently stated that people of European descent need to remember their own indigenous roots: "I do not want people to adopt Indian rituals because I want people to own their own rituals. I want them to come to ownership out of experiences that are real to them. Then I'll come and celebrate with them" (Cattaraugus Seneca John Mohawk, as recorded by Spretnak, 1991).

Indigenous Elder Apela Colorado (of Oneida and Gaul ancestries) advised me similarly when we began teaching together. As she commented years later: "For too long White people have been beggars at the doors of native ceremonies longing to be included. With their arrogance and sense of entitlement in place they refuse to investigate their Indigenous roots" (2014, p. xxi).

The idea of the recovery of indigenous mind and roots doesn't make much sense within the Western paradigm or within Western psychology. After all, the reference is to times hundreds and thousands of years ago. Consequently, it is easy to dismiss this notion out of hand as absurd.

However, for a variety of personal and political reasons, I was inspired by this challenge and possibility and felt compelled by my desire to establish a framework of egalitarian knowledge exchange among peoples outside of the paradigm of colonial appropriation and arrogance. Ever since I have worked to conceptualize the recovery process of indigenous mind. While this project has made persuasive sense to me for several decades now, I continued to have difficulty understanding and detailing the depth of what this process all entails. Something was missing. As it were, I was disturbed by a sense that there was more than what met my mind on the surface.

I have come to realize that to theorize the process of recovery of indigenous mind properly means, for example, revisioning the common understanding of the discipline of psychology, something that matters to me as a psychologist. Neither Indigenous philosophies nor quantum field theory—two seemingly different approaches that share important qualities—have impacted the field of psychology in significant ways, much to its detriment. This essay is an attempt to outline a few of the central coordinates of the depth of the recovery

> To theorize the process of recovery of indigenous mind properly means revisioning the common understanding of the discipline of psychology.

of indigenous mind process (a promissory note, as it were). And with it I develop a rudimentary framework for a transdisciplinary and integrative psychology.

Neither time, nor matter, nor mind, nor consciousness, nor place can be any longer understood in the terms the dominant Western paradigm offers (a paradigm that should have been impacted much more dramatically by quantum field theories, the most significant development within the Western paradigm). It is my good fortune that I can draw on contributions that have worked to undermine and expand this paradigm.[4]

VI

Round about the well of memory

I took Apela Colorado's advice and started the quest for my own indigenous roots, which included longer sojourns in Sápmi, the land of the Sámi people of the European Arctic, the only contemporary Indigenous peoples in Europe, as well as return travel to Germany. I visited Sápmi for neighborly knowledge trade since, in the midst of Fenno-Scandian modernity, shamanism and Indigenous presence are persisting. Dialogues with culture bearers and ritual engagement in places marked as sacred were the purpose of my trips.

I then, for a short while, lived on Iceland, because, as Jorge Luis Borges (1999, pp. 400 & 401) states succinctly and poetically:

Islandia
… Fría rosa, isla secreta
que fuiste la memoria de Germania
y salvaste para nosotros
su apagada, enterrada mitología …

Iceland
… Icy rose, secret island,
you were Germania's memory;
you saved for us
her snuffed-out, buried myths …

Living on Iceland was my way of connecting with ancestral memories that the island had saved. Here I unearthed what was buried, seemingly snuffed out, yet vibrant enough to flash back into my life, catalyzing a process of coming-to-presence in encounters with primordial and visionary dimensions while simultaneously catalyzing conceptualizations and inquiries beyond the conventions I had been trained in.

So here I stand, amidst the din of screams of nature violated and humans neglected, traumatized, and persecuted, my body bridging inside/out to my place of hope, an ancestral memory where the entanglement of mind and matter, imaginal and real, story and careful observation bring me to stillness and presence. This is the beginning point of a process that has communal origins and, once

> The beginning point of recovering indigenous presence has communal origins and ultimately, once again, requires a communal process.

again, ultimately requires a communal process. My personal starting place is in need of communal weavings that may obviate individualistic distortions.

The place of hope in my oldest ancestral root memories is a well by a life-giving tree where three women reach into the source of memory and re/generation, fertilizing the world with *aurr*, a fertile mass, a concrete entanglement of void and matter in the well, the concrete power of the imaginal; this is the dew that dabbles the dales, a creative and generative move, holo/sexual and erotic for sure, mind and matter appearing as time resists the simplistic corset of linearity.[5]

The three women reach into the source of re/generation and memory, catalyzing becoming (*Verðandi*) from exigent obligations (*Skuld*) as dark and light memory (*Urðr*) is re/collected. The three fertilize and inspirit the tree and the dales around as their pro/creative moves spread *aurr*, the riches of white dew, the catalyst of creation. Time manifests here not as progressive line, but as fateful movements, with flashes moving backward and forward, wealthy with potential for balancing acts. Prophecy was never about predicting the future but understanding the thick and multi-layered present during encounters with the past in horrifying and ecstatic primordial processes. Murakami's *Windup Bird Chronicles* (1998) and Jung's *Red Book* (2009) are examples of what the immersion in the well and primordial realms may offer; or, if you are inclined to travel the Greek way, hitch a ride with the goddess into the underworld, let Parmenides be your guide (Laks & Most, 2016; Kingsley, 2020). The three women, *Verðandi*, *Skuld*, and *Urðr* are at the center of my place of hope.

The three women appear around the well, its depth the access to re/generative primordial regions, memories and visions, re/configurations and remembrances. And then there appear three men.

One embodies ecstasy and poetry, *Oðr*, the oldest presence of *Oðinn*, two ravens on his shoulder, two wolves by his side and one eye sacrificed to depths of understanding and prophetic and utopian memory.

The second is *Hœnir*, the one who gave the light of reason and the dark of rationalistic encrustations, who knows of silence, passion, and ceremonial celebration.

And, importantly, the third appearing is the slippery trickster whose mischievous play loosens where obstruction and sclerosis have prevailed, an inevitable gender fluid presence by multiple names. Danger looms when our sense of self is incapable of self-irony and laughter about our rationalistic follies and grandiosities; this is when *Loki* may intervene to puncture our inflations.

The well of memory with its six presences is an un/certain place, un/real in its appearance as the imaginal breaches matter and matter breaches the imaginal; as mind and matter intra-act; the well of memory tends the world through at/tentions and in/tentions, balancing the fe/male and healing female (the erasure of female presences by heteropatriarchal narratives). In the background rises the tree of life, populated by other-than-human beings making their home in her, a multiplicity for sure, now oak, now larch, now ash, yet a certain presence reaching from the roots in the aqueous sources of the well upward to Polaris, the luminous appearance of un/certainty as it is wandering with the precession of the equinoxes, star knowledge transforming the understanding of memory and obligation as the stories of *Ragnarök* (the fateful moment for those who reign) portend challenges, obligations, and opportunities as the phenomena of reality appear in intra-active moves. [6]

It is the dew from the well, the *aurr*, that nurtures the tree of life, the world tree and axis mundi, which is inhabited by the squirrel of consciousness moving up and down the trunk, by eagle and hawk, by several snakes and a dragon at its roots, and four deer feeding on its leaves. On top of the tree stands *Heimdallur*, the guardian of the bridge into the starry realms (his role as guardian is to check on dissociative moves in the self, the losses of an indigenous mind process that now makes movements across the bridge treacherous). The well reaches down and the tree reaches up into our primordial memories and connections, altogether a different sense of time, a weaving of im/material tapestries and human presence in the world.

This is my place of hope and measure.

> My personal starting place is in need of communal weavings that may obviate individualistic distortions.

It is a place that arises from communal vision and that finds its completion in communal practice To attend to it means ritually embodying the bridging of mind and matter, of the imaginal and the literal, of inside and outside, spirits and material manifestations, archetypes throbbing and matter remembering.

Where I aim to stand in my practice is outside the mind territory I was raised in, outside the confines of embodiment I was trained in. This is a place not merely of disagreement or contradiction to prevailing paradigms and norms, the dialectics of its post/modern critical conversations, but a place wholly other and contained in its own sense of presence—an imaginal place and a literal multiplicity of places to re/turn to; a pregnant image of complexity fashioned into the appearance of simplicity.

Remembering the history of the betrayal of this ancestral memory is part of my healing work. This is not the memory of a stable image, as conventional historical understanding would suggest (such as an image presented in a book of history or mythology or even in a sacred text), but the intra-active engagement with heterogeneity through concrete intra-actions, ritual remembrances in the dense weave of the now.

When this image of the tree of life and the six presences is discussed by scholars of mythology and folklore, it becomes part of the world of modernity/coloniality where it is dismissed as early history, pre/modern, an irrational image of no importance to the world of modern science. In folklore seminars the story is a mythological curiosity which can only be understood as falsehood, now that myth mostly has come to mean untruth. It is part of a curious collection of mis/representations that are interesting as poetry and story, but irrelevant to contemporary reality, social practices, and understanding.

However, by stilling the vibrant process the image evokes, it has also been abused for fundamentalist and fascist purposes in contradiction to the process of visionary sovereignty it entails. The intentions of the victorious dominant forces are obedience, control, and belief, the stilling of any process bridging imaginal and everyday realities; this is the murder of visionary sovereignty and the enshrinement of conformity.

It is tempting to hold this image in a simplistic fashion, as part of a linear history that as lifeless memory then triggers nostalgia, sentimentality, and romanticism, the opposite of coming-to-presence. This is what can be seen in the paintings of Gauguin and Rousseau. Retro-romanticism and other dissociative moves enable the forces of acquisition to devour these fantasies for the purposes of profit.

Possibly one of the worst ideas humans ever had is purity in its various manifestations, the dissociative cut that creates a hypostasis of one pure element

> Attending to my place of hope means ritually embodying the bridging of mind and matter, of the imaginal and the literal, of inside and outside, spirits and material manifestations, archetypes throbbing and matter remembering.

over another, a colonial move denying entanglements (Shotwell, 2016); by contrast, among the more difficult ideas for humans to sustain, are unceasing process, complexity, paradox, and ambiguity while simultaneously striving for accuracy, integrity, and truth. Holding the image of the well and the six presences simplistically is ultimately life denying; by contrast, engaging with its complexity facilitates not only labors of remembrance, but it re/configures time, materiality, and mind/consciousness (as I will explore below).

> The woman of memory (Urðr) obliges me to provide an ethno-accounting of my presence on this land.

Holding the image of the well and the tree with fundamentalist purity empowers the forces of dissociation and enslavement. Holding this ancestral image in its complexity means acknowledging the complexity of my ancestral lines reaching from Northern Germany into the Alsace Lorraine where many Jewish people shifted to a Goyish identity, reaching east and northward, to shtetls in in the borderlands of Poland and Lithuania, and north from there. It means acknowledging not only where I come from but where I live now. It compels me to acknowledge that I am writing on the unceded traditional lands of the Pomo, Miwok and Wappo peoples in Northern California, that I am an immigrant and settler enmeshed with the consequences of a genocidal history and a history of enslavement..

And with this acknowledgment the woman of memory (Urðr) obliges me to remember meticulously the history of place, to provide an ethno-accounting of my presence on this land; to acknowledge the seemingly endless number of massacres in California (Madley, 2016; Atkins & Bauer, 2021), the violent history of settlement; the origins of names like Petaluma and the Indigenous stories of old and their renewal and contemporary telling (Sarris, 2017); it compels me to acknowledge the obligations that arise from my movement between places, from Northern Germany to Northern California; to acknowledge the ecstatic power of Óðr (Óðinn) to envision what presence might mean in all its complexity at this moment in time; to allow Loki to trick me into flashes of vision, to bust linear time into eddies of presence; to overcome one-dimensional rationality and to give integrative reason, precariously balanced between left and right hemisphere, a chance; all of these processes thus catalyzing *verðandi* (becoming), the manifestations of presence outside of the prison of linear causality moving through empty space, outside of the betrayal of memory for the sake of white supremacy and human exceptionalism.[7]

The three women by the depth of the well give access to historical and primordial memories. The three men at the point of anthropogenesis inspirit and give life to the first humans found as trees on the beach. And there is the central tree by many names and visions materializing: holy oak, ash, beech, rowan, elder, *Weckholter* (juniper), fir, pine, larch, *Irminsul, Yggrasil.* Its roots reach into the sources of un/knowing and re-membering, its top branches reach into the realms of rainbows by day and the milky way by night bridging multi-layered time and reality.

These are sources of science and imagination, the sources of nurturing conversations, the sources for balancing ourselves inside and outside, the sources of communal truths. This is the space in which time weaves and thickens in lines, cycles, and where remembrances flash up; it is far from empty, it is filled with presence, it is filled with potential and in/determinacy.

The fluidity and interplay of the motion of the three women and men is a visionary process, a transmotion (Vizenor, 1998, p. 15)[8] into potential and possibility as mind and matter intra-act, a natural sovereign motion and presence of the self interwoven with the worlds around.

The six are a ceremonial evocation, a shimmering presence and reality, the motion of remembering, of discerning obligations, of unfolding as trickery, ecstasy, as the depths of reason confront and plunge us (post)moderns into the potentials of presence. The interlacing of these movements creates certainty and unpredictability as vision and dream inspire. The foundational movement of the three women reaching into the well is a certain (holo)sexual and pro/creative move that catalyzes change and the possibility of balance. It generates the possibility of an emergent presence in place that is decolonial and affirmative of native presence all around as dark memories are ritually acknowledged.

"The void is a lively tension, a desiring orientation toward being/becoming … In/determinacy is not the state of a thing but an unending dynamism" (Barad, 2015, p. 396).

VII

Composting hopelessness

I did not grow up with the image of the six presences at tree and well, in fact, my shame and abhorrence of Old Norse mythic stories was intense in the aftermath of their Nazi abuses and the prior patriarchal and violent genocidal interpretations and uses of these stories. The thought of "going Viking" as rite of passage always gave me the shudders and my book of German mythology, printed in Fraktur font, so often regarded as "true German script" and the official Nazi font, was untouchable and remained unopened during my childhood; I was deadly afraid of contamination by poisonous ideologies. So I grew up with the conundrum of existentialist imagery and interpretations on the one hand and creative and nurturing inspirations from the natural world of the Northern German moors, marshes, sand dunes, and forests on the other.

One of the trees I grew up with was the bare tree center stage, as Vladimir, Estragon, Pozzo, and Lucky in Beckett's *Waiting for Godot* (1976) embodied the apparent absence of a God and the absence of any hope for rescue after concentration camps and the pervasive denial of the atrocities of the Shoah in Germany during those years.

The tree in the play has no leaves at its opening and Vladmimir and Estragon struggle to perceive it accurately: What is it? A tree? A bush? A shrub? A willow? At one point Estragon suggests: "Why don't we hang ourselves?" Of course, the promise of the arrival of Mr. Godot becomes a broken promise: "Mr. Godot told me to tell you he won't come this evening but surely tomorrow." In the second act the tree has four or five leaves, yet, despite this small sign of hope, Mr. Godot yet again fails to arrive.

In Berlin, at the time an island walled in and heavily guarded by East German and Russian military, I watched *Endgame* under Beckett's own direction, two of the characters residing in trash cans in an apparent pitiful state, another the servant, and the fourth the autocratic master.

For me, the bleakness of these plays depicted the hopelessness and darkness of the times accurately and viscerally. Sartre's *Huis clos* (No Exit) captured my mood inside the circle of the Berlin wall where East Germans trying to escape the dictatorship were regularly murdered; it captured my hopelessness by evoking an afterlife in which "*L'enfer, c'est les autres*" (Hell is other people). The ruins of the Second World War, holocaust denial, and an optimism solely grounded in the stunning economic progress of the German *Wiederaufbau* and *Wirtschaftswunder* did not inspire any hope in me; action reigned over introspection and self-confrontation.

Undetonated bombs from the Second World War were fished out of the river in front of our house on a weekly basis and we had to open our windows to prevent them from shattering in case of a blast. Teachers claimed they had not noticed their Jewish neighbors disappearing during the Shoah. And then the war ruins I walked by every day—all of this I held in my body.

This world of darkness, destruction, and denial entered my body, was incised in my body in cuneiform marks that required psychological digs for decipherment, carved in my bone as tumor and chronic pain. I had no language to adequately capture the depth of my experience and no mentor helped me forge words of release.

And not too far away the iron curtain where I played on the beach under the watchful eyes of East German guards toting machine guns. It did not represent the border to a more promising world, a place for hope, a Marxian utopia becoming real. In West Germany the East was thoroughly marked as bad and beyond any redemptive value or promise of a better future (see Neiman, 2019 for an excellent discussion). The optimism of the German economic miracle seemed fake and ungrounded to me and hopelessness in the face of political realities seemed nothing but an expression of realism. The striking socio-cultural ir/rationality and denial made pessimism seem a natural and sensible response.

The denuded center stage tree of *Waiting for Godot* was balanced by my own explorations of nature. The hobby, a bluish smaller version of a peregrine, screaming its piercing call on top of a pine tree embodied my hope for freedom and creativity. The seal and the herring gull I raised were companions that balanced the failure of Mr. Godot to show up or Hamm's autocratic directions on stage. Beethoven provided emotional release, comfort, and inspiration, but the mating cadences of the curlew soaring above the bog ultimately had more power in my heart. The scream of the arctic tern cut through hopelessness to levels of enticing beauty. *Red Tree* becoming *Horizontal Tree*, becoming Mondrian's compositions.

Along the way I encountered the skeleton of a dead boar and I was able to take its fang as medicine gift. Joseph Beuys had the courage to explain pictures to a dead hare and in 1974 he lived with a coyote for one week in the René Block Gallery in New York City to heal the psychological trauma of the history of the United States, because "a reckoning has to be made with the coyote, and only then can this trauma be lifted" (Beuys, 1990, p. 141).

When it came to words, Paul Celan's poetry suggested the necessity to wash words so that they can bear witness, a purification ceremony to enable remembrances. I followed his tracks, "written asunder," and in my imagination joined the conversation in the mountains where nature and memory can meet and heal (Celan, 1988; Hawkins, 2002).

Hopelessness and hope exchanged places in turbulent moves between my existentialist dark night journeys, in the touching of art and nature which provided soothing balms and flashes of inspiration. Often 'hope' and 'optimism'

> My childhood world of darkness, destruction, and denial entered my body, was incised in my body in cuneiform marks that required psychological digs for decipherment, carved in my bone as tumor and chronic pain.

my sense of self and presence that were reassuring and touched kernels of hope.

The healing balm of nature and my passion for art found an inspiring synthesis in seeing an image of a *Schimmel*, the German for white horse, on stage during one of Joseph Beuys' actions during the Frankfurt Theatre Festival (Tisdall, 1979).

I had just spent a night walking into the foggy and snowy hills behind my school, meandering in a landscape that led me through the process of abstraction as beech and oak transformed into geometric patterns—Mondrian's paintings in the forest; the lines of trees, hills, and path created abstractions of are understood to be synonymous, with the invocation of optimism an obligatory rhetorical move in U.S. political discourse, no matter the circumstance and commonly devoid of any analytical context. In my use of language optimism, as I experienced it in the German *Wirtschaftswunder*, its "economic miracle," is defined by its lack of engagement with the shadow, with the possibility of failure, the experience of moments of hopelessness and overwhelm, and the encounter with recalcitrant obstacles along the way. By contrast, hope by a different name arises from composting darkness. This darkness is what grounds it, gives it body, makes it palpable, and creates potential on the edges of imagination.

My existentialist despair about the political circumstances of my upbringing led to the emergence of hope that ultimately found its personal reality in the presence of the tree by the well and the three women and men in their unfolding movement catalyzing intra-actions of mind and matter and fertilizing the world with flashes of memory. It gave me growing courage to step where fear so often gets in the way. It has prompted me to try and to "try again. Fail again. Fail better" (Beckett, 1983) as I was struggling with the issues of what Indigenous science, philosophies, and ceremonial practices might mean for a white man today in the resolution of our conundrums and crises.

Žižek (2008) interprets Beckett's work depicting the inevitability of failure as opening paths to imaginative ways of utopian thinking. For me the darkness of German history, or Beckett's existentialism and experience of the Nazi occupation as a member of the French résistance (Morin, 2017), or Walter Benjamin's suicide in Port Bou as he was trying to flee his murderers (Eiland & Jennings, 2014)—all these pointed to my way *beyond* and *outside* utopian thinking as extension of a monolithic historicity; they point me to the remembrance of the deeper layers of Indigenous visionary sovereignty and a multi-layered sense of presence through the confrontation with darkness. Thus utopian thinking finds its grounding in the active working through of shadow material and the active remembrance and affirmation of decolonial islands.

The shimmering image of the well, the tree, and the three women and men is one of my guides out of the aporias of modernity/coloniality and into the sedimented origins of oppression and oppressed people, into indigenous practices of knowing and being that catalyze non-dissociative presence.

VIII

Severing ritual entanglements

Composting hopelessness with the help of ancient images requires an understanding of time and remembrance

> The shimmering image of the well is one of my guides into the sedimented origins of oppression and oppressed people, into indigenous practices of knowing and being that catalyze non-dissociative presence.

that is consistent with Indigenous ways of "beingknowing." Recovery of indigenous mind in a sense that is *meaningful for today* means reaching into the depths of what appears in remembrance.

How can remembrance work across time spans that often seem beyond the reach of any reasonable certainty or meaningfulness? How can memory be not merely a one-dimensional inventory of "facts" in the line-up of stories about victorious progress, useful as this may be? As long as one works within a framework of linear time and causality, any reach for depths outside the given constraints of historiography barely makes "sense" and suggests retro-romantic and nostalgic inclinations. [9]

The next sections inquire into the dissociative cuts central to the practice of linear time and contrast it with the thick present Indigenous traditions and quantum interpretations suggest.

Linear time and the notion of progress in modernity/coloniality, the accumulation of knowledge over time, suggest that anything Indigenous, even if it continues to be present (a surviving "remnant," a prehistoric island that should have been vanquished long ago), is remote and nothing but a chimera from times prior to the origins of linearity. If time is linear, empty, and homogenous, if it is filled with the linear progress of humankind, then the recovery of Indigenous knowledge, images, and practices can hardly be of significance.

The temporality of progress was enforced on the Crow and other Indigenous peoples. Prior to that—and as precondition—the sense of time changed in Europe with the rise of monotheism, the Enlightenment, and the notions of classical physics that were part of the emergent Western sciences. Clocks began to govern lives in the fourteenth century. First, the historical transformations, beginning particularly in the renaissance, effected in Europe the erasure of what is commonly labeled prehistoric, oral tradition, primitive, or tribal (as opposed to "the civilized"); this shift in consciousness and material practices enabled modernity/coloniality to work effectively on the erasure of Indigenous traditions all over the globe.

The ritual engagement with time as complex weave of a present thick with past and future was subdued in both cases by the regimen of clock time (in the European "centers" and subsequently in Indigenous worlds).

This shift and dissociative split can be called *the original trauma of "the West,"* resulting in a biopsychosocial configura-

> The notion of progress in modernity/coloniality suggests that anything Indigenous is remote and nothing but a chimera from times prior to the origins of linearity.

tion, continuing into the present, which might rightfully be described as ongoing process of posttraumatic injury. The chronic stress resulting from the separation from resources that nurture and balance the self can generatively be framed as traumatic process in order to understand the depths of its impact.

The separations during this original trauma are the normative split of the cessation of ongoing ritual engagement with the world. The old norms of mutuality, balancing, and ongoing storied process are now substituted by abstract rules of exchange and dissociative, objectifying forms of observation. With it comes an avoidance of remembrance, the world turns amnesiac.

And what is remembered now is flattened, remnant cardboard images retaining vague traces of what was profound engagement before the trauma. Research has shown (e.g., Harris, 2018) that these types of adversity, these disconnections

> *The original trauma of "the West" might rightfully be described as ongoing process of posttraumatic injury.*

and losses, these traumatic incisions consciously acknowledged or not, are passed on generationally through epigenetics. Normative dissociation thus was written into the flesh and manifests today through a wide variety of defensive and offensive symptoms ("white fragility") impeding the healing of racist histories.

The qualities of ritual engagement with the world (communally grounded, even when individually performed) are markers of social practices that create cultural worlds at odds with what modernity/coloniality demands of individuals. Rituals are "*symbolic techniques of making oneself at home in the world ... They structure time, furnish it*" (Han, 2020, p. 2). "Past and present are brought together into a living present ... Rituals are processes of embodiment and bodily performances ... Rituals create a bodily knowledge and memory, an embodied identity, a bodily connection ... Rituals are *narrative processes* that do not allow for acceleration. Symbols *stand still ...* Rituals contain aspects of the world, they produce in us a strong relationship to the world ... Rituals ... disburden the ego of the self, de-psychologizing and de-internalizing the ego" (pp. 8, 11, 13, 14).

Rituals at the well under the tree in the presence of the three women and men enact an intimate relationship with the world, they create stillness and depth of interiority beyond words; they connect into the depths of the presence through past and future, through the richness of mutuality, responsibility, alterity, and the impurities of origin.

The qualities of deep personal and communal ritual engagement had been central to the Crow world before colonization and just as they were central to European indigenous cultures. Ehrenreich's *Dancing in the Streets* (2007) tracks the shifts of celebratory festivals and rituals from balancing and healing to their use in the politics of control and the creation of conformity, spectacles to keep the populus deceived and thus oppressed.

Ritual engagement with the world and storytelling (including dream sharing) are communal activities. Freedom is only possible in community, it depends on the success and balance of my relationships with others: "'Only in community [with others does each] individual [have] the means of cultivating his gifts in all directions; only in the community, therefore, is personal freedom possible' ... being free means nothing other than *self-realization with others*" (Han, 2017, p. 3; initial quote from Marx).

Such freedom to self-realize can only be visionary as creative act in a specific place, it is the foundation of visionary sovereignty, the vision to move in imagination and to move in the body. The evocation of the vision of the well, the tree, and the six presences are an entanglement of mutuality, gifting, and visioning. It is both an imaginal move and the multiplicity of manifestations in different locales where oak, larch, and other trees are honored; an imaginal mindful intra-action and an embodied encounter with specific honored wells, springs, and lakes.

The movement of time changed as the circles of gift economies, i.e., exchanges based on concrete and personal intra-actions by the tree or the well, exchanges based in stories and rituals, were superseded by the abstract exchanges governed by currencies, by one-dimensional quantification, and profit maximization (Vaughan, 1997, 2015, 2019; Kailo, 2012).

Kailo defines the "gift imaginary" as worldview "that emerges from the values, social systems and ecosocially sustainable attitudes of people rooted in gift circulating cultures, old and new" (she cites the Haudenosaunee, the Sumatran Minangkaban, the Indian Khasi, and the South-Afrikan Khoesan as examples). What had been a cycle of mutual nurturance, utility, and stories shared over the exchanges—the Andean *criar y dejarse criar* (to nurture and be nurtured)—became a causal line of amassing abstract wealth that breeds greed for more wealth, a runaway addiction. Walter Benjamin, in 1921, called capitalism "a religion of pure cult, without dogma" which "offers not the reform of existence but its total destruction" (1996, p. 290-1; 1985, p. 102).

The significance of Karl Marx' analysis of the pathogenetic inner workings of capitalism, of alienation and exploitation, has not been diminished as it has been updated by Harvey (2014, 2018) and others. The self-colonization of Europe and the colonial disruptions the world over created dissociative norms

> *Normative dissociation was written into the flesh and manifests today through a wide variety of defensive and offensive symptoms impeding the healing of racist histories.*

through the destruction of rituals which split humans from nurturing interconnections with place, community, dreams, animals, plants, weather, mountains, and other relations, from the process of visionary sovereignty.

Normative dissociation is the runaway process that leads from crisis to crisis relinquishing the capacity to go beyond temporary band aids and reach for the recovery of ritual presence and ways of "beingknowing" that catalyze fundamental change.

The destructive power of rapacious capitalism is captured by Alan Ginsburg in his poem *Howl* (2006, p. 139), where humans sacrifice themselves at the altar of Moloch:

> Moloch the incomprehensible prison! Moloch the crossbone soulless jailhouse and Congress of sorrows! Moloch whose buildings are judgment! Moloch the vast stone of war! Moloch the stunned governments!

> Moloch whose mind is pure machinery! Moloch whose blood is running money! Moloch whose fingers are ten armies! Moloch whose breast is a cannibal dynamo! Moloch whose ear is a smoking tomb!

> Moloch whose eyes are a thousand blind windows! Moloch whose skyscrapers stand in the long streets like endless Jehovahs! Moloch whose factories dream and croak in the fog! Moloch whose smokestacks and antennae crown the cities!

> Moloch whose love is endless oil and stone! Moloch whose soul is electricity and banks! Moloch whose poverty is the specter of genius! Moloch whose fate is a cloud of sexless hydrogen! Moloch whose name is the Mind!

Ginsburg's personal and cultural lament, ruthless and dark as it is, has since been bested by the recent developments in capitalism, the heightening of normative dissociation and an increasingly narcissistic individualism. In Han's analysis "neoliberalism and financial capitalism … are implementing a post-industrial, immaterial mode of production … neoliberalism transforms workers into *entrepreneurs* … People are now master and slave in one. Even class struggle has transformed into an *inner struggle against oneself*" (2017, p. 5).

What before was a wrestle with alienation and exploitation out in the world now has been transformed into an internal arena that obscures the underlying dynamics of material relationships in the world. Where once were visions, dreams, imagination—the depths of interiority—there now are quantifiable data that can be sold.

"Today, we consume not only things themselves but also the emotions that are bound up with things … the aesthetic is colonized by the economic … Values such as justice, humanity or sustainability are exploited for profit … Moral values are consumed as marks of distinction. They are credited to the ego-account, appreciating the value of self. They increase our narcissistic self-respect. Through values we relate not to community but to our own egos" (Han, 2020, p. 5).

Everything now appears through the veil of psychology, the process of dissociation facilitates the vanishing act of material intra-actions and entanglements. The quantification and sale of psyche has entered the limelight of center stage. Han's statement can also serve as warning not to underestimate the powers of Moloch to absorb critical forces of protest and resistance, its symbols, and any solutions proposed outside of the prevailing paradigm.

> **Humans are denuded now, literally naked without the clothing of their natural interconnections, separated from the weave of nature, of dream, of totemic presences and imaginations.**

Profit voracity is its unrelenting hallmark as it continues to transform and reinvent itself while preserving the fundamental exploitative and alienating dynamics.

"Digital psychopolitics transforms the negativity of freely made decisions into the *positivity of factual states (Sachverhalte)*. Indeed, *persons* are being positivized into *things*, which can be quantified, measured and steered … Big Data has announced the end of the *person* who possesses free will" (Han, 2017, p. 12).

Emotions are for sale; self-disclosure is for sale; attention is for sale; charisma is for sale; symbols of protest are for sale ("change the world while drinking tea").

The normative dissociation of contemporary WEIRD societies (Western, educated, industrialized, rich, democratic; Henrich, Heine, & Norenzayan, 2010; Henrich, 2020), the ones that have pursued this path with the greatest rigor and vigor, manifests in multiple dimensions, but the power of Moloch, the abstract value of money, and the imperative to amass and concentrate more wealth, surely is among the causal factors that determine illusory and ungrounded hope or optimism. The pleasurable dopamine kick, often programmed to be addictive, regularly outmaneuvers serotonin processes of contentment and happiness.

The shallow now of the algorithmically determined pleasure devastates any complexity and layering of time, the depth of the well—the generative reach of the three women into the void and the creative play of the three men. Humans are denuded now, literally naked without the clothing of their natural interconnections, separated from the weave of nature, of dream, of totemic presences and imaginations. Denuded means being turned into an easily quantifiable item, psyche for sale. Gift economies, by contrast, established their equivalencies through the richness of personal history, connections, story, and obligations.

Now the gift economy with the tree of life and the well at its center, which helped maintain communal balance, has changed into a notion of "progress": humans are bereft of their natural interconnections, the weave of self into nature and nature into self, of self and dream, of self and totem.

What had been a lurching movement of presences enmeshed with each other became a linear movement of clock time moving forward in a compulsory causal straight line of progress leading into the future. Each step along this progression defines prior steps as ultimately dismissable—incomplete, inferior, or primitive.

IX

Flashes of remembrance

In 1940 the German philosopher Walter Benjamin wrote his *Theses on the Philosophy of History,* shortly before he suicided.[10] It ended up being his last major work and an important piece of his legacy. The themes of redemption, the remembrance of history in its completeness, and the critique of "homogeneous, empty time" (1974, p. 701, Thesis XIII[11]) are central to the theses as he orients to the possibility of liberated descendants.

> The remembrance of indigenous mind can be seen as a redemptive process with the potential of granting us our full past.

The writing of the *Theses* was motivated, as he told correspondents, "by the experience of his generation in the years leading up to Hitler's war" (Eiland & Jennings, 2014, p. 659). Mythic and theological notions are put in the context of politics and the understanding of history. "Only a redeemed mankind is granted the fullness of its past—which is to say, only for a redeemed mankind has its past become citable in all its moments" (Benjamin, 1974, p. 694, trans. Eiland & Jennings). He asserts that "history is the subject of a structure whose site is not homogenous, empty time, but time filled by the presence of the now" or *Jetztzeit* (p. 701, Thesis XIV).

Moments of qualitative and revolutionary change explode the purported continuum of history through awareness constelled in flashes of memory. The historian or historically aware person "takes cognizance of [the revolutionary chance for the oppressed past] in order to blast a specific era out of the homogeneous course of history" (p. 703, Thesis XVII).

In this sense the remembrance or recovery of indigenous mind (and similarly its ongoing performative affirmations by Indigenous peoples all over the world) can be seen as a redemptive process with the potential of granting us our full past, making it both "citable" and relevant for our future.

In the midst of our current crises, truly treacherous moments, we (post)moderns may actually grasp the past in greater fullness as it "flashes up in a moment of danger" (p. 694, trans. Eiland & Jennings, Thesis III). "For every image of the past that is not recognized by the present as one of its own concerns threatens to disappear irretrievably" (p. 695, Thesis V); such as the present fails to recognize Indigenous peoples present and past—they are of no concern for current socio-cultural and economic trajectories and this lack of recognition in the present threatens their disappearance.

These flashes of memory threaten to disappear when the present does not recognize itself in this moment of remembrance, when its difference cannot absorb the flash, when it dissociates because the flash points beyond the fictional line-up of victorious progress. Benjamin describes how these flashes of memory are triggered by crises and imminent dangers.

Benjamin talks about "flashing up" and seizing "hold of a memory as it flashes up in a moment of danger" (p. 695, Thesis V)—an evocation of the power and urgency of the moment—as something seemingly spontaneous and

> Indigenous rituals are among the tools to catalyze and invite such flashing up, such depth of clarity, connection, insight, and remembrance.

involuntary, lightning flashes as warning lights to remember. However, indigenous rituals inducing integrative states of consciousness (through ritual storytelling, chant, song, dance, fasting, or prayer) are among the tools to catalyze and invite such flashing up, such depth of clarity, connection, insight, and remembrance.

Benjamin's theses suggest that hope emerges only once we leave linear notions of history and its pressures to create unitary stories conforming to the ideologies of victors. Lightning flashes open vistas beyond the illusory and deceptive nature of the continuum of history, illuminations for the sake of liberation and visionary sovereignty. Any potential future now begins to make an appearance in different costume. Benjamin states that only those concerned with history and who are inspired by redemptive visions flashing up have the "gift of fanning the spark of hope" (p. 695, Thesis VI). The orientation should be down the line of descendants as image of "liberated grandchildren" (p. 700, Thesis XII).

Barad (2017), in an extensive meditative inquiry, has interpreted Benjamin's discussion of history within her framework of agential realism and quantum field theory, a dialogue with his *Theses* (originally published posthumously in 1942) and Judith Butler's (2012, 2016) discussion of Benjamin's final major work.

Both relativity and quantum theories have undone the prevailing assumptions about reality. The Newtonian worldview—that "equipped with unlimited calculating powers and given complete knowledge of the dispositions of all particles at some instant of time, [we] could use Newton's equations to predict the future, and to retrodict with equal certainty the past, of the whole universe ... [a] rather chilling mechanistic claim" (Polkinghorne, 2002, p. 1)—is in shambles, yet its power in the field of psychology and other disciplines continues undiminished. This is surprising given that these quantum scientific developments have their origins one hundred years ago or so.

Relativity and quantum theories have shown that reality is a field of interactions (or better: intra-actions) where entities or things are nothing but nodes in a web. The properties of these entities only become determinate once there is an intra-action. Entities exist only in relation to something else, not independently. "Everything is what it is only in respect to something else" (Rovelli, 2021, p. 199).

The assumed solidity of the world has disappeared. Our notion of time has been shown to be illusory: there is no singularity (time has a different rhythm in different places), no direction (no flow from past to future, continuity is contingent on our perspective), no independence (spacetime is embedded in the gravitational field), no present ("our present" is our bubble and does not extend throughout the universe), and no continuity (time is granular and discontinuous)—and yet: we live in a web of events.

"The events of the world do not form an orderly queue, like the English. They crowd around chaotically, like Italians. They are events, indeed: change, happening. This happening is diffuse, scattered, disorderly" (Rovelli, 2018, p. 96).

So time has been deconstructed: there is no single time; depending on where you are time passes differently; there is no universal time; time has no directionality, past and future are not part of the elementary equations of the world; the notion of a present no longer works. Instead of certainty we have probability. Reality is no longer what scientists were so certain it is, yet Newtonian assumptions continue to hold sway.

The assumptions of "orthodox, Western psychology," for example, continue to govern the content of mainstream psychology textbooks (see Tart's (1975) inventory of these assumptions that continues to be useful and pertinent). Of course, different quantum theories offer different interpretations, none of them as of now answering all the mysteries of quantum mechanics, yet some more persuasive than others.

Barad (2007) has offered an interpretation of Bohr's philosophy of quantum mechanics in her agential realism account. Any idea that we (post)moderns can place ourselves outside of our world as separated (scientific) observers, that we can be objective mirrors representing something that is going on outside independent of our inner worlds flies out the window. Our knowing practices are inevitably profoundly

> The Newtonian worldview is in shambles, yet its power in the field of psychology and other disciplines continues seemingly undiminished.

enmeshed in the world, they are part of the weave of world creation. Barad's "diffractive methodology is a critical practice for making a difference in the world … The agential realistic approach … eschews representationalism and advances a performative understanding of technoscientific and other naturalcultural practices … knowing, thinking, measuring, theorizing, and observing are material practices of intra-acting within and as part of the world" (p. 90).

Ontology, epistemology, and ethics are understood as inseparable. Knowing is a sociocultural and naturalcultural practice in which the knower is inevitably a part of culture and nature. "Making knowledge is not simply about making facts but about making worlds" and "objectivity is about being accountable to the specific materializations of which we are a part" (p. 91).

The ethical imperative of knowing practices then is accountability for how we (post)moderns are *making our worlds*. We can no longer claim the innocence of a distanced observer, but I have to acknowledge that my practice of creating facts makes and renews worlds. Instead of mirrored facts and "things" we now have phenomena, the results of specific intra-actions; phenomena, literally "appearances," do not exist prior to these intra-actions; reality is indeterminate until intra-actions create determinacies or phenomena (Bohr, 1958, p. 64).

Barad's interpretation of quantum field theory questions identity at any level and seems to leave us (post)moderns with a basket full of conundrums that ultimately constitute obligations for engagement with the world, an intimacy in which two agents are not distinct and separate in interactions, but are intimately constituted in *intra*-actions: "*Quantum*—an originary dis/continuity, not in space through time, but in the iterative intra-active constitution/reconfiguring of spacetime(mattering). Dis/continuity—neither continuity nor discontinuity but rather *cutting together-apart* (one move). *Intra-actions* cut togetherness apart, differentiate-entangle. *Intra-action*, no interaction. Causality reworked: cause does not precede effect, no subject/object; "subject" and "object," "cause" and "effect" are mutually constituted in and through intra-actions in "a 'holding together' of the disparate itself" (2017, p. 44).

This perspective deletes any notions of a separate observer or researcher, instead my presence in the world mutually constitutes the world I am inevitably

> We can no longer claim the innocence of a distanced observer, but I have to acknowledge that my practice of creating facts makes and renews worlds.

a part of—I am intimately connected in an ongoing *intra*-active process in which distinctions and differentiations are created, in which separation and togetherness exist in intimate simultaneity. When I make a distinction (paying attention to the tree I see or asking a research participant a question), I make a perceptual and material/embodied cut, I make a distinction while, at the same time, being an inevitable part of the constitution or materialization of the tree or the answer of my research participant.

It is important here to note that

"quantum phenomena are not restricted to some alleged "micro" domain" (Barad, 2015, p. 419), "quantum mechanics is the most successful and accurate theory in the history of physics, accounting for phenomena over a range of twenty-five orders of magnitude, from the smallest particles of matter to large-scale objects" (2007, p. 110). It is "a common misconception ... that quantum considerations apply only to the micro world" (pp. 109-110).

Rovelli (2021, p. 110) summarizes the relationship between Newtonian and quantum physics as follows: "Quantum theory *incorporates* classical mechanics and our usual vision of the world—as approximations ... The solidity of the classical vision of the world is nothing other than our own myopia. The certainties of classical physics are just probabilities. The well-defined and solid picture of the world given by the old physics is an illusion."

Indigenous science is the twin of quantum field theory. As described by Native scientists (Colorado, 1988, 1994; Bronson, 2004; Cajete, 2016), scientists always are part of the research process as they engage with the alive intelligence of nature; space and time are collapsed as past and present interweave; Indigenous science focuses on relationships with the goal of balance, i.e., normalcy. These notions of research, human beings, and nature are entirely compatible with quantum field theory. The twinship of Indigenous science and quantum theories is apparent when looking at the structure of Indigenous languages and the record of Indigenous storied inquiries and ceremonial proceedings (see Kremer 1996, 1997; see also Jaenke's article in this issue).

Barad, using quantum field theory, describes a sense of time that is multilayered, that has richness and thickness; this is a description of time akin to Indigenous understandings. She blasts open the prevailing understanding of linear time as notions of solidity and identity are deconstructed and multiplicity, alterity, and potential become foundational: "Quantum field theory radically deconstructs the ontology of classical physics ... Even the smallest bits of matter are an unfathomable multitude. Each "individual" always already includes all possible intra-actions with "itself" through all possible virtual others, including those (and itself) that are noncontemporaneous with itself. *That is, every finite being is always already threaded through with an infinite alterity diffracted through being and time.* In/determinacy is an un/doing of identity that unsettles the very foundations of non/being" (2015, p. 401).

The emergence of identity, of phenomena, now is understood as a radically different process that disrupts established lines of causality and linearity, that disturbs the established stories of history and scientific knowledge. The flatness or one-dimensionality of linear, empty time expands into thick layers of time, mutual causalities, and entanglements.

Indigenous science is the twin of quantum field theory.

Quantum field theory is the moment in Western science that allows it to encounter its twin Indigenous science anew and to bring its accomplishments into a healing context as flashes of remembrance allow what was to become what it could be.

Quantum theory reminds us of the realities of the thick now, also integral to Indigenous understandings of time and reality. "Temporal diffraction would be a really rich way to think of Benjamin's notion of *Jetztzeit,* or now-time. *Jetztzeit* is a crystallization of times, of multiple temporalities, blasted out of the continuum of history: a superposition of times—moments from the past—existing in the thick-now of the present moment. And in fact, according to quantum physics the past is always open and can be reconfigured, but never in a way that loses track (i.e., erases the trace) of all that has happened ... *a reconfiguring of time (spacetimemattering) itself*" (2017, p. 33).

This reconfiguration is a moment of healing the split of the original trauma in Eurocentered histories; dissociative practices, the norm in modernity/coloniality, are material practices that lack accountability and enforce interactions leading to hallucinatory visions of reality called "facts."

Quantum field theory is the moment in Western science that allows it to encounter its twin Indigenous science anew and to bring its accomplishments into a healing context as flashes of remembrance allow what was to become what it could be.

As mentioned, Benjamin talks in his theses about "flashing up" and seizing "hold of a memory as it flashes up in a moment of danger." This suggests a different relationship between past, present, and future and different notions of causality. He talks about flashes across time as awakening insight, comprehension, and understanding: the past and the present flash up in a meaningful constellation (rather than the past shining a light on the present or vice versa, as linear understandings suggest). These leaps are awakenings (Benjamin, 1982). The remembrance and affirmation of Indigenous presences, their flashing up creates new constellations for our future in the thick now.

Lightning occurs in ways different from the linear causality naked eye observations suggest. Closer analysis shows that lightning does not simply proceed from cloud to earth in a single direction. Instead, the electrical stepped ladder charges precede lightning as they gesture downward until close to the striking point. This then sends a spark cloudward which leads to the completion with visible lightning.

There is a seeming awareness at the center of this quantum communication in which sender and receiver relate to each other in a nonlocal fashion. "Lightning flashes have no truck with traditional conceptions of causality or a unilinear progressive notion of temporality. An arcing dis/juncture, lightning is a connective thread, a *luminous entanglement* ... an intra-action through which "this" and "that," "here" and "there," "now" and "then" are formed. *Lightning is a jagged dis/continuous "moving toward" with innumerable interruptions*" (Barad, 2017, p. 36).

X

Remembrance and sedimentations of time

Understanding history then as flashes of memory, as Benjamin does and, as I would contend, Indigenous peoples do, means the entanglement of past and present.

"The past remains open to what it might have been: 'What has been is to become'" (Barad, 2017, p. 36). In these flashes of remembrance the past may coincide with the present to such an extent that it comes-to-present, that it becomes recognizable (and citable, as Benjamin would have it). "There exists not-yet-conscious knowledge of the past that has the structure of an awakening when retrieved" (Benjamin, 1982, p. 491, fragment K 1,2 transl. from Benjamin, 1999).

Applying this understanding to remembrances of indigenous presence buried under the linearity of Eurocentrism, to the constellation of tree, well, the three women and men, and their animal relations, helps us (post)moderns recognize it as flash of awakening. It brings the past into the present so that it may become what it might have been—European Indigenous remembrance for the future.

This is the revolutionary potential, the remembrance of an indigenous science and praxis of presence, the remembrance of visionary sovereignty flashing up in the present dangerous moment. The constellation around the tree now is no longer an asphyxiated memory dissected in folklore seminars or celebrated in romantic fantasies; instead it awakens as the "red pill" of coming-to-presence presence (the potentially un/settling truths triggered by the red pill in the movie *The Matrix*, instead of the

> Remembrance of indigenous presence brings the past into the present so that it may become what it might have been.

contented ignorance the blue pill offers).

Benjamin's *Theses* address our understanding of history and progress. "Crucially then, Benjamin's methodology constitutes a *material intervention* into the making of time and history" (Barad, 2017, p. 37).

Similarly, the work (inquiry, research, and ritual practice) of recovery of indigenous mind, the remembrance of visionary sovereignty, the engagement with decolonial practices, is a material intervention into the making of time and history; it is not merely a process in mind or consciousness, no longer a fantasy or fantastical image. It never is merely psychological. Recovery of indigenous mind ritually re/constitutes our mind/matter intra-actions.

Quantum field theory, in Barad's interpretation, deconstructs time's homogeneity and emptiness, thus allowing for, among other things, temporal discontinuity, temporal diffraction, temporal entanglements and the condensation of time into an instant. "The past is not left behind, but rather, is diffracted through/in *Jetztzeit*, the now-time of the present moment" (2017, p. 37). For Benjamin the images flashing up are "offering the historical materialist a revolutionary chance in the fight for the oppressed past" (Barad, 2017, p. 37).

The flashing up of images of indigenous nurturing conversations and ritual presence offer the chance to break the progression of normative dissociation and to fight the history of self-colonization and modernity/coloniality. The trauma of normative dissociation at the root of modernity/coloniality is part of the creation of empty time and linear causality—but remove the dissociation and you remove linear understandings of history and now indigenous constellations flash up and can be remembered.

Butler (2012) discusses Benjamin's notion of remembrance, which "functions in an *inverse* relation to the progressive history he explicitly criticizes ... remembrance works *against* history, undoes its seamless continuity" (p. 102, emphasis added).

The contrast of the work of remembrance is with historical images lined up, forged into a cohesive march forward; this is a line-up in which indigeneity has been destroyed or, what Indigenous presence continues to assert itself, should have been destroyed.

The recovery of indigenous presence in European traditions then involves not only flashes of balance, but "a memory of suffering from another time, it is not exactly one's *own* memory; indeed, such a memory belongs to no one, cannot be understood as anyone's cognitive possession; it is circulating, shattered, lodged in present time; it seems to be a memory carried by things, or the very principle of their breaking up into pieces, perhaps in the form of part-objects, par-

> The trauma of normative dissociation at the root of modernity/coloniality is part of the creation of empty time and linear causality.

tially animated and partially inorganic and strangely divine; something flashes up from this nonconceptualizable amalgam, something that is decidedly not substance: light and shape, sudden, but also, oddly, chips exploding and lodging and flashing up" (Butler, 2012, p. 106).

The three women reach into the source of re/generation and memory and catalyze becoming (*Verðandi*) from exigent obligations (*Skuld*) as dark and light memory (*Urðr*) is re/collected. Part of what flashes up may be Hitler's genocidal distortions, colonial expeditions, witch hunts, Viking raids, missionization, crusades, lynchings, the ships of the Middle Passage, massacres, and more.

The recent physical recovery of pupils' graves at Canadian residential schools catalyzes flashes of remembrance that disrupt the story of "Canada" with Indigenous presence and suffering. Part of what flashes up may be rituals of balancing and healing that have been in hiding, stories that awaken to be re-told.

Benjamin asserts that "the true measure of life is remembrance" (from Butler, 2012, p. 111). Remembrance engages us (post)moderns with our collective shadows, the denied parts of history, with storytelling of suffering and listening to voices that need to be heard. Flashing up is not a mere flat image, it is a constellation that emerges from presence and performative practices with the potential to heal through the depths of remembrance in the thick now of indigenous presence. Remembrance creates wholeness and the possibility of a different world.

Barad (2017) elaborates: "The past is not fixed, not given, but that isn't to say that the trace of all memory can simply be erased. Memory is not a property of individual subjects, but a material condition of the world. *Memory—the pattern of sedimented enfoldings of iterative intra-activity—is written into the fabric of the world.* The world 'holds' the memory of all traces or rather: the world is memory (enfolded materialization)'" (pp. 47-48).

This provides the possibility of recovery of indigenous mind. Recovery, conceived as intra-active mind/matter endeavor, reaches into the material folds of history, it is the recovery of sedimentations in service of the oppressed, in the service of healing self-colonization. The constellation of tree and well with its presences is an image in nature.

Benjamin writes that "nature is Messianic by reason of its eternal and total passing away [*Verhängnis*]" (from Butler, 2016, p. 277). The constellation of hope and passion for cultural healing and redemption is in and of nature. Flashing up is an invocation for a remembrance of the suffering that the denial of indigenous roots in European traditions has caused, a suffering that has been exported as genocide of Indigenous peoples the world over.

Remembrance creates wholeness and the possibility of a different world.

Flashing up are also the images and sounds in caves, the communal tree with its six presences, standing stones, and rock carvings, the old ceremonies of *seiðr*, *útiseta*, *blót*, and others—images of balancing in a world of gift exchanges and multi-layered time.

Flashes of remembrance constellating memories of suffering and the potential for healing recovery imposes obligations and responsibilities. Knowing and being in a paradigm of normative dissociation, a mechanistic universe, enabled colonial endeavors, witch hunts, racist science, and other lethal misadventures. These are manifestations of disconnections and othering.

Recovery reaches into the material folds of history, it is the recovery of sedimentations in service of the oppressed, in the service of healing self-colonization.

By contrast: "Quantum entanglements are not intertwinings of separate entities, but rather irreducible relations of *responsibility*. There is no fixed dividing line between 'self' and 'other', 'past' and 'present' and 'future', 'here' and 'now', 'cause' and 'effect' … Entanglements are not a name for the interconnectedness of all being as one, but rather specific material relations of the ongoing differentiating of the world. Entanglements are *relations of obligation*—being bound to the other—enfolded traces of othering. Othering, the constitution of an 'Other' entails an *indebtedness* to the 'Other', who is irreducibly and materially bound to, threaded through, the 'self'—a diffraction/dispersion of identity. 'Otherness' is an entangled relation of difference (*différance*). Ethicality entails noncoincidence with oneself" (Barad, 2017. pp. 48-49; italics added)

The scientific practices of normative dissociation have left these relations of responsibility behind and fail to see their work of inquiry as relations of obligation; representing or mirroring "reality" obviates any sense of indebtedness to the 'other,' the *inter*action of two separate entities frees scientists from the accountability that bonds of *intra*-action obligate us to. This escape from responsibility enabled the (de)tour of modernity with its wonders and maladies. Quantum field theory affords modernity a turn from its addictive path where quantum theory and Indigenous science can meet in the thick now to actualize what the past can be in the future.

The work of recovery of indigenous mind (and continuing affirmation of visionary sovereignty of decolonial communities) means "taking responsibility to rework the past in the present (which is not the same as denying the past, but on the contrary, of being present to it on behalf of the oppressed and their erased histories)" (Barad, 2017, pp. 63-64). Vizenor's (2020) *Satie on the Seine* is an example of an artistic evocation of flashes of remembrance bringing the past into a healing present which addresses Native American genocide and the Shoah. The novel is the writing of a thick now in which the transformative potential of remembrance is made present through wild imaginings.

Quantum field theory, together with Walter Benjamin's conceptualization of history, has allowed us (post)moderns to understand the work of the recovery of indigenous mind beyond any romantic yearnings: Rather, it is living the responsibility to heal what has been oppressed and denied, the original trauma, the beginning of normative dissociation, the shift from a multilayered sense of visionary sovereignty and presence into the restraints of linear clock time, the linearity of time, history, and memory.

The image of well and tree with its six presences—*time moving and bursting with flashes of memory and presence*—evokes a process of mutual causality as memories of multilayered Indigenous time flash up and create lightning, helping us to connect with the presence of the sedimentations of time.

out of the linear restraints of time into the appearance, the phenomenon of the tree, the three women at source, the three men, and the animals around and about it. It is a shift in my intra-actions of mind and matter, of consciousness and body that facilitates embodied encounters beyond the masterful and thickly boundaried individualistic self.

Coming-to-presence bridges inside out and outside in. Presence tracks in flashes constellating the thick weave of time; tracks in intra-actions between mind and matter, tracks in synchroniza-

Snatches"). This is a published story (Anderson, 2016), but it flashes up now as memory and presence as the portals of sacred places on Maui and elsewhere facilitate re/connections with Indigenous mind.

I became part of this story's process when Apela Colorado shared it with me in conversation as we grappled with its deeper meanings. I received it as gift during this knowledge trade, and I am not merely grateful for it, but the story of *Manuakepa* has gripped and haunted me ever since.[12]

The setting of the story is the West Coast of Maui outside of what is now Lahaina. Its context is a world where the nurturing and balancing relationship with place, humans, and other-and-more-than-humans is guided by the ancient Hawaiian origin story, the *Kumulipo*. The villagers conducted their everyday and ceremonial activities governed by these original instructions.

> Quantum field theory affords modernity a turn from its addictive path where quantum theory and Indigenous science can meet in the thick now to actualize what the past can be in the future.

I have heard Natives talk about echoes across time that can be embodied, a process of mutual causality between ancestors and people living now.

Embodying the image of the tree of life is an act of balancing as memory, obligation, and unfolding create presence in a nurturing conversation, the gifting of humans to humans, the gifting of humans to nature, to more-than-humans, the gifting of nature to humans in a natural motion of visionary sovereignty. The image of the six around the ancestral well catalyzes a precarious tightrope walk and intricate dance, forever incomplete, yet complete in the visionary self humbly offering and dedicating themselves to the process of balancing. It is the natural motion between mind and matter that is captured in the imaginal presence of the tree. We humans live in a world of phenomena where both science and ritual action can hone our presence and perceptual skills.

XI

Confronting death

In my role as inquirer, teacher, and ceremonialist, one of my obligations is a coming-to-presence at my place of hope at the well under the tree. It is the flash of remembrance, the flash of stepping

tions of our different brain parts that plunge mind and consciousness into the depths of renewal and "beingknowing." The flashing up, the presencing of the tree materializes a place of hope and triggers gratitude as the intercalation of times catalyzes renewed ways of coming-to-presence in ceremony and inquiry. It opens possibilities to embody livable worlds of visionary sovereignty as the remembrance of shadow material

The outline of the story of Owl Woman is as follows: Invading warriors arrive in their canoes on the beach at the village of *Kapunakea* (White Spring). The villagers prepare to greet the strangers in their traditional way, but instead of the expected ritual exchange of greetings they are attacked and captured. The invaders then rededicate the temple of Owl Woman above the village, the *Heiau Haluluko'ako'a*, to the war god *Ku* and the first slain villager is ritually

> Remembrance requires commitment to initiation, to enter the dark passages of painful memories, and to confront death for the sake of our present evolutionary challenge.

is balanced in healing actions.

To enter this space is a tall order, for sure, whether for me with my Northern European ancestries or somebody with different ancestries. It requires commitment to initiation, to enter the dark passages of painful memories, and to confront death for the sake of our present evolutionary challenge. And to find the heart, the courage, to embody knowledge ceremonially.

On Maui there is an old story of Owl Woman *Manuakepa* ("Bird which

laid at the altar. They then scour the village *Kapunakea* for food and water and the invaders make plans for the next day to sacrifice the captives who have survived the attack.

Once the warrior chiefs and priests are asleep, Owl Woman frees the captives and they walk backwards quite a distance to the Owl Cave *Anapue'o*. Walking backwards, of course, is intended to confuse the invaders, but it is also a psychospiritual reversal and cleansing as the freed villagers begin an initiatory journey—a journey not of their choosing but the violence of the invaders determined the challenges and clarification of individual and communal intentions.

As they walk, their backwards tracks are recorded in the lava ash. Their escape route then leads them into an underworld journey through a lava tube ending in an encounter with *Moemoe,* the god of long sleep or death.

survival, but a journey that led to the embodiment of presence with soul, of presence woven into place through conversation with all relations.

The confrontation with deep sleep or death, *Moemoe,* is the choice between walking asleep in a soulless warrior culture, dissociated from stories, and practices that catalyze coming-to-presence. *Manuakepa* is the ruthless archetypal

historical moment, as confrontation with the dissociative paradigm of modernity/coloniality, a paradigm which makes war on Indigenous science, practices of coming-to-presence, and soul or spirit connection.

Jung, whose psychology in many ways struggles with Indigenous coming-to-presence from a Eurocentered perspective via alchemy and gnosticism, recognized the importance of historical roots and ancient cultural origins. He takes Odysseus' *nekyia* (Book 11), his descent into the underworld and his encounters with the spirits of the dead, as exemplary in his writings.

> The spirit of Owl Woman guided a journey that led to the embodiment of presence with soul, of presence woven into place through conversation with all relations.

At this point Owl Woman leaves the freed captives to confront death on their own, an inevitable encounter on any journey of initiation (in any true initiation the outcome is uncertain). *Moemoe's* cave opens into the ocean and, after their confrontation with death, the freed captives have to make their way through the waters to get to the village of *Kahapuloa,* their new place of ongoing ritual engagement with the sacred. They are able to reach this special place only in consequence of their initiation. Their embodiment of visionary sovereignty has been asserted, strengthened, and renewed.

Meanwhile Owl Woman returns to her village and demands that the invaders leave, but the warrior chiefs threaten her by stating that they would take her as a prize. *Manuakepa* then raises her arms and begins to chant thunderously, whereupon owls appear from all directions and attack the invaders. The chiefs and the warrior priest escape in a canoe, but it sinks just beyond the reef.

Owl Woman *Manuakepa,* a fierce feminine archetypal force, took the freed villagers on an initiatory journey, a life and death confrontation catalyzed by the warrior invaders, the disruption of ritual time, an event beyond their control. This is not a journey the villagers intended, it was not their choice, they were at the effect of the force of circumstance.

The spirit of *Manuakepa* had been part of the villagers' life and she had been honored at the temple, the *Heiau Haluluko'ako'a*; she guided the journey, which was not a journey of mere

psychopomp that guides the confrontation with the spiritual forces of the underworld. She triggered the purifying reversal of the war paradigm imposed on the balancing paradigm of the *Kumulipo,* she catalyzed their ritual presence in the thick now and led the villagers not only into the darkness of the underworld but to their confrontation with death.

It is important to note that *Manuakepa* leaves at this point, the completion of the initiation, the final steps, now put in the hands of each villager; they needed to rise to their initiatory challenge, they needed to complete without assistance.

After the confrontation with choice, with deep sleep and death, the survivors were then able to enter the village of *Kahapuloa* to embody in ritual and daily life the traditional teachings emerging from the Hawaiian origin story, thus

The *Manuakepa* story is an underworld journey, both externally and internally. *Externally* it is the movement through the darkness of the lava tube, entering the cave of *Moemoe,* and progressing through ocean waters and uphill to the place of lived integration. *Internally* it is the journey from personal fear of survival in the face of invaders to the confrontation with the impersonal forces of the primordial darkness, of death and deep sleep, and, finally, to the integration of the manifestations of the depths of impersonal forces into lived ritual practices in the village of *Kahapuloa.* The villagers accepted the chance offered by Owl Woman *Manuakepa.* They came to understand their obligations and responsibilities in their intra-actions with the world more deeply and committed more deeply.

It is difficult to overestimate the seriousness and severity of such primordial experiences where the outcome is far

> The initiatory encounter with death is outside of the tuition payment for a workshop in shamanic experience.

making the village sacred through their committed intra-actions guided by their original instructions. The life of balancing has been reestablished and, presumably, intensified as a consequence of the confrontation with the darkness of the warrior culture, the destructive force of an invading culture.

The encounter with the archetypal warrior god *Ku* and his representatives can be interpreted, in our current

from assured. The initiatory encounter with death is outside of the tuition payment for a workshop in shamanic experience and initiation.

Jung's discussions of primordial experience acknowledge their overwhelming quality. In fact, he talks about it as a "deep place like the crater of a volcano. My deep interior is a volcano, that pushes out the fiery-molten mass of the unformed and the undifferentiated …

He who enters the crater also becomes chaotic matter, he melts ... The formed in him dissolves and binds itself anew with the children of chaos, the powers of darkness, the ruling and the seducing, the compelling and the alluring, the divine and the devilish. These powers stretch beyond my certainties and limits on all sides, and connect me with all forms and with all distant beings and things, through which inner tidings of their being and their character develop in me" (Jung, 2009, p. 247)

The initiatory encounter with *Moemoe* is an encounter with primordial beginnings, forging connections with "what has been and what is becoming ... a part of matter and formation of the world" (p. 247). It is a profound engagement with the formative powers of reality, the process in which everything is moving, everything is an interrelated event. Time drops out of the equation, indeed, as conceptual husks are discarded and renewed; time is at a standstill as the thick now gets constellated afresh with consequences beyond the ritual encounter.

Jung (1966) comments that "the primordial experience ... is so dark and amorphous that it requires the related mythological imagery to give it form. In itself it is wordless and imageless ... It is nothing but a tremendous intuition striving for expression. It is like a whirlwind that seizes everything within reach and assumes visible form as it swirls upward" (pp. 96-97, para 151).

Indeed, on this initiatory material psycho-spiritual level we have dis/continuity and intra-actions cut togetherness/apart, differentiate and entangle, we have subject and object, cause and effect mutually constituted. In the face of death, *Moemoe,* assumptions are broken and renewed, disparateness and togetherness are part of the conundrum of the underworld journey in the lava tube.

Owl Woman *Manuakepa* is a familiar spirit to the villagers, the "mythological imagery" ritually encountered at the *Heiau Haluluko'ako'a*, the temple, and she manifests as psychopomp to guide the underworld journey into the "dark and amorphous" primordial experience of the villagers. The confrontation and challenge to commitment manifests

> The encounter with the impersonal forces of the primordial realms facilitates lives lived in community in the presence of archetypal spiritual forces.

as *Moemoe,* the god of deep sleep and death. The villagers not only survive this encounter with the paradoxes of darkness, the light in the dark, something which is beyond the personal, but they succeed in integrating this overwhelming encounter with impersonal forces by giving it visible form in their new village life. They have been seized by forces powerful beyond anything their personal power could control, and they bring it into the light of ceremonial practices, the labors of balancing and re-balancing.

Two points are worth reiterating: The first is that this is a communal experience. It begins with the destruction of village life and ends with renewed communal life in a different location. While each villager inevitably has to resolve their own confrontation with *Moemoe* as individual, the result is collective. The encounter with the impersonal forces of the primordial realms facilitates lives lived in community in the presence of archetypal spiritual forces, the external manifestation of internal initiations.

The second additional point worth emphasizing is this: Once *Manuakepa* has guided the villagers to *Moemoe's* cave, she departs. So far Owl Woman has taken charge of the lives of the villagers, but now that they are in the face of death, in the depths of primordial darkness, smelting into the experience of impersonal forces, they need to take charge themselves.

One can find a parallel in Silko's novel *Ceremony*, when the protagonist Tayo who suffers from "the witchery of the swirling darkness" (Wyman, 1973) which, in this particular case, manifests as posttraumatic stress injury, is led in a healing ceremony by the medicine man Betonie. At a certain point Old Betonie states: "It's up to you. Don't let [the forces of the witchery] stop you. Don't let them finish off this world" (p. 152). The villagers are initiated not just to survive, but stop the forces of the invading warriors, just as Tayo stops the witchery of the swirling darkness, the deadly virus of progress as Silko describes it at the center of the novel.

XII

Coming-to-presence at my place of hope

The stark choice presented to the villagers by *Moemoe* is the same our contemporary crises present us (post) moderns with. Are we (post)moderns willing to commit to the creation of livable communities in which we manifest our obligations and responsibilities to

> Are we (post)moderns willing to commit to the creation of livable communities in which we manifest our obligations and responsibilities to our fellow humans and other-and-more-than humans?

our fellow humans and other-and-more-than humans? In which we allow flashes of remembrance to constellate our healing coming-to-presence?

And what does this mean for me as settler on unceded Pomo-Miwok and Wappo lands, as part of a violent history of settlement that has yet to end? How do I hold the ancestral image of tree and well, part of my creation stories and original instructions, on land where my ancestors did not reside before me?

About twenty years ago I was in a ceremony with a circle of Native graduate students in one of the local roundhouses near where I live in California. The ceremony is led by local Pomo-Miwok Elders. As is customary, at the beginning we were asked to introduce ourselves by name and cultural identity.

I was called upon to start and immediately felt quite exposed since I was the only White person in the round. To be the first to introduce myself kicked up instant fear in me. I took the risk of introducing myself with the complexities of my cultural origins—as a river person, with my grandmother's and other family names; the places of my ancestral lines reaching from my birthplace around the Baltic Sea on my mother's side and down the Rhine Valley into the Alsace-Lorraine on my father's; I acknowledged the tribal peoples by the River Elbe where I grew up with the oldest names I knew. Once I had stood by my ancestry publicly something unexpected happened.

Having spoken my fear subsides, but I remain in a state of heightened attention. Then I notice two things coming together inside. My awareness settles into my body with startling comfort as ribcage and ribcage join. Out of the shift arises comfort, not merely the cessation of anxiety. A novel sensation spreads. My physical being and who I think I am merge and meld into a new form of congruence. Somatic consonance. The reunion of fragments. It is a homecoming. This is the label I attach to the joining of story and story. Homecoming. The dizzying interior space of one ribcage encounters reassurance in the vertiginous riches the other offers. Homecoming. An insufficient word for sure, romantic. Homecoming as process, being at home in an unfolding process of conversation. This homecoming is also shocking, since I have never been there. Yet no other word describes my feeling of coming-to-presence more accurately.

The ritual I was part of is what allowed me to make home, what helped me heal my shame of German history, the Shoah, witch hunts, and violent patriarchal distortions. It helped me confront the history of California missions and the innumerable massacres of Native peoples throughout the state.

I have fasted for the tree and for raven messenger, I have made offerings on sites of concentration camps and massacres. I now stand un/comfortably, with some confidence and some shame, at the dangerous intersection of remembrance of my own ancestral roots, the acknowledgment of the Native peoples where I live, and the possibilities of personal and cultural meeting in a balancing process. Standing at my ancestral place I hope to increase my capacities to hold the innumerable conundrums discussed, to dwell in hope when hopelessness appears.

The image of the tree evokes a sense of self and collectivity that is heterogeneous and includes humans, non-humans, and other-than-humans or more-than-humans. It is an image beyond and outside the Anthropocene, an image for the post-human world. The image and the movement of mind, matter, and time it evokes, is non-anthropocentric.

Apffel-Marglin (2011) describes ceremonies or rituals as "actions that create continuity in the sense of weaving or reweaving livable common worlds" (p. 163). It is a weaving to create and regenerate livable worlds that in their origins are connected with specific ecologies and histories. Ritual or ceremonial action in whatever form is designed "to synchronize the awareness of different participants—humans, non-humans, and other-than-humans—enabling them to weave each other into a continuous world, a regenerated world" (p. 164).

This is a worldview and performative practice that supersedes the modern worldview in which the observer and the observed, facts and values, ethics and praxis are neatly separated. Instead we can come-to-presence of the weaving of *intra-actions*, movements of nurturing and being nurtured, *criar y dejarse criar*, where all the components of what constitutes reality and evokes reality are not givens, but parts of an *intra-active* conversation creating presence.

The tree and the well, the three women—*Verðandi*, the Woman of Becoming, *Skuld*, the Woman of Obligation arising from sedimentation, and *Urðr*, the Woman of Remembrance—and the three men—*Oðr*, holding intention and inspiration, *Hœnir*, holding the process of reasoning and the mysteries of silence, and Loki holding chance and indeterminacy—together with the animals about the tree and the bridge leading from the top of the tree into other worlds as the roots of the tree open to primordial experiences—these are images from my ancestral communal universe.

These origin and creation stories "are the most important accounts any society can tell itself about itself" (Nabokov,

2015, p. IX). They constitute original instructions, "sacredly revealed, repositories of ultimate truths, and arbiters of existential questions." They are humanly, creatively created connections between worlds that need to be maintained through ritual participation. They emerge from a profound intimacy with the surrounding world, the local ecology. They have the powers of re/generation and healing.

Cosmos and non/human, mind and matter, past and present are intra-acting. The ancient Indo-European root for wholeness and integrity is *kailo-* (Lincoln, 1986) and the work of healing and balancing means engaging with a process of coming-to-presence. Knowing my ancestral tree and well and all the beings around it opens the chance to become part of constellating flashes of healing memories on settled land. The *aurr* lifted by the three women from the well then becomes obligatory remembrance which inspired reasoning can chance to embody.

My "homecoming ceremony" shifted my conversations with Indigenous acquaintances, friends, and colleagues. Stories shared became part of an egalitarian knowledge trade in initiatory encounters.

Standing atop one of the Pueblo katsina mountains, I shared my ancestral image with the Acoma Antelope Priest I encountered on his pilgrimage to make offerings to the spirits. I shared it with a Patwin medicine man in the Central Valley of California. In these and other situations the conversation shifted from the uneasy rub between Indigenous and modern/colonial paradigms to a shared space of mutual recognition through ancestral imagery. These conversations were initiatory conversations for me, conversations in which I surely was the much younger brother.

Flashes of memory, whether in dreams, during inquiry, or as a result of ceremony, connect our emotional and rational brain parts in this labor of remembering and presencing. Together with the riches of traditions and ceremonial or ritual practices they facilitate bridging, afford opportunities for a re-inspiriting of indigenous understandings or original instructions of humans living in a particular place.

Such re-inspirations honor traditions, those of local provenance and those that have migrated into a place, by confronting not just needs for personal healing, but collective shadow material, thus renewing traditions in wild (as in: connected to wilderness or nature), creative inspirations and imaginings that re-member and en-vision the future using our "natural reason," i.e., "an active sense of presence, the tease of the natural world in native stories" (Vizenor, 2003).

Our present collective pathologies—as manifest in individuals, communities, and ecologies—may find healing remedies in the rub between personal dreaming and visionary experiences, between ancestral stories of place and migrations, and between practices committed to resolving personal and collective shadow and traumas into creative and imaginative presences that heal. Such work addresses historical violations not for the sake of revenge but the healing of a restorative justice for the future. This means bridging our dreams and ancestral stories into the history of place. For its success such a practice can never be merely individualistic, but it needs to welcome, invite, and strive for communal dialogue and conversation (a dialogue between multiple communities in one place).

Thus traditions may be renewed and grounded in deep dreaming with ancestors and memory of place. Such practice supersedes scientism and religious or spiritual fundamentalisms by bringing the indigenous science contained in each tradition into a life that honors the spirit of inquiry for the sake of human freedom and creativity.

Our initiatory and evolutionary challenge is to bring the parts which modernity/coloniality mistakenly thought could be safely left behind, forward into full presence. The twins Indigenous science and quantum field theory can help us correct pathological thinking as the smooth linearity of time progressing is exploded by flashes of remembrance constellating a depth of presence and obligation to life largely forgotten by non-indigenous people.

Moemoe, the god of deep sleep and death is staring in our face. And in this, there is hope.

Coda

The boy, his back leaning against the well under the tree, he stretches his bow and aims into the chasm that circumscribes his presence. The arrow carries his wondering, unknowing incised in his flesh.

Images: Jürgen Werner Kremer

> Our present collective pathologies may find healing remedies in the rub between personal dreaming and visionary experiences, between ancestral stories of place and migrations, and between practices committed to resolving personal and collective shadow and traumas into creative and imaginative presences that heal.

Endnotes

1. Vizenor (1998) describes visionary sovereignty as follows: "The sovereignty of motion is mythic, material, and visionary, not mere territoriality, in the sense of colonialism and nationalism" (p. 183). "Sovereignty as motion and transmotion is heard and seen in oral presentations, the pleasures of native memories and stories, and understood in the values of human and spiritual motion in languages ... The sovereignty of motion means the ability and the vision to move in imagination and the substantive rights of motion in native communities" (p. 182).

2. Bloch was not appreciated by the fundamentalist orthodoxies perpetrated behind the Iron Curtain, his discussion of spiritual traditions was not appreciated. He ultimately had to leave the GDR, where he had voluntarily settled after World War Two, and live in West Germany.

3. Gratitude to Leny Strobel for conversations that facilitated my insights.

4. In my first attempts to conceptualize this framework as participatory or shamanic concourse (Kremer, 1992) this was not the case and, although the general idea still holds, it was rather incomplete. Let me begin by tracking my inquiry and quest here in broad brushstrokes.

5. For extensive references that form the basis of my description here, please see Bjarnadóttir & Kremer, 1998/99.

6. In other traditions, the *Lighting of the Seventh Fire*, or the end of the Mayan calendar identify similar challenges and opportunities.

7. Marvel's (2021) television series *Loki* can be interpreted as the struggle between the modern colonial control of the timeline by the "Time Variance Authority" to prevent the threats of time variants.

8. Vizenor (1998, p. 15) describes "transmotion" as follows: "The connotations of transmotion are creation stories, tometic visions, reincarnation, and sovenance; transmotion, that sense of native motion and an active presence, is *sui generis* sovereignty."

9. This section leans heavily on Barad's (2017) discussion of time, incl. her use of Walter Benjamin's theses on history (1974) and Butler's (2012) discussion of Benjamin's Messianic politics. Rovelli's (e.g., 2016, 2018, 2021) interpretation of quantum theory have also been helpful.

10. This and the subsequent were catalyzed by Karen Barad's *What Flashes Up: Theological-Political-Scientific Fragments* (2017), I gratefully acknowledge this source of inspiration.

11. Unless otherwise noted, all translations of the *Theses* are by Harry Zohn.

12. I am indebted to Apela Colorado for sharing unpublished material of her work in progress.

References

Adorno, T. W. (1980). *Minima moralia (Gesammelte Schriften 4)*. Suhrkamp Verlag.

Akhtar, A. (2020). *Homeland elegies*. Back Bay Books.

Anderson, M. (2016). *The storied places of West Maui*. North Beach – West Maui.

Apffel-Marglin, F., with PRATEC. (1998). *The spirit of regeneration*. Zed Books.

Apffel-Marglin, F. (2011). *Subversive spiritualities*. Oxford University Press.

Artaud, A. (1983). *Die Tarahumaras. Revolutionäre Botschaften*. Rogner & Bernhard.

Atkins, D. B., & Bauer, W. J. (2021). *We are the land – A history of Native California*. University of California Press.

Barad (2007) *Meeting the universe halfway*. Duke University Press.

Barad (2017). What flashes up: Theological-political-scientific fragments. In C. Keller & M.-J. Rubenstein (eds.), *Entangled worlds*. Fordham University Press.

Barad, K. (2015). Transmaterialities. *GLQ: A Journal of Lesbian and Gay Studies, 21*(2), 387-422.

Baudrillard, J. (1993). *The transparency of evil*. Verso.

Beckett, S. (1983). *Nohow on*. Grove Press.

Beckett, S. (1976). *I can't go on, I'll go on*. Grove Press.

Benjamin, W. (1974). *Über den Begriff der Geschichte (Theses on the philosophz of history), Gesammelte Schriften Band I(2)*, pp. 691-704. Suhrkamp Verlag. Translation: H. Zohn, (1968), *Illuminations*, Schocken Books.

Benjamin, W. (1982). *Das Passagen-Werk. Gesammelte Schriften Band V*.

Benjamin, W. (1985). *Kapitalismus als Religion*. In: *Gesammelte Schriften Band VI, pp. 100ff*. Translation from *Selected Writings* (1996), The Belknap Press of Harvard University Press.

Benjamin, W. (1999). *The arcades project*. The Belknap Press of Harvard University Press.

Beuys, J. (1990). *Joseph Beuys in America*. Four Walls Eight Windows.

Bjarnadóttir & Kremer, 1998/99 The cosmology of healing in vanir Norse mythology. In: H. Kalweit & S. Krippner (eds.), *Yearbook of Cross-Cultural Medicine and Psychotherapy 1997*, 127-176. Germany: Verlag für Wissenschaft und Bildung.

Bloch, E. (1977). *Das Prinzip Hoffnung (The Principle of Hope)*, Gesamtausgabe 5 (3 volumes). Suhrkamp.

Bohr, N. (1958). *Atomic physics and human knowledge. The philosophical writings of Niels Bohr, Vol. 3*. Ox Bow Press.

Borges, J. L. (1999). *Selected poems*. Penguin Books.

Bronson, M. (Ed.) (2004). *The language of spirituality. ReVision, 26*(3).

Butler, J. (2012). *Parting ways*. Columbia University Press.

Butler, J. (2016). One time traverses another: Benjamin's "Theological-Political Fragment". In: C. Dickinson & S. Symons, *Walter Benjamin and theology*. Fordham University Press.

Cajete, G. (2016). *Native science: Natural laws of interdependence*. Clear Light Publishers.

Celan, P. (1988). *Poems of Paul Celan* (Transl. M. Hamburger). Persea Books.

Cixous, H. (1993). *Three steps on the ladder of writing*. Columbia University Press

Colorado, A. (1994). Indigenous science and western science – a healing convergence. Presentation at the World Sciences Dialog I. New York City, April 25-27.

Colorado, A. (1988). Bridging Native and Western Science. *Convergence, XXI*(2/3), 49-67.

Colorado, A. (2014). The ceremonial stepping stones of ethnoautobiography. In: J. W. Kremer, *Ethnoautobiography*. ReVision Publishing.

Cox Richardson, H. (2021, April 30). Letters from an American.

Ehrenreich, B. (2007). *Dancing in the streets*. Holt.

Eiland, H., & Jennings, M. W. (2014). *Walter Benjamin – A critical life*. The Belknap Press of Harvard University Press.

Forbes, J. (2008). *Columbus and other cannibals: the Wetiko disease of exploitation, imperialism, and terrorism*. Seven Stories Press.

Fukuyama, F. (1992). *The end of history and the last man*. Free Press.

Fukuyama, F. (2018). *Identity*. Farrar, Straus and Giroux.

Ginsburg, A. (2006). *Collected poems 1947 – 1997*. HarperCollins.

Han, B.-C. (2017). *Psychopolitics*. Verso.

Han, B.-C. (2020). *The disappearance of rituals*. Polity.

Harris, N. B. (2018). *The deepest well*. Houghton Mifflin Harcourt.

Harvey, D. (2014). *Seventeen contradictions and the end of capitalism*. Oxford University Press.

Harvey, D. (2018). *Marx, capital, and the madness of economic reason*. Oxford University Press.

Hawkins, B. (2002). The washing of the word, the washing of the world: Paul Celan and the language of sanctification. *SHOFAR, 20*(4), 36 – 63.

Henrich, J. (2020). *The weirdest people in the world*. Farrar, Straus and Giroux.

Henrich, J., Heine, S. J., & Norenzayan, A. (2010). The WEIRDest people in the world? *Behavioral and Brain Sciences, 33*(2-3), 61-83.

Hillman, J. (1975). *Re-Visioning Psychology*. Harper.

Hillman, J. (1985). Notes on white supremacy: The alchemy of racism. Spring, 29-58

Jung, C. G. (1959). *Aion*. Princeton University Press, Bollingen Series.

Jung, C. G. (1966). *The spirit in man, art and literature*. Princeton University Press, Bollingen Series.

Jung, G. G. (2009). *The Red Book*. W. W. Norton & Company.

Kailo, K. (2012). Ecospiritual Action and the the Gift Imaginary. In: Brenda Cranney and Sheikla Molloy (eds.), *A Union of Spirituality and Politics - Woman studies: an Introductory Reader*. Inanna Press

Kingsley, P. (2020). *Reality*. Catafalque Press.

Kremer, J. W. (Ed.) (1997). Indigenous science. *ReVision, 19*(3).

Kremer, J. W. (Ed.) (1996), Indigenous science. *ReVision, 18*(3).

Kremer, J. W. (1992). The dark night of the scholar. *ReVision, 14*(4), 169-178 & Whither dark night of the scholar? *ReVision, 15*(1), 4-12.

Laks, A., & Most, G. W. (2016). *Early Greek philosophy. Western Greek Thinkers, Part 2*. Harvard University Press.

Lear, J. (2006). *Radical hope*. Harvard University Press.

Lincoln, B. (1986). *Myth, cosmos, and society*. Harvard University Press.

Madley, B. (2016). *An American genocide*. Yale University Press.

Mignolo, W. D. (1995). *The darker side of the renaissance*. The University of Michigan Press.

Mignolo, W. D. (2011). *The darker side of Western modernity*. Duke University Press.

Mignolo, W. D., & Walsh, C. E. (2018). *On decoloniality*. Duke University Press.

Mishra, P. (2020). *Bland fanatics*. Farrar, Straus and Giroux.

Mohawk, J. (1991). As recorded by C. Spretnak.

Morin, E. (2017). *Beckett's political imagination*. Cambridge University Press.

Murakami, H. (1998). *Windup Bird Chronicles*. Knopf Doubleday.

Nabokov, P. (2015). Introduction. In: *The origin myth of Acoma Pueblo*. Penguin.

Neiman, S. (2019). *Learning from the Germans – Race and the memory of evil.* Farrar, Straus and Giroux.

Polkinghorne, , J. (2002). *Quantum theory.* Oxford University Press.

Rovelli, C. (2016). *Seven brief lessons on physics.* Riverhead Books.

Rovelli, C. (2018). *The order of time.* Riverhead Books.

Rovelli, C. (2021). *Helgoland.* Riverhead Books.

Sarris, G. (2017). *How a mountain was made.* Heyday.

Shotwell, A. (2016). *Against purity: Living ethically in compromised times.* University of Minnesota Press.

Silko, L. M. (1977). *Ceremony.* Penguin.

Simpson, L. B. (2020). *Noopiming.* University of Minnesota Press.

Tart, C. T. (1975). Some assumptions of orthodox, Western psychology. In: C. T. Tart, *Transpersonal psychologies.* Psychological Processes.

Tisdall, C. (1979). *Joseph Beuys.* Thames and Hudson.

Tomasello, M. (2014). *A natural history of human thinking.* Harvard University Press.

Vaughan, G. (1997). *For-giving.* Plain View Press.

Vaughan, G. (2015). *Homo donans.* VandA. epublishing.

Vaughan, G. (Ed.) (2019). *The maternal roots of the gift economy.* Inanna.

Vizenor, G. (2003). *Wordarrows.* University of Nebraska Press.

Vizenor, G. (2020). *Satie on the Seine.* Wesleyan University Press.

Vizenor, V. (1998). *Fugitive poses.* Lincoln, Nebraska: University of Nebraska Press.

Wyman, L. C. (1973). *The red antway of the Navaho.* Museum of Navaho Ceremonial Art

Žižek, S. (2008). *In defense of lost causes.* Verso.

Impermanence
   –for Emrich

This morning, I wake to greet the 69th
season since my birth. Young trees
outside my urban hut are arrayed with

fragile newborn leaves, shedding the
last withered leaves of winter, all dancing
in the breeze. To the East, the

newborn sun rises above the ridge of
Sonoma Mountain as a giant white
egret glides gracefully along the base,

just beyond brown wintered pastures.
Beyond the greening horizon, monks and
laymen sit like Buddhas, chant sutras—

minds emptied, stroll the temple grounds
amid newborn riots of delicate pink
cherry blossoms on the path to Suzuki-

roshi's shrine. Spring prematurely
born in depths of winter, signs of
transience everywhere: even (global)

climate can change.

               —*R.L. Boyer*

Created by the United Nations General Assembly in 1980, the University for Peace trains future leaders to explore and formulate strategies and practices to address the causes of problems affecting human and global wellbeing.

The Master of Arts Degree in Indigenous Science and Peace Studies (ISPS)

This program examines the traditions of Indigenous peoples of the world and their generations-tested ways of making peace and balancing societies, offering a roadmap to prosperity that respects individual and collective rights, local development models and environmental solutions.

IS IT FOR YOU?

- Do you want to help solve the global crises facing humanity by transforming outdated paradigms?

- Are you inspired to learn how Indigenous knowledge and Western science can be employed across disciplines and professions to transform crises and conflicts, and build peace?

- Do you want to spend a year studying in an academically challenging environment, at a global university with students, faculty, and Indigenous Elders from around the world?

WHAT WILL YOU LEARN?

Steeped in Indigenous Knowledge Systems and methodologies, the Master's Degree in Indigenous Science and Peace Studies (ISPS) will train you to be an insightful researcher and practitioner who understands the central issues that impact diplomacy, policymaking, and community work.

- Learn a synthesis of indigenous scientific research and theory relevant to the transformation of conflicts.

- Gain a diversity of perspectives that impact peace, justice, security, sovereignty, and reconciliation.

- Obtain detailed knowledge of the United Nations System and related institutions, procedures and instruments that affect decision-making regarding Indigenous peoples and traditional knowledge.

This course enables students to become more effective policymakers, community workers, diplomats, activists, and communicators who create change to renew life on earth.

**For more information, go to www.upeace.org/programmes/indigenous-science-and-peace.
To apply, go to www.upeace.org/pages/apply-admission.**

The main campus of the University for Peace is located in San Jose, Costa Rica

Loving Life

Karen Jaenke

Balance

I am the kind of person who likes to first comprehend the Whole, in order to best know how to engage with it—the Whole of the human psyche, with the full range of subjective states that humans experience; the Whole story of humanity's existence on the planet; the Whole of life and its hidden secrets of vitality; the Whole of the cosmos and its essential principles and processes. Undeniably, this need to know, to discover the secrets of the Whole, stems from the radical shattering of Being that occurred at my beginnings. The scattering of myself at birth into so many shards in turn gave birth to a longing to gather the fragments back into a Whole.

With this bit of autobiographical context, let me affirm that the foundation for my hope resides in this relentless search for holistic understanding, together with the intention of aligning my personal existence with the greater Whole. So here, I take the reader on a journey to Hope, via the winding path of seeking to comprehend the Whole, along with sharing my method for placing my own existence in alignment with the greater Whole. For surely there is no better lifejacket in this outrageous adventure of life than orienting one's being toward the greater Whole. Life is something akin to a river-rafting trip, with calm spaces of floating and gliding, interspersed by dangerous white water rapids, when moment-to-moment survival can become uncertain.

Since the journey to comprehend the Whole is an ambitious undertaking, with meandering tributaries diverging from yet leading back to the main current of Wholeness, let me share the final destination of this expedition. Simply put, our hope dwells in loving life. And loving life means aligning our personal lives with the dynamic principles of vitality and creative energy that flow equally through the cosmos and the vessels of our own bodies.

Yet our human predicament on this planet today is so dire that objective,

---

Karen Jaenke, Ph.D. has served as Chair of the Consciousness & Transformative Studies Masters degree program at National University (formerly John F. Kennedy University) since 2013. In 2016, she launched and built the online modality for the Consciousness & Transformative Studies program, giving this cutting-edge program global reach. In 2021, she added to this leading-edge curriculum a Coach Training Program certified by the International Coaching Federation. Formerly, she served as Director of the Ecotherapy Certificate Program at JFKU (2011-14) and Dissertation Director at the Institute of Imaginal Studies in Petaluma, CA (2001-2008). An Executive Editor of ReVision: Journal of Consciousness and Transformation, she has edited journals and published articles on the topics of Imaginal Psychology, Shamanism and the Wounded West, Earth Dreaming, and Places of Hope, as well as numerous articles on dreams and consciousness. A repeat presenter at the International Association for the Study of Dreams, Society for the Study of Shamanism, and Science and Nonduality conferences, her creative vision synthesizes dreamwork, indigenous ways of knowing, subtle body awareness, living systems theory, and flow states..

scientific touchstones are needed to guide our personal and collective journey forward. Living systems theory can guide us in knowing, in an objective and practical sense, how to love life.

Let me begin with a personal story of how I arrived at adopting living systems theory as a personal practice. A number of years ago, while working as director of an Ecotherapy graduate program, I was actively imbibing, as a steady diet, the latest news of ecological devastation. This news, now so ubiquitous, continuously cast forth dire statistics, such as:

- Since 1970, humanity has wiped out 60% of mammals, birds, fish and reptiles, an annihilation of wildlife that threatens civilization itself.
- Since the Paris agreement was signed in 2016, the world has seen the five hottest years on record. The vast and growing consumption of food and resources by the global human population is destroying the web of life.

Ingesting this cataclysmic news as a regular meal can quickly submerge one in depression, despair and apathy, tinged by fear and guilt. And if we know one thing about ourselves as a species, we are rarely inspired or energized towards creative action by the darker emotions. Humanity will only find motivation for sustained meaningful action through positive emotional states, like joy and pleasure. We need access to natural sources of joy and pleasure that support and empower us to live and act in alignment with the needs of the planet. For humanity to make sacrifices and adopt sustainable lifeways that accord with planetary wellbeing, our innate constitutional need for pleasure must be tapped. The intersection of human well-being with planetary well-being is the sweet spot.

Amidst my depressive dilemma of drinking in the doomsday news of impending ecological collapse, a new thought suddenly appeared. "The Earth is a living system, and so am I. If I desire planetary wellbeing, then my own wellbeing as a living system surely must receive equal attention. By attending to my own balance as a living system, I learn about the requirements for planetary balance." Human microcosm and planetary macrocosm, intrinsically intertwined as living systems, together thrive or fail according to an underlying set of dynamic principles. In this simple formula, I found an initial ray of hope.

Amidst our planetary crisis, with the COVID-10 pandemic as a symptom and warning of civilizational imbalances, I found a new way forward by orienting myself according to the principles of living systems theory, which inform us about the vitality and dynamism of all

> Our human predicament on this planet today is so dire that objective, scientific touchstones are needed to guide our personal and collective journey forward. Living systems theory can guide us in knowing, in an objective and practical sense, how to love life.

living systems—from the tiniest cell to the cosmos as a whole. Within this unifying framework of self and Earth, co-joined as living systems, my first obligation became balancing myself as a living system. This self-balancing could then serve as a touchstone for my attitude and actions towards all other living systems, including the Earth. Thus a personal inquiry was born: what does it mean to relate to oneself as a living system?

The approach of aligning my own life with the principles of living systems bestowed hope and bore early fruits.

I applied the living systems approach in the workplace, in my position as a program chair in the university setting. Understanding the academic program that I was overseeing as a living system, with an eye to the health of the Whole, I sought to welcome feedback from all parts of the system—especially students and the larger university system. Over a number of years, this led to the dramatic growth in student enrollments at a time when many programs at the university were shrinking and disappearing. The takeaway lesson was that applying living systems theory to immediate contexts can guide a pathway towards growth and well-being.

Typically, living systems theory is not applied to the individual human life, nor to the processes of human subjectivity, nor has it been considered as the basis for a spiritual or transformative practice. My turn towards living systems theory as a guide for living parallels a disturbing sense that the trajectory of human civilization as a whole is dangerously distant from the mark of sustainability. Most current human systems, largely rooted in egoic consciousness rather than a thoughtful surrender to the principles of balance, cannot be relied upon to generate well-being across the planet. My despair about the course of human systems and civilization prompted this turn towards the intelligence of nature.

A recent dream depicts my desire to approach the thoughts of nature. In the dream, I am visiting a handsome,

> The intersection of human well-being with planetary well-being is the sweet spot.

articulate man who is a successful architect, designing tiny homes for compacted spaces. While he aspires to an Ivy League MBA, he lives in an underground grotto with a waterfall, and has befriended a bear who visits him there. Seeing their congenial relationship, I am not afraid. Then the bear transforms into a bear-man, with hybrid features of both.

The intimate contact with the bear in this earthy underground space, the friendly, non-fearful, non-otherizing attitude between man and bear, and the interchangeable features of bear and man,

SUMMER/FALL 2020   35

all together suggest an intimacy with nature, a human capacity for instinctual knowing and comfortability within nature. I awoke from the dream in a most blessed place, encompassed by a vitalizing fountain of energy, pleasantly percolating throughout my mind and body.

With the dream is a sense of an animate, creative intelligence infusing my entire body. The intelligence of nature is like this, infused into every particle of being, while perpetually generating aliveness.

While the man in the dream possessed the upper world markings of success and status, what intrigued me was his deep unconventional ties to the underworld. Translating the constructs of the upperworld and underworld onto the plane of the human body, the upperworld corresponds to the upper body, while the underworld corresponds to lower body. This underworld is accessed as human consciousness descends into and circulates through the lower recesses of the body. I shall return to this notion of consciousness circulating throughout the entire body, and its role in bestowing natural pleasure, towards the end of this piece.

While the dream conveys the feeling tone of what I am seeking, in this article I draw mostly upon rational, upper world understandings of the intelligent design of nature, since today, humanity lives and thinks largely in the categories of the upper world. With the narrowing time frame for correcting our human maladaptation to the ecology of the planet, the rigor of a scientifically-grounded approach is sorely needed. Comprehending the basic principles of living systems offers an initial step, preceding a second step of rigorously applying these principles to the individual human life.

A living system is defined as an integrated Whole whose essential properties cannot be reduced to those of its parts; the properties of the system arise from the interactions and relationships between the parts. Furthermore, in the systems view, the world is an integrated Whole rather than merely a collection of separate entities, with recognition of the fundamental interdependence of all phenomena. A main premise is that each individual component of a system impacts and is impacted by every other component of the system. Thus, change at any one point eventually influences the total system, along with its component parts.

Why Living Systems Theory?

Beyond my personal experience, there are any number of objective reasons why living systems theory offers a beacon of hope to humanity at this time. In the words of Fritjof Capra:

> In the coming decades, the survival of humanity will literally depend on our ecological literacy, on our ability to understand the basic principles of ecology and to live accordingly. None of our global problems—energy shortages, environmental degradation, climate change, economic inequality, violence and war—can be understood in isolation. They are systemic problems, interconnected and interdependent. What we need is system solutions… The systems approach is a powerful tool that can make all the difference. This is a lesson we can learn from nature" (2019).

Capra then asks, "If we have all the knowledge and technology to build a sustainable world, why don't we do it?" The answer to this question very much depends on appreciating the deeper sources of human motivation, which cannot just entail an appeal to rationality and morality, but must tap deeper into the wellspring of imagination and affect, especially joy and pleasure. Neither the darker emotions of fear, despair, and guilt, nor a purely rational or moral approach to doing the "right thing" are sufficient motivating drivers for human beings. The sustained motivation and action now needed to turn the tide of our current societal and ecological crises can be derived from contacting natural

> The sustained motivation and action now needed to turn the tide of our current societal and ecological crises can be derived from contacting natural wellsprings of vitality, and the cascade of positive emotions that personal wellbeing generates.

Mergansers on the bay

wellsprings of vitality, the cascade of positive emotions that personal wellbeing generates, as well as the energizing potential of shadow work.

Living systems theory is above all, a life science, discerning the hidden laws of vitality, while being grounded in the scientific enterprise that aspires to objectivity. The living systems framework has been tested and fruitfully applied to a wide range of scientific disciplines. The emergence of systems thinking in the early 20th century catalyzed its progressive spread across scientific disciplines—from ecology, to biology, to cybernetics, to computer science, to mathematics.[1] Simultaneous to these developments, the new physics of the 20th century ushered in a complementary worldview. Overturning the earlier Newtonian focus on solid material particles, quantum physics discovered that at the subatomic level, nature does not show us any isolated building blocks, but rather a complex web of relationships among the various parts of a unified whole. Subatomic particles display dynamism, continually changing into one another, in a continuous, fluid dance of energy. Moreover, subatomic particles turn out to not be discrete grains of matter but probability patterns and interconnections, in an inseparable cosmic web that includes the human observer and his or her consciousness (Capra, 2014).

In the 20th century, systems theory emerged as a coherent theoretical framework uniting the various scientific disciplines, by describing the dynamic principles of all living systems as well as the basic operations of the universe at all levels of organization from the micro to the macro. With all the major biological, physical and social sciences fruitfully adopting living systems theory, the elevation of systems theory to the status of a comprehensive scientific framework is justified through its unique capacity to integrate disparate disciplines—in comprehension of the Whole. Living systems theory offers a unique coherent framework, providing a unifying scientific theory and comprehensive approach to all sciences (Capra, 2014).

Yet consciously embracing living systems theory necessitates overturning our standard view of the world. The mechanistic metaphor that dominated the scientific worldview throughout the last four centuries of the modern era today is being replaced by this holistic and ecological worldview, with a change from seeing the world as a machine to seeing the world and life as a network. The former Newtonian focus on substance and matter is giving way to a living systems emphasis on pattern, form, and relationship, leading to notions of order, organization, relationship, interdependence, and balance (Capra, 2014).

When cracks appear in the edifice of manmade institutions, and in times of escalating societal turbulence, reassurance and stability can be discovered by remembering our elemental roots in nature, the enduring foundations of life. The primordial features and functions of natural living systems, as distinct from the scaffolding of human civilization built atop it, offers a ground of hope in the substrate that governs life itself. Since the human body belongs to nature, cultivating intimacy with the dynamics of our own bodies offers a portal to kinship with the natural world and the deep intelligence coded into billions of years of evolutionary history.

Contemporary living systems is also heir to an ancient tradition, the time-honored wisdom of indigenous peoples. Both living systems theory and indigenous knowledge are anchored in the core principle of balance. Other terms signifying balance are equilibrium, coherence, sustainability, vitality, well-being, and harmony.

Oneida elder Apela Colorado introduces the term *indigenous science* to highlight the life science of balance practiced by indigenous peoples. "Just like western science, indigenous science relies upon direct observation; there are tests to ensure validity and data are used for forecasting and generating predictions.... Unlike western science, the data from indigenous science are not used to control the forces of nature, instead, the data tell us ways and means of accommodating nature" (Colorado, 1994).

Colorado identifies nine tenets of indigenous science.

1. The indigenous scientist is an integral part of the research process and there is a defined process for insuring this integrity.
2. All of nature is considered to be intelligent and alive, thus an active research partner.
3. The purpose of indigenous science is to maintain balance.
4. Compared to western time/space notions, indigenous science collapses time and space with the result that our fields of inquiry and participation extend into and overlap with past and present.
5. Indigenous science is concerned with relationships, we try to understand and complete our relationships with all living things.
6. Indigenous science is holistic, drawing on all the senses including the spiritual and psychic.
7. The end point of an indigenous scientific process is a known and recognized place. This point of balance, referred to by my own tribe as the Great Peace, is both peaceful and electrifyingly alive. In the joy of exact balance, creativity occurs, which is why we can think of our way of knowing as a life science.
8. When we reach the moment/place of balance we do not believe that we have transcended—we say that we are normal! Always we remain embodied in the natural world.
9. Humor is a critical ingredient of all truth seeking, even in the most powerful rituals. This is true because humor balances gravity. (Colorado, 1994.)

It is worth noting that humanity's oldest science, indigenous science, indicates

> Any authentic hope must come to terms with the dark history our species, our destructive propensity accompanying our planetary conquest.

that the attainment of balance confers positive subjective states—vitality, peace, joy and creativity.

Living systems theory, along with its ancient predecessor, indigenous science, are sciences of balance. Yet before delving deeper into the underlying principles of balance, let's consider humanity's long departure from shared lifeways that sustain balance, producing today's ecological predicament, our greatest impediment to hope.

A Brief Tour of History: Human Transgressions Against the Law of Life

Any authentic hope requires a holistic assessment and reckoning with our species' history, inclusive of its shadow aspects. Grappling with the shadow—the part of ourselves that we don't readily see, acknowledge, or admit into consciousness—leads towards a holistic comprehension of our species, rather than a partial one. So before reviewing the basic elements of living systems theory, I wish to step back, and take stock our species history as a Whole, undertaking a fearless inventory of our human transgressions against the web of life, leading to today's ecological calamities.

Confronting the shadow side of humanity is not without pain; it's much easier to divert our attention and focus solely on the many extraordinary things human beings have accomplished. But at this critical juncture in history, we need a complete, rather than partial, story about our species. The dark side that we don't admit into consciousness holds tremendous power over us. Only by consciously confronting the full impact of our species' history on the planet can we hope to shift its trajectory into a hopeful future for all.

Many scientists believe the Earth is entering a sixth mass extinction, the first to be caused by a single species—ours. Recent analyses indicate that *Homo sapiens* has destroyed 83% of all mammals and half of plants since the dawn of civilization. Moreover, even if the destruction were to end now, it would take 5-7 million years for the natural world to recover (Carrington, 2018).

Mass extinction is not new news; but what may be new is how long human ecological destruction has been going on. According to evidence amassed by Uval Noah Harari, the First Wave Extinction began not a few hundred years ago in the industrial revolution, nor even 12,000 years ago with the agricultural revolution, but 70,000 years ago with our hunter-gatherer ancestors, as part of the Cognitive Revolution—a dramatic growth in the human brain (2015).

According to Harari, the human alteration of habitats and the extinction of other species has come in three waves. The First Wave Extinction began with the Cognitive Revolution—a stunning emergence of new ways of thinking and communicating between 70,000 and 30,000 years ago (Harari, 2015). This dramatic increase in our cognitive abilities brought a revolutionary explosion of inventiveness. Around 70,000 years ago, *Homo sapiens* began inventing boats, oil lamps, bows and arrows, needles, art, religion, commerce and social stratification (Harari, 2015). The boost in cognitive ability brought increased technological innovation, accompanied by new levels of environmental impact. These three developments—cognitive ability, technological innovation, and ecological destruction—appeared together in quick succession.

> Our desecration of species and habitats has been with us for most of the history of our species and constitutes our species shadow. With each increase in human abilities and inventiveness came a parallel increase in calamitous effect.

The "genetic mutations of 70,000 years ago changed the inner wiring of the [Sapiens brain, enabling us] to think in unprecedented ways, to invent unparalleled tools and technologies, and to communicate using altogether new type of language" (Harari, 2015, p. 21). The Cognitive Revolution, a defining moment in our species history, conferred three new types of communicative abilities, along a continuum from concrete to abstract thinking:

- the ability to transmit larger quantities of information about the surrounding natural world, which allows for planning and carrying out complex coordinated actions, such as hunting
- the ability to transmit larger quantities of information about Sapiens' social relationships—in a word, gossip—allowing for cohesive social groups up to 150 individuals and social cooperation on a scale far surpassing any other species
- the ability to transmit information about things that do not exist in physical reality, such as art, tribal spirits, nations, human rights, legends, myths, gods, religions—in other words, the ability to imagine. Sharing myths enables large numbers of strangers to psychically bond and cooperate, inducing rapid innovation of social behavior, while accounting for why Sapiens rule the world (Harari 2015, p. 37).

Myths or shared imagined realities function like social glue, binding together large numbers of individuals, thus allowing for unprecedented social cooperation, well beyond the prior wandering bands of 150 individuals (Harari, 2015). The creation of social constructs or imagined realities gave rise to the dual reality of humans – objective physical reality and the imagined reality of culture, allowing Sapiens to rapidly transform their social networks to now include strangers, to coordinate wide-scale economic activities, and to modify behaviors, within the short span of merely a decade or two. This ability to invent fiction enables Sapiens to fabricate more complex realities, further elaborated by each new generation (Harari, 2015).

With the birth of these new cognitive capacities, 70,000 years ago hunter-gatherers began completely reshaping the ecology of our planet—long before the first agricultural village was ever built. "The wandering bands of storytelling Sapiens were the most important and most destructive force the animal kingdom had ever produced" (Harari, 2015, p. 62). Long before the industrial and agricultural revolutions, "Homo sapiens held the record among all organisms for driving the most plant and animal species to extinction…[with] the dubious distinction of being the deadliest species in the annals of biology" (Harari, 2015, p. 74).

Prior to 70,000 BC, all human species lived exclusively on the Afro-Asian landmass. But "following the Cognitive Revolution, Sapiens acquired the technology, organizational skills and… vision to break out of Afro-Asia and settle the remaining Outer World" (Harari, 2015, p. 63). The first remote place to be settled was Australia about 45,000 years ago. Until then, humans' effect on their environment had been negligible. But within a few thousand years, "The settlers of Australia… transformed the Australian ecosystem beyond recognition" (Harari, 2015, p. 65). Across the continent primordial food chains were broken and rearranged, and 23/24 Australian large animal species soon went extinct, along with a large number of small species (Harari, 2015).

Wherever "people settled another part of the Outer World" (beyond the Afro-Asian land mass), it was followed by large scale ecological disaster, with a long list of victims. Everywhere the first to go extinct were the large mammals.

At the time of the Cognitive Revolution, the planet was home to about 200 genera of large terrestrial mammals weighing over 100 pounds. By the time of the Agricultural Revolution, only about half remained. Homo sapiens drove to extinction about half of the planet's big beasts, long before we invented the wheel, writing or iron tools (Harari, 2015, p. 72).

Everywhere humans went, the large mammals were wiped out in a short time, followed by many smaller species. Harari refutes the common counter-argument that

Sunset

climatic factors were responsible for the rapid demise of species, rather than homo sapiens, since the same pattern of devastation occurred over and over again each time humans migrated into a new habitat. The historical record points painfully to the destructive impact of our species, making "Homo sapiens look like an ecological serial killer" (Harari, 2015, p. 67).

This now all too familiar ecological tragedy replays across the entire planet. The tragedy opens with a scene showing a rich and varied population of large animals, without any trace of humans. In scene two, Sapiens appear, evidenced by a human bone, spear point, or perhaps a potsherd. Scene three quickly follows, in which men and women occupy center stage and most large animals, along with many smaller ones, are gone (Harari, 2015, p. 72).

Sapiens unrivaled cognitive abilities enabled us to conquer the world. Yet this is just the familiar half of the human story, widely told and celebrated. The fact that our damage to the web of life began not 12,000 years ago but 70,000 years ago, calls for a serious reassessment of *Homo sapiens.* Our desecration of species and habitats has been with us for most of the history of our species and constitutes our species shadow. With each increase in human abilities and inventiveness came a parallel increase in calamitous effect.

Any authentic hope must come to terms with the dark history our species, our destructive propensity accompanying our planetary conquest. In our generation, this long history of ecological destruction culminates in an unsustainable future. But to change course, we must first consciously confront this species shadow—our radically destructive propensity. The dire situation of our present world means that everything we do now must be done with great awareness or we could all be gone. It is not enough that a small segment of the human race takes up the challenges. Collectively we must wake up together, initiating a radical transformation of the destructive impetus of our species. We must now learn to live in harmony with the planet.

Livings Systems Basics

As our manmade institutions and lifeways fall into disarray, breakdown or outright collapse, a trustworthy place for hope rests in orienting ourselves to the primordial designs of nature, with their 14-billion year generative track-record. Moreover, our collective straying from these natural laws to impose a manmade world on top of the natural one, constitutes a direct causal line to our present predicaments. But we can turn to nature's systemic intelligence as a guide for restoring alignment with the codes of creativity and vitality inlaid within the deep structures of the universe.

We inhabit a universe filled with structures that display self-organizing dynamics. "Form-producing powers are latent everywhere in the universe," according to Brian Swimme and Thomas Berry (1992, p. 70). The systems that compose the organization of the universe are "cosmological orderings of the creative display of energy" (Swimme & Berry, 1992, p. 72).

We can observe these elemental patterns that allow life to arise and thrive. As a code of life, living systems theory offers a trustworthy path to correct our human misalignment with the larger web of life. Since the dynamics of living systems precede and supersede the manmade edifice of human civilization, turning to the fundamental operations of living systems provides a path to re-align our human habits with the Law of Life.

Every system within the universe participates, in nested fashion, within larger more encompassing systems.[2] The web of life consists of networks within networks, an elegant fractal of nested relationships. This *nesting of systems* implies that systems exist in a dynamic, interactive relationship with their surrounding environment. Indeed, all structures in the universe are dependent upon the conditions of their encompassing systems for their birth, and thereafter on the continuing exchange of energy and information, known as *inputs* and *outputs*.[3]

It is easy to grasp that the "existence of any structured thing requires [the input of] energy... both for its formation and for its perdurability. [Physicists] refer to this fact as the second law of thermodynamics... Any physical system closed off from new energy will eventually decay" (Swimme and Berry, 1992, p. 52).[4]

Additionally, systems entail the interplay of two opposite tendencies—an integrative tendency to function as part of a larger whole (the afore-mentioned nesting of systems), and an internal self-assertive or self-organizing tendency to preserve individual autonomy. "Things in the universe resist all efforts to reduce their presence in the world. Even at the level of elementary particles, we find this irreducible reality of the individual" (Swimme and Berry, 1992, p. 52). Once a new dynamic center is born from the matrix of other pre-existing systems, its sustenance depends on its own self-organizing powers that resist encounters that might push it towards extinction. Each living system faces the challenge of balancing "itself in the midst of generative and degenerative processes" (Swimme and Berry, 1992, p. 283).

Alongside an impetus towards self-preservation, there is a "tendency in all things towards the fulfillment of their inner nature" (Swimme and Berry, 1992, p. 53).[5] There is no way to understand the unfolding of an organism in interaction with its environment and its own genetic inheritance without taking into account this internal template, or developmental tendency, towards fulfillment of innate potential (Swimme and Berry, 1992). In living systems theory, this impetus towards self-realization is called *autopoesis*, literally self-making, while in human beings it is called *individuation*. All things in the universe, in their own subjectivity, are pervaded by inherent tendencies toward the fulfillment of their potential" (Swimme and Berry, 1992, p. 53). *Autopoiesis* then refers to the interiority and unifying principle of an organism or system, designating the living qualities of "subjectivity, self-manifestation, sentience, inner principle of being, voice and interiority" (Swimme and Berry, p. 72).

Additionally, a prerequisite for the continuance of a system is its ability to maintain a steady state or steadily oscillating state, known as *equilibrium* (Kuhn, 1974).[6] The parts of a system are coordinated to maintain the balance of the whole, while the properties of the parts derive their purpose from the organization of the whole. Participation in *feedback loops,* or information processing, is what enables a system to maintain equilibrium.[7]

Feedback loops are the foundation of systems, controlling the behavior of a system over time, and influencing systems in one of two directions, either magnifying changes or buffering against them. *Negative feedback loops,* which serve to diminish the direction of change, enable a system to maintain its present equilibrium, making it more stable. *Positive feedback loops,* on the other hand, amplify changes in a system, driving a system from its initial baseline, making it more unstable, potentially leading either to runaway exponential growth or decline and demise.

A key concern with climate change is that a rapid succession of environmental changes can activate multiple reinforcing feedback loops, resulting in a runaway situation, making the planet no longer inhabitable in a short amount of time; i.e., greenhouse gases generate warming temperatures leading to melting ice, resulting in less reflection of the sun's heat back into the atmosphere plus rising sea levels, along with extreme weather events that further destroy habitats.

Finally, while systems can be either open or closed, the health and longevity of a system requires openness, that is accepting input from the environment, and using this input to create output, thus acting on the environment.[8] While closed systems only maintain or decline in organization, open systems tend toward higher levels of organization. Open systems are inherently adaptive, learning and growing from their interactions with the environment, thereby readjusting to environmental changes in order to survive, or even thrive. Thus,

> As our manmade institutions and lifeways fall into disarray, breakdown or outright collapse, a trustworthy place for hope rests in orienting ourselves to the primordial design of nature, with its 14-billion year generative track-record.

a heightened degree of interactive participation in feedback loops can propel a system into an optimal state of functioning, vitality and wellbeing.

The Information Processing of Living Systems

As noted, open systems engage in exchanges of energy and information with their environment, leading to flourishing. Miller defined information as "the degrees of freedom that exist in a given situation to choose among signals, symbols, messages, or patterns to be transmitted" (1978). Living systems theory leads to the radical notion that matter itself participates in information-processing. It is intrinsic to the very nature of matter to process information.

Information exchanges and information processing are radically fundamental to the universe.[9] Everything in the universe, from the simplest particle, to complex molecules, through the plant world, the animal kingdom, and finally the human being, participates in the interactive exchanges of information-processing.[10] Information processing includes everything that happens, or changes, in the universe.

With the evolutionary emergence of neural structures in the animal kingdom, information-processing receives a tremendous boost in capacity and complexity. And the subsequent development of the large human brain and finely-articulated nervous system bestows a further quantum leap upon information processing.[11] Human information-processing is so highly developed and unique that it confers the name of our species, *homo sapiens*, the knowing or conscious ones.

Along with the steady stream of stimuli coming in from the environment, our nervous systems are constantly streaming a flow of internal information, transmitted from the sophisticated inner workings of our mind-body circuitry.

Living system

Through disciplined mindfulness and meditation practices, we can develop heightened awareness of these subliminal signals, or internal feedback loops, thereby enhancing our functioning as living systems.

Within the animal kingdom, humans possess a super upgraded consciousness potential, inclusive of self-reflective consciousness—the capacity to observe ourselves and our inner subjective processes.

Kelly Bulkeley elaborates on the meaning of the human capacity for meta-cognition, or self-reflection:

thinking about thinking, awareness of awareness, knowing that one is knowing. In other words, metacognition involves the mind considering itself, stretching out the time between perception and action, taking its own processes as objects of thought. It also includes pondering one's options ("should I do this or that?"), making plans for future action, monitoring one's inner feelings, and regulating the expression of desires and wishes (2008, p. 79).

Today's looming challenges call for the actualization of this meta-cognitive capacity for self-observation, both as a realization of a latent species potential, but also to avert the dire consequences of unconscious human behavior.

Attunement to one's internal stream of information-processing allows for vital awareness of the implicit dynamic processes that potentiate the animate world. Awareness of one's own subtle processes attunes us to the hidden processes of other living beings. Cultivating heightened awareness of the subliminal subtle signals infusing one's own living system transforms a human being into a refined instrument, capable of sensing and adjusting to the delicate balances that sustain wider living ecologies. From a place of inner discrimination, our meeting and greeting the world—which is a composition of living systems—is informed by the primary reference point of self-as-living-system. Awareness of one's own subtle processes attunes us to the hidden processes of other living beings and systems.

At the heart of relating to self-as-living-system is the practice of increasing one's participation in the information-processing of feedback loops, both external and internal. Intentional engagement with feedback loops generates increased adaptability, vitality and wellbeing. By refining the practice of self-reflective consciousness, and participating in external and internal feedback loops, humans can become optimally thriving living systems, attuned to and living in harmony with the natural environment.

Participating receptively in feedback loops shifts the central metaphor of the human enterprise—from imposing human will onto reality—to entering into deep conversation with reality.[12] Simultaneously, by attending to all available feedback loops, active and receptive modes of being come into a balanced relationship. Humans can relate to the environment as an information-rich, communicative intelligence. Respecting the world as a living, communicative partner shifts one's fundamental mode of relating from an objectifying I-It

> Participating receptively in feedback loops shifts the central metaphor of the human enterprise—from imposing human will onto reality—to entering into deep conversation with reality.

stance—so damaging to the planet—to an honoring I-Thou.

Humans not only possess a capacity for self-reflection, but according to today's necessities, an ecological imperative to do so, in order to avoid the hyper-destructive tendencies made possible by our large human brain. If the powers of our extraordinary information-handling abilities do not include self-observation, mindfulness and inwardly-directed attention, and instead are entirely outwardly-directed towards outer conquest of the physical world, we risk, as the ecological record indicates, becoming a collective monstrosity ravaging the planet, callous and impervious to the subtle, intangible dynamics that actually animate life.

The practice of balancing one's own living system generates a sensitizing, self-regulatory restraint that reduces blind action and violence towards other living systems. Developing the know-how to balance my own living system brings more awareness to the dynamics of balance generally, attenuating humanity's otherwise vastly destructive propensity.

My approach follows a Confucian logic regarding the primacy of engaging with self-as-living- system, as a precursor for relating respectfully and mindfully to other living systems: "To put the world in order, we must first put the nation in order; to put the nation in order, we must put the family in order; to put the family in order, we must cultivate our personal life; and to cultivate our personal life, we must first set our hearts right" (Confucius, n.d.).

Internal Feedback Loops

One of the few critiques leveled against living systems theory concerns its omission of the analysis of subjective phenomena" ("Living Systems", n.d.). Here I wish to address this gap in living systems theory, by applying living systems theory to subjective human processes. So I pose the question: *what does it mean to adopt living systems theory as a personal framework for living?*

Conscious participation in feedback loops, along with the discipline of self-observation, balances the human self, with the concomitant blessing states of flow, harmony and joy. I highlight three specific internal feedback loops that humans can choose to actively engage with, leading to a refined balancing of self-as-living-system. Engagement with the internal feedback loops of affect regulation, dreams and bodily signals reveals how the framework of living systems theory can be applied to subjective phenomena, thereby countering the main critique of living systems theory.

Bridalveil Falls

Affect Regulation

Emotions are a gift of evolution bestowed upon mammals to increase our responsiveness to our environment, with the fullest repertoire found in humans. Emotions operate as an internal signal system designed to alert us to changes in our immediate environment, in order to increase our survival responsiveness and adaptability. For example, fear alerts us to potential danger; anger alerts us to perceived injustice; grief to loss; shame to violations of personal integrity.

Affect regulation refers to the ability to modulate one's emotional experience, thereby steering clear of the twin challenges of repression on the one hand and explosive reactivity on the other. Affect regulation entails the ability to modulate one's emotional state while adaptively meeting the demands of the environment and the necessities of the moment. High affect regulation involves a capacity to flexibly adapt to a range of stressful situations and draws on executive and cognitive functions. Executive functioning refers to a set of cognitive processes necessary for the intentional directing of one's behavior and actions.[13]

By contrast, dysregulation occurs when we are triggered and overwhelmed by our emotions, leading to either over-reactions or going numb. With dysregulation, we are unable to remain present to the current moment. Typically, our unintegrated emotional history is the culprit behind these states of emotional overwhelm. Excessive emotional reactions offer clues to unprocessed experiences from the past.

Mindfulness meditation is extremely helpful in improving affect regulation. A broad array of research over the past two decades supports the claim that mindfulness meditation confers beneficial effects on physical and mental health, enhancing cognitive performance and self-regulation, including attention control, emotion regulation and self-awareness (Tang, et al., 2015). As a metacognition skill, mindfulness practices cultivate a neutral observer of our subjective states. This "witness consciousness" allows us to create a space or pause between our emotional reactions and our responses, thereby opening the possibility of redirecting negative emotions in positive ways that are creatively responsive, rather than inimical, to the needs of the moment.

Affect regulation is a self-regulatory capacity that draws upon a subset of skills: a) learning to be aware of and accurately identify our various emotional states; b) allowing our emotions to inform us of the present situation and our internal responses; and c) channeling the affective energy behind our emotions so as to act in socially appropriate or even creative ways.

Dreams

Mammals have been dreaming for 80 million years, making dreaming another evolutionary invention with a self-regulating and survival function. In addition to the value of affect regulation for the waking state, our dreams provide an additional internal feedback loop that seeks to harmonize the conscious and unconscious sides of the personality. According to depth psychology, the typical personality development of modern persons undergoes a fundamental bifurcation between the conscious side of the personality—those aspects we are aware of and readily identify with—and a deeper stratum of unconscious material that is at once personal and collectively-shared. The personal unconscious, acquired during one's lifetime, includes unacknowledged psychological material that is unique to the individual, while the collective unconscious includes ancestral and cultural memories, along with instinctual patterns and universal archetypes common to all of humanity. According to Carl Jung, our dreams oscillate in the fecund space between the conscious and unconscious sides of the personality, seeking to bring about a reconciliation and balancing between the two.

Jung describes the regulating and compensatory function of dreams in terminology akin to the language of living systems theory. The psyche is a self-regulating system that maintains its equilibrium through the activity of dreaming. For Jung, the chief function of dreaming is psychological compensation, in that dreams correct and compensate the excesses of the ego's waking standpoint. When the waking ego becomes too one-sided, or represses unconscious material, dreams emerge to highlight the imbalance and guide the individual towards wholeness and integration. For example, when a person becomes narcissistically over-inflated, dreams compensate by offering humbling self-portraits. When we are too impressed with our own goodness and moral righteousness, our dreams surface our darker impulses. So when Jung talks about the compensatory function of dreams, it's a system's attempt to establish better flow, better integration between the conscious and unconscious sides of the modern personality.

While dreams seek to maintain a dynamic balance between the conscious and unconscious, for this function to be fully actualized, the waking self also needs to participate by consciously processing dream contents, thereby allowing this balancing and integrating function to be realized. When engaging with a dream, we can ask: What conscious attitude does this dream compensate? By listening to our dreams, and learning the symbolic language that dreams speak, we bridge conscious and unconscious sides of our personality, resulting in greater internal coherence.

> The energy body or subtle body is the human faculty that mediates the perception of seamless interconnectedness between self and world.

Conversely, if we ignore significant dream messages, the dream symbolism and accompanying emotions tend to intensify, becoming more extreme, as the unconscious psyche escalates its efforts to gain our attention.

Body Knowing

Through the highly-articulated human nervous system, human bodies are exquisitely-refined instruments that can sensitize us to the embodiment of other life forms. According to Arnold Mindell, the body is replete with luminous signals

Nicasio tree

and meaningful information waiting to be apprehended and unfolded (1985). Mindell maintains that the body communicates information through multiple channels, including bodily feelings, visual imagery, auditory voices, and kinesthetic movement. A profound reservoir of subtle sensation and subliminal perception is available through the body's various modes of knowing, allowing us to refine our body awareness and responsiveness to life.

Body signals communicate information about the internal environment of the body as well as the external environment. Bodily sensations like discomfort, tension, nausea, and constriction, offer signs of stress or perturbation. Listening to and heeding these signals, as a subtle feedback loop, can lead to a harmonization between mind and body, with increased inner coherence. In contrast, when body awareness remains undeveloped, and in the absence of the full discriminating potential of the body, our interactions with the world can become obtuse, even reckless.

Bodily intelligence is an integral dimension of our being, a conduit for all our experiences, yet in the Western context, we are often encouraged to ignore or override the body, numbing physical sensations, and leaving the mind-body connection undeveloped. Numbing is a default strategy used to defend against the overwhelming experience of trauma. In trauma, our consciousness tends to dissociate from the depths of bodily knowing, instead perching on the surface of the body. The habits of Western culture in turn reinforce this superficial surface perception, rather than the depth perception of true embodiment.

So it is important to distinguish between the traumatized body and the natural body. The traumatized body suffers from dissociation and zones of numbness, conveying an armored and mentalized version of the person. The natural body is touch with the streaming of internal sensations and energy and is generally open to new experience. The consciousness associated with the trauma body, also called the pain body by Eckhart Tolle (1999), lives on the surface, cut off from the deeper built-in, natural sources of pleasure that full embodiment confers. Thus, the trauma body tends to seek outward sources of pleasure, being prone to dysfunctional addictions, pursuing immediate pleasure where it can get it. Unhealed trauma and widespread fixation on external sources of pleasure by billions of people collectively tax the natural resources of the planet.

Shifting from the trauma body to the natural body requires attending to the energy body, a subtle source of internal feedback. The notion of the energy body derives from a worldview that apprehends the energetic basis of reality, as attested to by indigenous peoples, mystics and contemporary physicists alike. If one accepts that energy is the underlying essence of the cosmos—that the objects we see and interact with are actually energy posing in different forms—then logically, the human body is also, by extension, most fundamentally energy.

The energy body or subtle body is the human faculty that mediates the perception of seamless interconnectedness between self and world. The subtle body, recognized in esoteric spiritual teachings around the world, refers to the psycho-spiritual proclivities arising from a subtle anatomy, loosely associated with the anatomy of the gross physical body. The subtle body is composed of energy centers and channels, which can exist either in an open, flowing state or a contracted, blocked, knotted state. The underlying openness or blockages within the energy body significantly influence our perceptions of the world.

By attending to the patterns of contraction and expansion within the subtle body, we tap into the most refined feedback loop available to our species. Constrictions in the body indicate frozen, numb processes, while open flows of energy signal an optimal state of aliveness and vitality. Tracking the contractions and expansions in the subtle body enables the mind to transmute frozen energy into flowing energy and to align at the deepest level with the movements of life force energy.

The quality of subtle attention required for tracking shifts within the energy body is akin to noticing the movement of air across one's skin. Yet since the standard orientation of Western consciousness is towards physically-observable phenomena, consciousness must undergo a radical reorienting and training in order to observe the micro level of reality. Subtle reality is a significant blind spot for most modern people. Our general lack of awareness of subtle reality means that we fail to notice initial signs and incipient processes of disturbance and imbalance.

To briefly recap: intentionally cultivating awareness of one's emotional life, dream life, and energy body brings

Bridalveil Creek

engagement with internal feedback loops, leading to a more refined attunement to self and world. Balancing the primary living system of self enables us to relate to other living systems from a balanced center. Conversely, neglecting these internal feedback channels leads to imbalances and disturbances that cloud our consciousness, burdening our interactions with projection, entanglement, and unnecessary conflict.

External Feedback Loops

In addition to cultivating awareness of internal feedback processes such as affect regulation, dreams, and the energy body, we can approach the world-at-large as a feedback loop, as a living, communicative partner. Rather than objectifying the world as an entity to be willfully subdued, or a resource to be extracted for our own pleasure, the world can be engaged from a stance of respectful listening. World phenomena provide a potential source of feedback that clarifies our participation in the larger life process.

Arnold Mindell (2015) regards the world-at-large as a living channel of meaningful information and source of wisdom, a view also held by Native American traditions. The material world emanates non-verbal communications, picked by those who are attentive. We can recognize and respect the Earth and environment as wise teachers that send messages and lessons through its rivers, stones, and stars. In addition, we can attend to incongruities, discord in relationships, and social conflicts, considering these clash points as places of imbalance calling for a different kind of response—an imaginative response of largess—in order to restore balance and harmony.

By listening to the natural and man-made environments, we voluntarily participate in feedback loops that redress and rebuff our egocentrism, making possible a refinement in our way of being. The world responds differently to interactions conducted from a balanced psyche versus an imbalanced one. Whereas stances of dissociation and dysregulation tend to activate clash points with the world, balance naturally generates openings into connection and flow.

Attending to internal and external feedback loops admittedly requires a disciplined approach to life, while fostering a high degree of self-possession, inner coherence and self-intimacy, along with a harmonizing movement in one's outward relations. Feedback loops are living communications; and respectful mutual communication forms the heart of intimacy. Possessing oneself internally brings freedom from a need to possess externally—people, objects, the fruits of the Earth. Moreover, this disciplined path of balance generates surprising openings to hidden, secret forms of pleasure, intimacy, and joy.

The Pleasurable Future of Humanity

To briefly recap, living systems are open self-organizing life forms that interact with their environment. Living systems are sustained by flows of information and matter-energy. According to the originator of living systems, Miller, matter-energy and information always flow together. The more integrated a system is, the more feedbacks and information flow occurs among its parts. Conversely, if any of these flows are blocked, a system's vitality will decline precipitously.

Thus, since every living system's very sustenance depends on participating in exchanges or flows of information and energy-matter with its environment, we can affirm that flow is an overarching quality of living systems and indeed, of the universe itself.[14] Restated, flow is a continuous, ongoing process of all living systems. By contrast, in dying systems, flow of matter-energy and information is decreasing. In other words, flow emerges as an intrinsic property of living systems.

Flow facilitates ongoing systemic integration, internal balance, and balance between internal and external dimensions. Systems have a natural impetus towards flow, balance and integration, three interconnected processes. Flow states and systemic integration in living systems are subjectively satisfying and objectively insure survival and well-being.

Now let's consider the specific way that flow manifests among humans. In humans, the tendency towards flow, balance and integration is named by Rogers and Maslow as self-actualization. Yet self-actualization does not occur automatically; it requires our active participation. Intentional participation is required to integrate conscious and unconscious sides of the self. Notably, what disrupts this natural tendency towards flow in humans is trauma. So whenever trauma has occurred, healing, integrative processes and practices must be engaged in order to re-establish flow. When human systems are open, in balance, and free of (unresolved) trauma, they tend towards flow.

It is worth recognizing that the modern human condition tends to be a traumatized condition, and an unexamined traumatized condition, in which access to and awareness of flow has been severely disrupted. Due to trauma's pervasiveness, it is often assumed to be normative, rather than a distorted, aberrant condition. Addictive tendencies then commonly take over to offer quick, temporary relief to the constrictions of trauma and deprivation from natural flow. By contrast, in Apela Colorado's description of systemic integration and interconnectivity within indigenous cultures, the joy of balance and flow arises a normative feature of intact native lifeways.

Flow states in humans have been extensively researched and discussed in positive psychology, yet the larger context of flow within all living systems has not been made (Jurgen Kremer, personal communication, May 28, 2020). Human flow states offer a specific example of the wider quality of flow within all living systems.

> A proper state of balance with life, attained through conscious participation in internal and external feedback loops, bestows a natural delight, the celebrated joie de vivre.

Our bodies contain a natural, built-in self-gratification system that is activated during high degrees of internal and external synchronization, known as flow. Mihaly Csikszentmihalyi (1975) first introduced the term "flow", defining it as "the holistic experience that people feel when they act with total involvement." Flow occurs when one is totally absorbed in and focused on the task at hand, engaging with confidence in meeting a challenge that entails a modest stretch of one's abilities.

People in a flow state typically feel that they are performing at the best of their ability with effortless control and ease (Csikszentmihalyi, 1997, p. 29). Concentration is so intense that there is no attention left over to think about anything irrelevant, or to worry about problems. Self-consciousness disappears and the sense of time is altered. Flow states are extremely enjoyable and gratifying, carrying their own intrinsic motivation and fulfillment, independent of external reward. While human consciousness naturally undergoes fluctuations, this state of optimal performance accompanied by euphoria can potentially be cultivated by anyone in any situation, wherever there is deep absorption in meeting a challenge and intrinsic enjoyment of the activity.

Flow includes nine main elements:

1. there are clear goals every step of the way;
2. there is immediate feedback to one's actions;
3. there is a balance between challenges and skills;
4. action and awareness are merged;
5. through deep concentration, distractions are excluded from consciousness;
6. there is no worry of failure;

> In addition to experiencing flow through high-level performance activity, another more mysterious possibility exists, experiencing internal flow states. Internal flow occurs when awareness joins with the subliminal flow of subtle energies through the body.

7. self-consciousness disappears;
8. the sense of time is modified;
9. the activity becomes autotelic, carrying intrinsic motivation and purpose (Csikszentmihalyi, 1996, p. 111).

States of flow occur in the presence of high inner coherence and harmony between internal and external dimensions. They also tend to catalyze further

Moonrise

integration of the self, "because in that state of deep concentration consciousness is unusually well ordered. Thoughts, intentions, feelings, and all the senses are focused on the same goal. Experience is harmony" (Csikszentmihalyi, 1996, p. 41). Flow, known by athletes as "being in the zone," enhances life-satisfaction, performance, and well-being.[15]

Learning how to access flow states bestows physical and cognitive benefits. Consciousness plays a role in facilitating these states, functioning "as a clearinghouse for sensations, perceptions, feelings, and ideas, establishing priorities among all the diverse information" (Csikszentmihalyi, 1990, p. 24). As conscious beings, we can direct conscious events such as thoughts, sensations and intentions, giving us the power to organize our consciousness towards the coherence that is conducive to flow (Csikszentmihalyi, 1990, p. 40). "The optimal state of inner experience is one in which there is order in consciousness" (Csikszentmihalyi, 1990, p. 6).

In addition to experiencing flow through high-level performance activity, another more mysterious possibility exists, experiencing *internal flow states*. Internal flow occurs when awareness joins with the subliminal flow of life energy through the body. This pleasurable unity between conscious awareness and the underground stream of life force energy becomes possible through a high degree of conscious attunement and synchronization with internal and external feedback loops.

Akin to the underground water tables and water flows deep within the earth, the human body contains a little-known underground stream, attested by esoteric spiritual and scientific traditions alike. Spiritual traditions recognize a stream of energy flowing through the human nervous system, detectable in certain non-ordinary states of consciousness and through the cultivation of mindfulness and spiritual practices focused on the body. In the Indian Tantric spiritual tradition, this channel of subtle energy, called *kundalini*, refers to a spiritual energy or life force closely associated with the spinal column. Western science identifies an anatomical parallel, a clear, colorless fluid found in the brain and spinal column known as the cerebrospinal fluid, involved in experiences of internal flow. While ordinary consciousness is oblivious to this underground river of energy, consciousness can be trained to perceive and experience these subtle pleasurable sensations of vitality.

Kundalini experiences, which are internal flow states, signal optimal functioning of the human living system, with heightened experiences of vitality. This optimal state of thriving is intrinsically pleasurable, in sharp contrast to survival-oriented, defensive modes of consciousness that accompany egocentric states. The emergence of internal flow states suggests a mind-body system in optimal balance.

Internal flow states arise as the conscious personality becomes aligned and synchronized with the life force energy, during high levels of inner and outer coherence. As the conscious mind surrenders its defensive and restrictive egoic patterns, it can mindfully merge with the deep energy streams that circulate throughout the human nervous system. Awareness drops into the interior channels of vibrational energy that bestow a subtle yet tangible pleasure in simply being alive. Conscious harmonization with one's personal share of cosmic energy, as it flows through one's own bodily being, confers profound attunement and intimacy with the vital essence of life.

A proper state of balance with life, attained through conscious participation in internal and external feedback loops, bestows natural pleasure and delight, the celebrated *joie de vivre*. The learned capacity to harmonize oneself—through actively attending to internal and external feedback loops—generates more frequent access to this optimal, hopeful state of being. Flow states arise in situations of thriving and flourishing (as distinct from being in survival mode).

An ancient spiritual tradition that resonates with the path of flow and my own approach to hope—the practice of synchronizing one's personal life force with the universal creative energy—is Taoism. The Tao, distinct from the countless "named" things, denotes the essential underlying order and energy of the Universe that gives rise to the countless "named" things. The *Tao* refers variously to the ultimate principle and natural order of the universe; the way, path or proper way of existence; to ongoing practices of attainment; and the state of enlightenment or fullness of being that is the outcome of such practices. This way of "life," ungraspable by the mind, is instead realized through the lived daily experience of attuning to the flow of energy within and without. According to the *Tao Te Ching*, Verse 21, "The Master keeps her mind always at one with the Tao; that is what gives her her radiance." (Lao Tze, n.d.).

All photography by Karen Jaenke

Endnotes

1 The systems approach first emerged in the 1920s with ecologists studying food chains and food cycles. Then in the 1930s, biologist Ludwig von Bertalanffy developed general systems theory. In the 1950s, the application of living systems theory to cybernetics and information processing emerged, with Gregory Bateson as one of its highly-original synthesizing voices; meanwhile systems thinking began to influence engineering and management in solving practical problems. The 1960s-70s brought the formulation of complexity theory and nonlinear dynamics; with the development of computers, it now became possible to model the nonlinear interconnectedness of living systems. In the 1980s and 90s, a proper mathematical language for living systems emerged.

2 For example, the atom is nested within the molecule; the molecule within the cell; the cell within the organ; the organ within the organism; the organism within a family; the family within the tribe; the tribe within its ecological niche; the ecological niche within the planet; the planet within the solar system; the solar system within the galaxy; the galaxy within the universe.

3 *Inputs* are the movement of matter-energy and information from the environment into the system, and all developments in the universe require the input of energy. Conversely, outputs are the movement of matter-energy and information from the system to the environment. Both inputs and outputs involve crossings of the boundaries that define the system.

4 The birth of new autopoietic structures depends upon the conditions of the universe for their origin, that is, upon the larger systems in which they are nested.

5 This tendency towards self-preservation is variously referred to in physics as *quantum tendencies*, in biology as epigenetic pathways folded into a particular ontogeny, and in cybernetics as the *autopoiesis* of a coherent system (Swimme and Berry, 1992, p. 53).

6 When all forces in a system are balanced to the point where no change is occurring, the system is in a state of *static equilibrium*. By contrast, *dynamic* (or steady state) *equilibrium* exists when the system components are fluctuating, yet the system as whole still hovers around its baseline.

7 Feedback occurs when outputs of a system are routed back as inputs in a chain of cause-and-effect that forms a circuit or loop. The system can then be said to *feed back* into itself.

8 In a *closed system,* interactions occur only internally among the system components but not with the environment.

9 Every change in the universe can be viewed as a type of information processing. Even the interactions of elementary particles engage in a type of interactive exchange or information processing

10 The processes of cognition are embedded in and synonymous with the processes of life. Hence, as living systems theorists Varela et al. (1991) point out, mind and matter are not two separate things; rather mind is infused within the body all along. Thus the ancient mind-body problem of Western philosophy, and the contemporary mind-body split, dissolve with the recognition that all living beings and all matter process information.

11 Information-processing, sentience and consciousness refer to three related phenomena existing along a continuum. Information processing is a basic capacity, present in all of matter, referring to the receiving and transmitting data in interaction with the environment. Sentience refers to the capacity to feel, perceive or experience subjectively, and is a minimalistic way of defining *consciousness.* In Western thought sentience is typically attributed to all animals possessing neural structures. The highly-developed, complex neural structures of humans make us hyper sentient, conscious, with abilities to process a fantastical range of different types of information.

12 Conscious participation in feedback loops means cultivating receptivity to internal and external messages, thereby also countering a bias of Western culture towards unilateral egoic-action. Willful action is tempered by listening to the steady stream of internal messages (as provided by emotional states, body sensations, nighttime dreams, and the energy circuits of the subtle body).

13 Basic executive functions include cognitive processes such as attentional control, cognitive inhibition, inhibitory control, working memory and cognitive flexibility. Higher-order executive functions make simultaneous use of multiple basic executive functions and include reasoning, planning, fluid thinking, problem-solving.

14 I want to thank Jürgen Werner Kremer for the discussion on this issue (Kremer, personal communication, May 28, 2021)

15 Athletes, referring to flow states as "being in the zone," experience "joyful movement, effortless exertion, fluidity, expansion," and a "connectedness to the cosmos" (Lloyd, 2015, p. 24). The harmony of senses, awareness, and action enables the athlete to perform and compete at a heightened ability, often performing at their best while in flow.

References

Bulkeley, Kelly. (2008). *Dreaming in the world's religions.* New York, NY: New York University Press.

Capra, Fritjof and Luisi, Pier Luigi. (2014). *The systems view of life: A unifying vision.* Cambridge, UK: Cambridge University Press.

Capra, Fritjof. (2019). *The Heart of the Matter: A Systems Approach for Achieving the UN Sustainable Development Goals.* https://vimeo.com/336717769

Carrington, Damien. (2018, May 21). *Humans just 0.01% of all life but have destroyed 83% of wild mammals – study.* The Guardian. https://www.theguardian.com/environment/2018/may/21/human-race-just-001-of-all-life-but-has-destroyed-over-80-of-wild-mammals-study)

Colorado, Pamela. (1994.) "Indigenous science and western science: A healing convergence." Presentation at the World Sciences Dialog I, New York City, April 25-27, 1994.

Confucius. (n.d.) "Confucius Quotes." Good Reads. https://www.goodreads.com/quotes/58081-to-put-the-world-in-order-we-must-first-put#:~:text=To%20put%20the%20world%20in%20order%2C%20we%20must,life%3B%20we%20must%20first%20set%20our%20hearts%20right."

Csikszentmihalyi, M. (1975). *Beyond boredom and anxiety: Experiencing flow in work and play.* San Francisco: Jossey-Bass.

Csikszentmihalyi, M. (1990). *Flow: The psychologoy of optimal experience.* New York: Harper & Row, Publishers, Inc.

Csikszentmihalyi, M. (1996). *Creativity: Flow and the psychology of discovery and invention.* New York: HarperCollins Publishers.

Csikszentmihalyi, M. (1997). *Finding flow: The psychology of engagement with everyday life.* New York: Basic Books.

Harari, Yuval Noah. (2015). *Sapiens: A brief history of humankind.* New York, NY: Harper Perennial.

Kuhn, Thomas. (1962.) *The structure of scientific revolutions.* Chicago: University of Chicago Press.

Lao Tze. (n.d.) *Tao Te Ching.* Verse 21. Retrieved October 20, 2020 from https://www.harinam.com/tao-te-ching-verse-21-the-master-keeps-her-mind-always-at-one-with-the-tao-that-is-what-gives-her-her-radiance/

"Living Systems." (n.d.) Wikipedia. Retrieved November 27, 2020 from https://en.wikipedia.org/wiki/Living_systems#:~:text=Theory%20Living%20systems%20theory%20is%20a%20general%20theory,was%20intended%20to%20formalize%20the%20concept%20of%20life

Lloyd, Rebecca. J. (2015). From Dys/Function to Flow: Inception, Perception, and Dancing Beyond Life's Constraints. *The Humanistic Psychologist,* 24-39.

Miller, James Grier. (1978.) "Living systems: The basic concepts." Retrieved May 30, 2021. http://www.panarchy.org/miller/livingsystems.html#Anchor-44867

Mindell, Arnold. (1985). *Working with the dreaming body.* London, UK. Penguin Books.

Swimme, Brian and Berry, Thomas. (1992). *The Universe Story: From the primordial flaring forth to the Ecozoic Era—A celebration of the unfolding cosmos.* San Francisco, CA: Harper SanFrancisco.

Tang, YY., Hölzel, B. & Posner, M. The neuroscience of mindfulness meditation. *Nature Reviews Neuroscience* 16, 213–225 (2015). https://doi.org/10.1038/nrn3916

Tolle, Eckhart. (1999). *The power of now.* Novato, CA: New World Library.

Varela, F. J., E Thompson, and E. Rosch (1991). *The embodied mind.* Cambridge, MA: MIT Press.

Revitalising Hope Through the Power of Story

Paul Callaghan

I magine a world with no poverty. Imagine a world with no hunger. Imagine a world with no homelessness or crime, where all people have all they need to live a long life of wellbeing mind, body and spirit.

Some people think this kind of world is a forlorn hope, more a vision of fantasy than reality. They might suggest humanity has a history of not being overly humane ... that history shows us that humans have always been in conflict ... that it is our nature to fight and hurt each other ... that it is impossible for us to live in harmony and unity. This thought is understandable but wrong.

Paul Callaghan is an Aboriginal man belonging to the land of the Worimi people which is located one hour north of Newcastle, NSW, Australia. Paul has held a number of senior executive positions in his career and has qualifications in the disciplines of surveying, drafting, commerce, training, executive leadership, company boards and executive coaching. He is about to complete a PhD in Creative Practice at the University of New England. His most important learning however, has been through going bush with Elders. Paul is a motivational speaker, a story teller, a dancer and an author. His book entitled *iridescence - Finding Your Colours and Living Your Story* was published in 2014 and his new book *The Dreaming Path* will be published September, 2021. These books provide insights on how the modern world can benefit from the wisdom of Aboriginal Elders through an increased understanding of Aboriginal culture and spirituality.

Brewarrina fishtraps (Powerhouse Museum Sydney)

The utopic world outlined in the opening paragraph existed for over 3,000 generations in a country now called Australia. It is not the purpose of this article to prove this assertion, but I can assure you, the evidence is there if you know what to look for.

I write as an Aboriginal person connected to my traditional culture, the old ways and the old spirits. I am not bounded by the standards for truth and evidence demanded by the dominant Western culture.

True wisdom is found when the constraints of logic and measurement are exposed and acknowledged ... and replaced by expansive thought that is allowed to flow unhindered by the need to dot i's and cross t's. Hope thrives when rigidity of thought dies.

In much the same way work-life balance has become a catchcry of a world that has become seduced by consumerism and materialism; we need to realign the construct of knowledge to one of technical- spiritual balance.

This balance was mastered by Aboriginal people tens of thousands of years before the Megalithic Temples of Malta (5000 BC) or the Pyramid of Djoser (3000 BC) were built.

Although Aboriginal people have engineered significant rock structures (scientists suggest Brewarrina fish traps to be approximately 40,000 years old), our Old People have always considered the building of relationships and knowledge of far more importance than the building of material structures.

The ability to ensure a way of life that embodied wellbeing and contentment through meaningful relationships and pedagogical excellence was underpinned by an ontology captured in the English word *Lore*, which can be defined as a *body of knowledge, stories or traditions that is passed down from members of a culture usually by word of mouth.*

The Aboriginal meaning of the word *Lore* is more accurately and respectfully captured in the Aboriginal word *Ngurrampaa* which can be translated in English to mean, *"my responsibility to care for my place and all things in my place above all things."*

Before the white sails appeared in Sydney Harbor in 1788, over 500 diverse Aboriginal clans throughout the land were united by this overarching responsibility. The knowledge of how to uphold the *Ngurrampaa*, the *Lore* was provided through story in its various forms including dance, song, art and narrative.

The emphasis on the arts as the basis of knowledge and learning is a stark contrast to the Western world focus on science, mathematics and engineering. (The Australian government has recently reinforced this edict through a shift in the cost of university degrees whereby art students are forced to pay far more than students in the technical areas).

This way of thinking is destined to continue the erosion of wisdom in our society. Instead of expansive thought that upholds the sacred responsibility *to care for our place and all things in our place for future generations* we see narrow, one dimensional thinking focused on economic health over 3- to 5-year time horizons.

It is therefore no surprise we are living in a world where the social determinants of a healthy earth are being severely undermined leading to symptomatology that includes:

- The extinction of myriads of animal and plant species
- Global warming
- Pollution of the land, waterways and air
- Pandemics
- Destructive weather events

> In the Aboriginal way of thinking, all things have spirit … all things are born … all things die … and all things are connected.

- Disastrous bushfire events
- Famine
- A lack of parity in wealth distribution leading to an overrepresentation of poverty, illness, violence, incarceration and homelessness in many parts of the world

In the Aboriginal way of thinking, all things have spirit … all things are born … all things die … and all things are connected.

We have stories that teach us about all these things, including how the plants, the trees, the insects, the furred animals, the reptiles, the fish, the birds, humans and all living things are born of the one mother, Mother Earth, making us all brothers and sisters.

In Aboriginal spirituality, humans (and all living things) are no different to a tree. For a tree to flourish, it needs to grow in rich and fertile soil. As humans, we also need to grow in rich and fertile soil. The *Lore*, understanding our responsibility to care for our place and all things in our place for future generations, gives us this soil. The *Lore* is the incubator of love and hope. The *Lore* is the gateway to the path of wellbeing. If we forget the *Lore* or fail to acknowledge and uphold the universal truths it contains, our soil becomes barren. In barren soil we stagnate individually … we stagnate as a community … we stagnate globally. By ignoring the wisdom handed to us by those who have come before us, we create a desert where life withers and eventually dies.

The catalyst of positive change, the means to creating rich and fertile soil, is as simple as it is profound. Its essence is captured in the comment below by Uncle Paul Gordon, an Aboriginal Elder and *Lore* Man.[1]

> In our stories, everything started from country and our people went out throughout the world and over time their skin changed, language changed, *Lore* was forgotten.
>
> In 1788 some of the forgotten children came back.
>
> Now children you are home. You need to awaken and listen to your Elders.
>
> It is time for you to learn what you have lost.

In essence, what Uncle Paul is saying is that all of us need to reconnect with the *Lore*. The way we do this is to

> Hope is only powerful if built on wisdom. Wisdom is created from knowledge. Knowledge is shared through story. Story is built from *Lore*.

reconnect with Elders and to reconnect with story.

Hope is only powerful if built on wisdom. Wisdom is created from knowledge. Knowledge is shared through story. Story is built from *Lore*.

The story below has been created by me based on traditional Aboriginal Dreamtime Stories but in a way that incorporates a modern context. Hopefully it gives you an insight into the power of story as a vehicle for opening up minds and creating dialogue and conversations that will change the world.

The Hurdle

Witjagit the father emu smiled down at the animated bundles of feathers that were jumping up and down with excitement.

Witjagit was excited as well. He was also a little bit sad.

He had sat on the nest for 56 days without eating or drinking until each of the eggs had hatched. He had spent four months teaching them how to look after themselves including how to gather food and how to follow the *Lore*. It was almost time for them to leave his side, for him to let them go to find their own Dreaming Path, to walk their own footsteps without him.

'Now children, before we start, I want you to take one last look at this camp that has given us all we need for so long. This is the *Lore*.'

The emu chicks stood quietly in a circle as Witjagit prayed.

'To our sky creator *Biaimii*, our mother, Mother Earth and the Spirit Ancestors who look over us, we give thanks for this place that has fed us, protected us and shared with us for so long.'

There was silence for a minute or so. A gentle breeze arose from nowhere, creating a gentle rustling in the tree tops and fluffing up the feathers of the children to make them look even cuter.

'Aah. Feel that children. The Old Spirits send their blessing. We can now go.'

Witjagit was pleased they were finally moving, but he didn't tell the children why. His good friend Gaaku the kookaburra had warned him two days before that Batjigan the dingo clan had recently crossed the river into Witjagit's country.

Throughout the day the group followed the songline Witjagit had been given when he was young. The songline guided them to sacred places where Witjagit shared story, song and dance.

The chicks learned about the Father,

Emu with chicks

the Mother and the Spirit Ancestors. They learned about the importance of sharing and being humble, loving and respectful in all they did. Above all, they were taught the importance of caring for their place and all things in their place.

Time ceased to exist as the children listened to their father and the Elders he introduced them to on the way. In what seemed like the blink of an eye, the sun was starting to spread red, orange, violet and pink fingers of love on the western horizon.

'Father, this has been the best day of my life,' one of the chicks said in an upbeat voice. 'But now I am so hungry.'

Witjagit laughed softly. 'Yes. It has been a wonderful day Gapirr and over this hill we will find some lovely quandong fruit. And tomorrow, I will take you to a beautiful waterhole where you will meet many of your cousins.'

The chicks squealed as one.

'We must have the best father in the world,' another chick said as they followed their father's long legs up the ridge. When they reached the top of the ridge, Witjagit's large eyes blinked rapidly as his beak opened and closed and his large chest heaved in and out. Where once there was bush as far as the eye could see, there now was red sand with no trees, no plants and no life in sight.

'Oh well. We can do without tucker for a night I guess,' one of the chicks said. The sadness in her voice wrenched at Witjagit's big heart.

'The fruit trees are gone Marruy. I am not sure why. But there is no need to worry. If we walk along this ridge, we are bound to find some other food.'

After finding plenty of food as promised, the chicks were soon sleeping soundly. As the full moon rose, Witjagit looked into the bare space before him and felt fear start to seep into his spirit.

The golden glow of the pre-dawn warned Witjagit of the approaching hot day. 'Off we go children. We will be at the waterhole before we know it.'

The group moved quickly through the landscape, quietly and with purpose. Every now and then, unnoticed by the chicks, Witjagit would look behind as the subtle throb of fear started to cloud his head with negative chatter. The chatter became even louder as he recognised the fence ahead of them.

'But Father, what shall you do?'

'Oh Marruy. Ever the worrier. You and the others just need to make your way to the waterhole and introduce yourself. You will find plenty of family there to make you feel at home.'

One by one, Witjagit lifted each of his children in his mouth and gently dropped them over the other side of the fence.

Kookaburra

Dingo

Quandong tree

'Off you go now.' Witjagit said with a laugh. 'I will be with you before you know it.'

The chicks made their way to the waterhole, taking great care not to look back as instructed by their father ... all that is ... except Marruy who noticed the shadows of the dingoes making their way towards where her Father stood waving.

'Your long legs cannot keep us away forever old man,' Batjigan sneered.

'You are right,' Witjagit replied in a voice that was strong and clear. 'But I know that I am being watched by the Old Ones, and they will find a way to protect me if I believe. So I will use my long legs as long as I need to.'

Throughout the night, Witjagit kept the dingoes at bay, his desire to see his children once more giving him strength and purpose he didn't know he possessed. Although his head told him he would die in this place, his spirit told him all would be well.

A yelp of pain shattered the darkness left behind by the long-descended moon. Followed by another ... and another.

'Who is there?' Witjagit's voice was both elated and scared.

'There is no need to be fearful my

Kangaroo

brother,' a soothing voice said. 'I am Bundaa of the kangaroo clan. Maruuy told us of her worries and we have come to get you.'

The gentle light of the sun's first rays outlined the silhouette of a large kangaroo. Witjagit could see he was surrounded by many others as hot tears flowed from his eyes.

'You cannot know how thankful I am that you have come to my aid. And I am truly relieved that my children are safe.'

'They are safe indeed ... and full of water and food.'

'I am very thirsty myself so without wanting to be disrespectful, I must follow this fence line until I can cross it and join you at the waterhole.' Witjagit noticed the kangaroo shaking his head and his heart sank.

'That will take you many sunrises my brother, and you will surely perish before you make it back. But do not worry. Many think us kangaroos are just good for jumping over things like these stupid fences, but we also have very strong arms. We will join our arms and fling you over this fence but make sure you curl yourself into a ball as we throw you. We don't want your long legs or neck getting caught.'

And that is what they did.

Witjagit was soon reunited with his children. That night, a big corroboree ceremony was held by the waterhole. Old friends and new friends came together to share story, song and dance around the fire long into the night. The next morning, the emu family gathered with the animals to say goodbye.

'Thank you for what you have given us,' Witjagit said. 'You have shared much knowledge ... you have shared much wisdom. You have given us special memories and life-long friendships. But most of all, you have showed us to never, ever, ever give up hope.

The story above might be considered a contemporary Dreamtime Story. The word dreamtime creates an unfortunate inference that the narrative is some kind of fairy tale created to entertain and having no bearing with reality in this contemporary world.

This kind of thinking could not be further from the truth. If you look closely at this story, it provides keys that open many doors of insight and conversation relevant to day to day modern life. Themes include:

- Responsibility
- The role of parenting
- Stereotyping
- Gratitude
- Spirituality
- Understanding danger (imagined versus real)
- The importance of learning
- The importance of Elders
- The importance of children
- Environmental vandalism
- The need to care for the environment
- Greed
- Hope
- Selflessness
- Belief
- Finding the strength within
- Unity
- Kindness
- Resilience
- Thinking creatively
- Accepting help
- Celebration
- The importance of relationships

There are probably more themes a reader can harvest from this one short story, which is also an important aspect of dreamtime stories ... the learning that comes through the story will differ for each person hearing it. The main reason I wrote this story however, wasn't about the themes I have outlined. It was to demonstrate that the sharing of story is a powerful mechanism for creating positive learning, messaging and conversation that is much needed if we are to turn the current negative aspects of the world around and build on the positive.

There are many good things in this world. By fusing them with the wisdom of the ancients, a new hybrid of thought and action can be generated that learns from the past, prepares us for the future and enables us to dance in the present.

In the Aboriginal way of thinking, we are conceived in love, born in love, are surrounded by love and eventually leave our bodies to travel back into the spirit world which is a place of love.

If we are able to truly embrace this concept of universal, unconditional love, we will walk meaningful footsteps that are infused with gratitude for what we have (as opposed to envy for what we want). In a mindset of gratitude we are more able to share (goodwill, knowledge, spirit and material things), providing a platform of meaning that enables us to care for our place and all things in our place. In this space, hope will flourish.

Hope can be defined as an optimistic state of mind that is based on expectation of positive outcomes with respect to events and circumstances in one's life and the world at large.

For Aboriginal people, the infusion of spirituality into all aspects of daily life created a way of thinking where hope was so ubiquitous as to be invisible. It is a sad reflection of modern society that we need people to become 'hope ambassadors' in attempt to foster and grow this diminishing resource.

The Old People say that *when we leave this world behind all we leave behind is our story ... so make it the best story possible.*

In traditional times, every individual was given the knowledge and support to achieve this. Once upon a time the world as a collective was living a good story.

Right now, many individuals aren't living the best story possible.

Right now, the evidence (scientific, statistical, observative, spiritual) suggests the world is living a tainted story.

It is not too late to turn this around and enable the world to once again be a good story. We owe this to those who have come before us and we owe this to those who will come after us.

I have not given up hope.

Endnotes

1 Callaghan. P, Gordon. P, (2014). Iridescence – Finding Your Colours and Living Your Story.

---

blessing

be blessing of bone—supple as tree in the purity of storm
be storm—raining ripped roofs over the pride of brick
be stone as whiskey in the belly—like hot truth
be the wing of sun-seeking geese crying over the hurt of tomorrow
be in each other's eye
be like the smoke of time-shrouded sorrow
be between the bullets of teeth
be over all the fingers of lost, seeking cheeks of understanding
be like jazz in hand, like blues in heart, like song of nowhere
      bursting now into a thousand possibilities
be the rap of revelation, the interruption of assimilation, the stove of cooked isness—
      burning black recipes
be amen of street-corner at midnight, the coffee of nose at dawn
be without the end of narrative in the middle of your neighbor's tongue
be the joint of metaphor blowing white up the vein of community
be the bond of syncopation
be the cut across the body of same
be the note between the lines
be calabash of ancestor eyes
be the now of nirvana on the thigh of desire
be tomorrow today
      like a trope rioting truth
      like instinct
      like a verb from the third eye
      like blood in heat
      like a word over the void
      like the groan of knowledge inside the groin of despair
be that
be it
be all
be where   the one shouts many
beware   being unaware
be   be   be   be
bop.

—*jim perkinson*

Hope Summons:

Meditations on An-Other-World Seeing

S. Lily Mendoza

Agusan Marsh Wildlife Sanctuary, site of one of author's reflections. (Photo by Jojie Alcantara)

I remember reading Vera de Chalambert's piece, "Kali Takes America: I'm with Her" (2016) in the aftermath of Trump's election in 2016 and being struck by the counter-intuitive insight: we need to let Holy Darkness have her way with us, that it's only in Kali, the Hindu goddess of destruction, that our illusions of false hope can fall away that then prepares us for the ministrations of the Divine Doctor. And how much we need those ministrations! A xenophobe, narcissist, misogynist, White Supremacist, climate change denier, pathological liar, taking hold of the biggest bully pulpit in the world. And this after decades of unrelenting neoliberal plunder and business-as-usual indifference to ice caps melting and ecosystems collapsing. And then like a kamikaze exclamation point—a virus pandemic, upending everything that the civilized world had taken for granted as "normal."

The Dark Night of the Soul—the work of the Underworld—seems to be our nearly ubiquitous course today as a species. When Canadian singer-songwriter Leonard Cohen was interviewed at the release of his fourteenth studio album, *You Want It Darker*, he was noted to have remarked that, contrary to what many had interpreted as an expression of hopelessness, his album was really about "offering ourselves up" when the "*emergency becomes articulate*" (in de Chalambert, 2016, emphasis added). But emergency doesn't just come into speech on its own—was my thought reflecting on his meaning. For that to happen, something other than the default condition of emergency has to become apparent as well; otherwise, all we get is a seamless experience of catastrophe in moving from one exigency to the next. There is need for a contrast apparition, a vision of something different in order to bring the given state of emergency into stark relief.

I am someone who, for decades now, has been compelled by an alternative report on the world to what might be called "the prize winning story" of civilizational triumph (Kremer & Jackson-Patton, 212-217), in which human beings are represented as having at last conquered the world by gradually, over the course of millennia, wresting their fate from the maw of barbarism, backwardness, and precarious living (unlike those that cannot but bow to the "will of the gods"). Within the logic of this much venerated story, the constant state of emergency that has come to define the

---

Dr. S. Lily Mendoza is a full Professor of Culture and Communication at Oakland University in Rochester, Michigan. She is known for her pathbreaking work on the politics of indigeneity and critique of modernity, in particular, within the Philippine diasporic and homeland context. She has published widely around questions of identity and belonging, cultural politics in national, post- and trans- national contexts, race and indigeneity, and, more recently, on ecology and questions of meaning in the face of climate change and eco-systems collapse. She currently serves as the Executive Director of the Center for Babaylan Studies, a movement for decolonization and indigenization among diasporic Filipinos.

modern condition—the sense of there never being enough time, resources, energy, wealth, etc.—is hardly seen as such, but simply the price that must be paid for *homo sapiens*' triumph.

The reasoning goes this way: we were made for *this*—for endless advancement, for accelerating progress, for the hard-fought assemblage of ever better ways "full humanity." In that colonized view, life on the land was "eewww" (!)—no better than animal-like existence, conjuring images of dirt, pitiful privations of subsistence living, and back-breaking labor just to eke out a living. Who in their right minds would want such? Hands down, we choose the prize winning story (of modern convenience, sur- felt like an ancestral visitation from a time before my own existence.

I speak of that transformative moment as one that now allows me to find the emergency of our time keenly articulate in every fiber of my being. The progressive story I had swallowed whole, sugar-coating a violence that now begins to appear global in scope, no longer shapes my longing. It rather grates within like jagged glass, its contradictions and impossibilities broken open by an older and deeper vision whose wisdom gives stark warning. There is no vaccine for what we have unleashed on the earth, no "normal" to return to that is not itself more deadly than the virus we currently suffer. Our moment is indeed "emergent" like apocalypse, disclosing a doom that could well spell not only our own end as a species but a terminus for much of the rest of life on the planet. In the gloom of such we may well try to persuade ourselves that it is the moments just before daybreak that are darkest. But if dawn is to come, its clemency will be Indigenous, a deliverance not new, but ancient as the sun, as recurrent as seed.

In ancient Indian prophecies of the Eagle and the Condor in both North and South "America" (cf. SOTA, 2013), we are told that the intelligent, powerful, masculine energy of the Eagle from the North that invents, explores, and makes things happen will once again—after its separation by the advent of Euro-colonialism—reunite with the feminine, more intuitive, energy of the Condor from the South that feels as the Earth Mother feels, that seeks interconnection with all beings. When that time comes, the question for the rest of us is whether or not we will become part of the throng that will "offer themselves up," as Leonard Cohen's "You Want It Darker" album intones. If and when the emergency finally becomes "articulate" to us as emergency, and not simply business as usual, will we rise up to the demand?

> But if dawn is to come, its clemency will be Indigenous, a deliverance not new, but ancient as the sun, as recurrent as seed.

to live. And, although the price of this "progress" is sometimes lamented as regrettable, it is deemed "nevertheless worth paying" (Wolloch, 2013, p. 108). Hence, emergency simply becomes the air we breathe. Without an alternative story, we indeed flounder, but just grit our teeth, make do and (all too often) ask no further questions. But this narrative begs challenge. It is neither natural nor inevitable.

My own schooling in an alternative story irrupted into my life unexpectedly a few decades ago. It happened, quite unwittingly, in a seminar at the University of the Philippines where I was doing graduate studies, serving as a watershed moment in my life that now frames all my subsequent transformative journeying. This life-defining moment, the overturning of the conventional, received worldview and the uncovering of layers of richness and subtle beauty rooted elsewhere that I had not known previously except in my bones, has become the foundation of my hope today.

The title of the course was "The Image of the Filipino in the Arts," taught by an ethnomusicology professor who brought into the classroom samples of the works of art of the Philippines' various Indigenous tribes—their fabrics, weaving designs, basketry, dances, epic chants, architecture, etc.—and what they expressed by way of a different mode of being in the world. That first-time encounter with indigenously-authored beauty opened me up to a whole new world—one only peripherally glimpsed in my colonial upbringing as a world we, Filipinos, had to leave behind if we were ever to "advance" and come into our plus production, and mesmerizing technological wonders).

In that class, however, I was smitten. I fell in love, awestruck not only by the beauty of Indigenous design, but by the ritual subtlety and cosmological complexity of the worlds that gave birth to such brilliant artistic creations. Here were peoples whom I had only heard talked about previously as "*napag-iwanan ng panahon*," "left-behind by the times." Yet, the effect of that first-time encounter with their different way of being as revealed through their works of art was a quickening of what British mythologist Martin Shaw calls "bone memory."[1] Like a lab-raised chick shuddering when a hawk-shaped shadow is passed overhead in the lab when it has never seen a hawk before and does not shudder at other shadows, I, too, responded with bodily tremor. But from recognition the opposite of fear! Walking out of every class session, heaves of emotion and copious tears would overwhelm me, flooding me with homecoming relief after what had seemed like an interminable exile from my own Indigenous soul—the consequence of years of unrelenting psychic disconfirmation through colonial tutelage growing up. Bones shook and re-birthed flesh; hope for myself and for a different kind of world began to make themselves

> There is no vaccine for what we have unleashed on the earth, no "normal" to return to that is not itself more deadly than the virus we currently suffer.

In what follows, I share three meditations coming out of my schooling into the alternative story I mention. My hope is that they might help in throwing into sharp relief the arbitrariness of our modern civilization's emergency and its naturalization as "just our given human condition." The message is simple: Things don't have to be this way. The meditations come out of my journaling entries as I reflect on a number of rare opportunities to spend a stretch of time with the Condor peoples in my home country, the Philippines—those who still live and carry memory of life outside the roiling emergency. Though unspared of its effects (and in fact the recipients of its worst impacts), they remain remarkably grounded in the summons of that alternative world that they, and their ancestors before them, have sought to keep alive through generations. They are the Earth peoples, the rememberers. And I smile recalling all that they have taught me. Whatever tinge of hope I have, whatever possibility of a different future I can imagine (different from that augured by the architects of the not-yet articulate emergency already here), I owe to their witness.

Agusan Marsh Diaries

Journal Entry #1

There are no words to describe the magic of our time in Agusan Marsh, a wildlife sanctuary in the Southern Philippines in the island of Mindanao where a Manobo tribe lived in a floating village called Sitio Panlabuhan. There were three of us women, namely, Grace Nono, head of Tao Foundation,[2] and Mila Anguluan and I, elder-collaborators from the Center for Babaylan Studies,[3] who were self-commissioned to do an advanced reconnaissance of places we might include as part of the programming for a gathering called *Pamati*, a Visayan word meaning "to listen." It was a meeting of Philippine tribal elders and youth learners (both local and diasporic) scheduled for the following year. The Agusan Marshlands presented a good opportunity, given its proximity to the main gathering venue in Bunawan where Grace's family's ancestral home was located.

The tree sentinels and water lilies at the Agusan Marsh. (Photo by Jojie Alcantara)

Our trip began with a three-hour boat ride going from Bunawan to the site with the accompaniment of new friends from the local community in Agusan del Sur. Catching sight of the floating village of Sitio Panlabuhan was breathtaking, with children skillfully rowing slender *bancas* (small dug-out canoes) on their own, and community members welcoming us ever so warmly.

Entry into the village (comprised entirely of houses and structures floating atop either cut bamboo or big plastic barrels) meant parting the thick stretch of water lilies as we approached the village area. Now and then our competent rowers would step out of the boat into the shallow waters to stir the boat through the lush green. We're told that crocodiles routinely inhabit the waters but that only the domesticated ones (!) eat humans. That's because there are unwise people who take baby crocs as pets, putting red bead necklaces around their necks as identifying tags and getting them accustomed to being fed instead of letting them learn to hunt for food on their own. The day comes when their "owner" fails to feed them and they go hungry, and that's when they take the first flesh they could find, often an unsuspecting human. The natives know this and thus refrain from messing with the wild creatures that actually command respect in their own right. (They also know not to go to regions in the water known specifically as their abode, placing well-defined limits on human habitation.)

Punctuating the floating landscape, or rather, waterscape, were tall thin trees with trunks curiously covered with long downcast leaves, standing silently like noble sentinels guarding the place with a watchful eye. One wonders how tall these trees really were—how far into the water the trunks extended before they hit solid ground. Everything here is alive. Looking out from the balcony of the main building structure, one is overtaken with a sense of awe at the beauty of it all—with Father Sky[4] kissing the gentle waters on the horizon as the stately tree sentinels looked on. Occasionally, a splash here and there announced the presence of finned relatives, although, increasingly, village folk lamented the destruction of their kind by the recent practice of illegal fishing that used *kuryente* to electrocute or shock these living creatures into paralysis, thus making them prone to easy capture. Often even baby ones get killed and those that manage to escape become sterile, their reproductive capacity rendered permanently nil. This practice drives the fish away, we're told, and makes life harder for the people of the sitio who rely mostly on fishing for their sustenance.

When we arrived, Datu Boyet, the president/elder of the Tribung Manobo of Sitio Panlabuhan, performed a simple but moving ritual requesting the spirit guardians of the place to grant us safety and protection as we visited, assuring them of the goodness of our intentions. We had come prepared with the requested items for ritual offering: sweet candy, biscuits, rum, beer, Royal Tru Orange (!), coins (one from each of us), cigarettes, and lit candles. Invoking first the *Ginoo* (supreme being), then the *Amigos* (spirit ancestors/guardians of the place), Datu Boyet made humble supplication in his native tongue for our gifts to be accepted. Then the drinks were poured out into the water, the biscuits and candy as well. Lastly, we were asked to throw in the coins while silently reiterating our personal reasons for coming.

It must have been the sincerity of the words spoken, or the spirit with which Datu Boyet prayed, but the tenderness of the ritual so touched me that I was moved to tears. Amazing how such a simple gesture of asking permission served as a cautionary announcement, reminding one of local conviction that courtesy was required to come, not as a tourist, but as a guest, humbly seeking the sufferance of one's intrusion from the beings of the place—the waters, the land underneath, the trees, the fishes, along with the human hosts. Later, everyone was invited to share in what remained of the drink, candy, and biscuits, with the kids only being allowed to partake of the Royal True Orange, not the rum, or beer. (Whether such items were innovations from the surrounding commercial culture, I had no chance to figure out for sure. But not unlike in other parts of the world where commercial items of commodified intrusion (like Coca-Cola) are taken up in Indigenous genius and re-deployed, alongside more native offerings, in service of respect (cf. Nelson, 1997)—and some such even taking on the aura of magic or a fetish—I could only imagine so).

In the afternoon, it rained hard and the water rose a bit. After it stopped, we decided we wanted to go check out the *langgam* (migratory birds) that we were told liked to come through that area, but that really come from places far away as none of them were native to the place. Datu Boyet obliged and, again, we reveled in being out on the water, this time, bird-watching.

We had brought our own food for lunch and dinner—chicken and pork adobo prepared by Grace's expert cook, Arcing, the trusted caretaker of her family as far back as Grace could remember. Manang Diding, who had a PhD in Home Economics,[5] with the assistance of her med tech daughter KKen (Kiken), made sure everything was laid out just so. It was quite a feast by candlelight. The marsh took on an eerie feel as night fell slowly and all you could see were the shadows of the tree sentinels in the not too far distance.

Since there was no electricity, we decided to head early for bed, as our "civilized" bodies reluctantly eased into Nature's circadian rhythm. Our hosts had laid out sleeping mats on the floor with mosquito nets—Mila, Grace, and I under one large mosquito net, and Nang Diding and Kken in another. As usual, Mila was out cold right away while Grace and I yakked away sharing life journeys. Then it was time to sleep even for us.

When we awoke early the next morning, the whole marsh was solid green! The water lilies had closed in and formed one big giant island, stopping only short of the long bamboo demarcation barrier placed at the entrance of the water village. The transformation was magical—mud and water taken over in a single night by a breathing emerald carpet! It isn't for nothing that marshlands have been called the "kidneys of the Earth" (in the way forests are described as the

> The transformation was magical—mud and water taken over in a single night by a breathing emerald carpet! It isn't for nothing that marshlands have been called the "kidneys of the Earth."

Author's visit to the floating village of Sitio Panlabuhan of the Tribung Manobo, Agusan Marsh with host tribal Elder Boyet and other community members. (Photo by Grace Nono)

Banca ride to and from the Agusan Marshlands with Grace Nono. (Photo by KKen Toyong)

"lungs of the Earth"). Besides serving to strain out upstream pollutants, they filter "muck" into vibrant beauty, granting "nearly a billion human denizens a bounteous living by way of farming, fishing, tourism, or transportation and serving as 'nursery' for around 40 percent of the world's species" (Gibbens, February 2, 2021).

Our hosts caught and broiled *gurami* and *dalag* and donated a giant cucumber from their floating garden and also cooked the rice that we brought with us. The *sawsawan* (sauce) was *sili* (hot pepper), *suka* (vinegar) with *toyo* (soy sauce) and chopped onions. We decided to eat right at the bamboo platform outside instead of inside the structure and again, what a feast!

Then it was time to go to the next village by Lake Mihaba, also on the marsh. En route, we stopped to greet Datu Dinagat, whom we caught finishing the building of a nice boat all by hand. He was trusted by both the insurgent NPA (New People's Army) and the military, an unusual feat, and was a strong leader in his community.

The village of Lake Mihaba was a different story altogether. Arriving there next, we found a sense of depression and deprivation that we didn't find in Datu Boyet's Sitio Panlabuhan. The people also complained of illegal fishing by those they call "techno killers" (the loggers, the miners, the illegal fishers, etc.) but it seemed that, in their case, they've had nowhere to go with their grief and anger. Not surprisingly one of us caught a whiff of alcohol on the resident *baylan* (shaman) who performed a ritual for our entry into the area that included, this time, use of a sacrificial chicken (that we had supplied), along with the usual candy, biscuits, coins, cigarettes—and this time we had to "offer" apologies, as we had already used up the rum, beer and Royal Tru Orange in the previous sitio. It was a hard place for us and we all felt the heaviness when we debriefed afterwards. The other community had exuded joyful wholeness and spiritual strength despite their challenges, but this one was different. Modern aggression had left its usual mark.

Then it was time to go home—another three hours on the *banca*. This time, we were all mostly quiet and exhausted—and feeling it especially on our butts (!) from sitting on hard planks of wood for long periods. Our guide, a boy merely eight- or nine-years old, sat at the front end of the banca. I had noticed him even earlier on, on our way there, sitting quietly the whole time, looking out at the marsh. His presence reflected the waters themselves—clear, fluid, undisturbed. And I was struck by the sudden recognition: no need to worry about kids like him getting hooked on drugs or needing gadgets to distract them from boredom. Their untrammeled capacity to engage with their own Wild "home" granted them an entrancement and fascination unparalleled by artifice or substance. They lived in the kind of ecstasy for which all of our species is designed.

Sakahang Lilok Organic Farm, Tanay, Rizal. (Photo by Lester Valle)

Once back into town, we stumbled into another juxtaposition of emergency and its alternative—the story of ceaseless crises versus the longing for more natural fluidity and mutuality. The crisis was at the immediate doorstep. It turned out that Grace had been dealing for some time with an encroachment problem on her parents' land where a developer had begun cutting meters into their property. So as soon as we got to her house, we again hopped on a tricycle—this time to the barangay captain's office to request a stop order to the construction going on until further investigation. Luckily, the barangay captain was more than happy to oblige.

On the other hand, the next morning, Mila and I were supposed to head back to Butuan City for our flight back to Manila later that day when Grace decided we'd pay a courtesy call on the president of the State Agricultural College of Bunawan. So off we went on another tricycle, only for her to realize it was only seven o'clock in the morning and no one was at the office yet, so back we went to have breakfast, then back again to the president's office where we were welcomed warmly. When I mentioned that I teach culture, communication, and Indigenous studies, the president immediately said that's the kind of program he wanted to build in his college! Ancestral yearning is never far under the surface! And so we brainstormed a bit and committed to helping develop a curriculum for teaching, research, and extension.

The bus ride to Butuan City where Mila and I were to take our flight back to Manila left me with much to mull on, my heart filled with a mix of dread and longing. And looking out the bus window only amplified the feeling starkly. Here were huge logging trucks loaded with murdered tree beings all along the way! More grief! How long could Earth-loving peoples keep watch over the land and waters and preserve the beauty they revered intact? Revisiting those moments for this writing, I am struck by a recently encountered article. "When a wetland disappears, it's like pulling a linchpin out of a healthy environment," says National Geographic correspondent Sarah Gibbens (February 2, 2021). Fifty years since the Ramsar Convention in Iran to protect wetlands, "more than 35 percent of the world's wetlands have been drained for urban development or agriculture, polluted, paved over, or lost to sea level rise," she adds.

Pamati Summons

Journal Entry #2

How to capture in words seven days of glorious communing with Indigenous elders and fellow urbanized participants and with the lush vegetation, waterfalls, springs, and mountains of Tanay, Rizal[6] and the sacred mountains of Apo Banahaw, and Mariang Makiling? This is the longest time I've been away from my laptop and cellphone screens, thanks to the forbidding distance from civilization (and perhaps to the energies of the sacred mountains for which human-made electronic signals were no match?).

It was the second *Pamati* gathering convened by Tao Foundation and its co-hosts[7] in the summer of 2017. Those of us modern-schooled, and no longer living on the land came to listen, to learn from the elders, to have our bodies and souls remember the old ways again.

Writing this, I feel a deep sense of gratitude to our gracious venue hosts—Sakahang Lilok Organic Farm, Nature Villa Banahaw (c/o traditional healing arts practitioner Boy Fajardo), and the Philippine National High School for the Arts at Mt. Makiling, a publicly-funded school for gifted youth artists (courtesy of alumna Grace Nono and Director Vim Nadera, whom I finally got to meet in person for the first time). To Sakahang Lilok I owe special thanks for teaching our bodies to fall in love again with the simple deliciousness of (mostly) plant-based slow-food cooking and the totally respectful and sensible concept of zero-waste living (where even our human waste becomes "*ambag*"/useful contribution for other earth beings). I was grateful, too, for the permeable walls and bamboo structures of our sleeping quarters that allowed the elders' contagious laughter and loud uninhibited bantering to wake us up in the early morning, sometimes even before dawnbreak—the one thing I'd probably miss the most from this year's gathering!

I imagine this is how it must have been when we still lived embedded in the generosity of the natural world and in the face-to-face sociality of our Indigenous villages: waking up to the first rays of Grandfather Sun whose westward trek is aided by the cacophonous voices and toothless laughter of elders (and the running about of happy children's feet); ordinary conversations spontaneously breaking into song or poetry at a moment's inspiration (I will miss Datu Makalipay and Manong Rodolfo's mellifluous duets of love songs!); work life spared of tedium by the rhythmic accompaniment of song to motion and/or the trading of *tsismis* (gossip); young people's bodies naturally synched up to the rhythms of nature's circadian clock and quick to take to the beat of gongs, drums, and other native instruments—the energy of dance and movement climbing up their spine and out their nimble limbs without so much as effort or trying. And when death, sickness, or conflict occurs, the gathering of the whole village to grieve, deliberate together, and perform rites of healing and/or reconciliation.

Pamati gave us but a tiny taste (a "*patikim*") of that earth-based life that we all used to know (and perhaps, to a degree, still know in our bones) before a part of our species had the (supposedly) brilliant idea of breaking away and building a culture (purportedly) "more advanced" and unconstrained by the collective necessities of village-and land-based living. And indeed, given my overly domesticated body, a part of me, like an addict in withdrawal, craved, while at Sakahang Lilok, the usual comforts of unhampered electricity, sanitized flushing toilets, and piped in water supply (that didn't remind one of the preciousness of water and the deleterious effects on the ecosystem of the water

The Philippine High School for the Arts at the foothills of Mount Makiling (view of Makiling partially obscured by cloud cover in the background). (Photo by Gino T. Manalastas)

closet and the toxic chloro- and hydro-chlorofluorocarbons and other greenhouse gases from air conditioning).

So much so that by the sixth day, when we got to the Imeldific structures (yes, designed by the famed "patroness of the arts" herself—Imelda Marcos, the grandiose, shoe-loving wife of the former Philippine dictator Ferdinand Marcos!) of the fully air-conditioned executive suites of the Makiling Philippine National High School for the Arts where we were to close out our gathering, it was as though the drug-starved neurons of the ease-addicted civilized body instantly started firing, having finally found their "stash."

Alas, whatever pleasure the initial "hit" brought, it wasn't long before grief's reality check followed suit. The feeling was akin to what my hubby and I had once experienced in a five-star hotel stay in Bangkok (courtesy of a conference host), where, upon entering our luxury room and lighting a ritual candle to pay homage to the new place and taking note of the exquisite wood paneling, the stone, and metal that graced the tastefully designed interiors, we found ourselves imagining what grandmother tree (or rock or iron) had to be sacrificed and forcibly taken from its wild abode to be tamed and reshaped for another purpose by human ingenuity. In the lavish executive lodgings of the School for the Arts, I likewise wondered what sort of ritual permission and honoring, if any, were performed in the building of these luxury structures that allowed one the glorious panoramic view of the nearby Mount Makiling from the unalloyed convenience of one's individual veranda.

I cry now writing these reflections, realizing once again my own domestication that causes my "oh-so-civilized" body to flinch at the slightest bit of discomfort and to revel—despite awareness of the cost to other beings and to life itself—at the (mostly non-ritual[8]) invention of modern conveniences. When I heard one elder ruefully remark on what he thought was their mountain's "relative disadvantage and undesirability" in comparison to the sleekly paved Mt. Makiling foothills, I knew I wasn't alone in my discord. But as if to affirm the complex relations between human-tamed and wild places, another elder replied, "*Pero mas malakas pa rito ang energy ng mountain namin*" ("But the energy of our [wild/untamed] mountain is even stronger than this one").

There have been many learnings for me. Despite the limitations of the framework of Pamati (that artificially brings together in the span of eight days a roughly equal number of Indigenous elders and Indigenous root-seeking urbanized Filipinos both in the homeland and abroad for mutual listening), there is something powerful even in such a brief encounter. For the younger urbanized participants, the copious tears and heartfelt expressions of gratitude to the elders for their unstinting generosity in sharing their gifts and stories and for the sense of community created is testament to the need for such initiatory opportunities for mutual encounter. For the elders, to find such openness of hearts and eagerness among the urbanized participants for a taste of what they had to offer was deep affirmation of their sense of self—in contrast to the racialization and devaluing of their ways of being that is just their default experience living cheek-by-jowl with mainstream culture. The mirroring back to them by the younger participants of what they still have—the memory of how to live in a good way on the land that the young ones have lost and are only now seeking to recover in a world of amnesia—creates a fertile ground for mutual love and transformation. "I see you," they seem to say to each other—and in that deep seeing and affirmation of generations is the seed of wholeness, healing, and recovery of well-being.

I saw this in the eyes of the students of the Philippine National High School for the Arts, elite young scholars all, that we were privileged to engage on the last day of our gathering. Here were students schooled almost exclusively in the Western arts (what were deemed "the real arts" worth learning, not the dubious so-called "arts" of "primitive" peoples like those gathered with us at *Pamati*). I saw during our time with them the hunger in these students as they listened to the testimonies of our own young participants. And as they joined the workshops conducted by the different groups of Indigenous cultural masters, we saw them gamely try their hand at native instruments (kulintang, gong). We witnessed them move their bodies to the vigorous guitar rhythms and dance steps of the Ayta and to the graceful movements of the Maguindanaon *kuntao* (martial arts). We saw their curiosity to learn about the Indigenous healing arts (hilot, herbal/plant medicine) from the elder practitioners.

Even after the formal plenary where each group reported on their learning experiences, a number of students persisted in playing the various native instruments. One 15-year-old student came to me unable to hold back her tears, sharing her grief at being forcibly severed from what she recognized as her gift of "third-eye" seeing that she said she possessed from a very young age, of being able to connect deeply with nature spirits, and of being friends with unseen beings, until her parents, now Christian, performed a ritual to close up that third eye and effectively banished her spirit guides from her. This she now experiences as a deep loss. She said the testimony of one of the diasporic youth who shared her story of being deemed "mentally ill" from her possession of a similar gift (until she was able to find Indigenous teachers who helped her make sense of her experience) resonated deeply with her.

Such resonances were many at the conclusion of our time together. As well, questions and struggles of where now to go with this kind of rich learning and experience. A lot of our process in the

Building of a Manobo Tinandasan Hut using no nails. (Photo by Lester Ngawit Valle)

Completed Manobo Tinandasan Hut. (Photo by Lester Ngawit Valle)

co-convening group has answered to the proverb "we make our way as we go along" knowing the kinds of times we live in—dire times of climate change, species extinction, ecosystems collapse, war and more war.

For me, that "way" has especially been portended by the example of another antique people, whose starkly apocalyptic encounter in 1976 with the planet's capacity for fierce disruption of any human pretense to control has been remarkably detailed by shaman-initiate, Martín Prechtel (2012). On February 4 of that year, a 7.5 magnitude earthquake had decimated many mountain villages in Guatemala (ultimately killing more than 31,000 and displacing more than 180,000). Prechtel had survived the initial tremor and then had set about trying to bring relief (food and water) to stranded highlanders, when he and fellow volunteers came upon the gathered remnants of five villages in the upland environs of Cuchumaquic. Some 300 people were huddled out in the open in extended family groups, exhausted, famished, and in pain, convinced the world was ending everywhere, but resolved to live their last moments together with all the beautiful honorifics and respectful courtesy they exhibited in everyday life under normal circumstances. Prechtel much later wrote:

> [T]hey had come to pass the world's end at the place all Mayans, every village and tribe, know as their rumuxux or the "umbilicus of the world." They wanted the symphony of their thousand years' struggle to live in the arms of the corn seed's earth to end here where it had begun: at the place of their mutual origins. In this way they themselves would become spiritual seeds and their passing become temporal humus from which the Divine could regrow a world beyond their own time. In their parallel understanding of vegetation and human culture, they wanted to be rooted in the Earth's memory of their having been there, even if they as humans had to disappear. After all, all the mythologies said that they as people had themselves sprouted from a time previous to any of our own presence, and like seeds had resprouted themselves from the compost of a world of previous human failures. (P. 46-47)

The trick was not to seek the fantasized comfort or the falsely anchored dependability that civilization promises. Instead of the illusion of security, it's better to get good at riding out [Earth's] motion like a bone cell heaving in the ribs of Her breathing chest—and heaving She was. (P. 25)

Their witness was and is astonishing—putting virtually every "modern" reaction to similar kinds of emergency to shame. There was no frenzy, no opportunism, no crazed hysteria seeking self-preservation. There was just calm acknowledgment of an irreducible magnificence that would continue to grace this world's wild fierceness of motion and life whether death would come quickly or wait another time. The example is epochal and for me, epic. I feel this is a time when, like the people of Cuchumaquic, we no longer come together "just to have a better chance at survival" but rather to learn to prepare for a time beyond our own, to sow seeds of love for the Holy in Nature that can resprout after the dying or even something as radical as extinction.

Offering Ourselves Up When the Emergency Becomes Articulate

Journal Entry #3

It has been a remarkable year—full of endings and new beginnings, the shock of unexpected death (and near-deaths) in the family, the deep tutelage in grief and survival and the many questions why. Yet the world goes on, and I go on—taking up new mantles of responsibility, learning new roles, letting go of old struggles, and stepping in faith into new ways of being that, soon enough, the body recognizes as really old and familiar.

"Written in the bones," the Wise Ones would say, from ancestry long forgotten, but not finally extinguished. It is these embers of old ways of being that now demand hallowing in this new season of life—capped ceremoniously in the homeland by the gift of ritual cleansing by an elder from the North, a communal celebration of Ayta brothers and sisters in the Plains, and, finally, the witnessing of power, spirit, and resurrection (of Indigenous memory) in a gathering of healers and elders in the South that I have yet to find words to fully describe.

I have glimpsed life-giving beauty—the building of a Manobo *tinandasan* hut using no nails, with each piece of bamboo, nipa, or rattan, sang to and praised before harvest until permission is granted, master builders still retaining memory of the old way of doing things;[9] people who co-exist and honor the crocodiles on their marshlands as the Spirit Guardians of the waters (in stark contrast to the town Mayor's bloodlust upon capturing—and eventually killing—the crocodile Lolong, touted as the largest in the world); a woman Indigenous leader being ministered to in ceremony by Muslim *patutunong* healers so she could finally accept her calling to become a healer herself; native youth taking up the mantle of leadership in fighting corporate encroachment of their ancestral lands; the laughter of *Manangs* and *Manongs* as they told their stories, and the beautiful chanting of other elders in response.

It is these kinds of encounters—with our Indigenous Peoples and those working on the ground alongside them—that now serve as the homeward beacon for me. Just like native peoples everywhere else around the globe threatened by the relentless incursion of the now globalized initiative of extraction into their territories, our own Indigenous kin in the Philippine homeland struggle bravely to keep their beautiful ways of being alive amidst the assault. The grief (at their beleaguered condition) compels, but so does the grace, beauty, and courage of their spirit.

I have studied—and written—extensively about indigeneity ever since the start of my decolonization journey, but not until recently have I allowed my body to be part of that process of knowing in any significant way. "You cannot exit one cultural formation without entering another," I hear my hubby, James Perkinson, say. To me, that "other" would no longer be just the "nation"—land of my birth and home country prior to diasporic exile. To the extent that the national cultural formation (urban, modern, schooled, civilized) re-enacts on its cultural "others" (rural, Indigenous, unschooled, "unwashed") the same colonizing logic imposed upon it by its foreign oppressors, it is just as culpable of the ongoing genocide and oppression of its internal unassimilable (Indigenous) "others."

The crisis of our time—whether of climate change, species extinction, dying oceans, or disappearing forests and marshlands—is rooted finally in our civilized world's insistence on separating itself from the Earth womb whence we all come from. The slow-cooking required by that Earth life in crafting lives of ritual subtlety, beauty, and nuance brooks no shortcuts, and no time-saving gadgets and other lords of efficiency; rather what it calls for is a kind of diligent tending befitting a courtship relationship with the Divine Life-Giver. Face-to-face with the Condor peoples still living and accepting both the gifts and vicissitudes of Earth-based living, I could only echo Prechtel's (2012) sentiment when, confronted with Cuchumaqic's astonishing counter-example in the face of mortal hunger and decimation, he says:

> At least the few of us...who could see it knew that both we and the civilization we came from were the starving ones, searching all our lives to be fed by this indescribable thing that the world we were born from could not comprehend, much less maintain. (P. 61)

He calls that thing we're starving for "seeds of peace." Real peace (or what I would call rest from our modern lives' ceaseless striving), he reminds us,

> ...cannot be obtained, taken, bought, or stolen, nor can it be bestowed. This kind of peace was always there; it just had to be accepted and lived, if even for a few minutes. This peace said that people were not here to succeed in taking over the world; they were here to feed the beauty of being a human to the Holy in Nature. By keeping such seeds alive we become beautiful enough to keep the Holy alive. That [is] peace. (P. 61)

Today, I no longer just want to "study" the *katutubo* [indigenous], but to strive to become at least partially reshaped in their image (without thereby fooling myself that I have become "Indigenous" myself). Entering into some kind of ongoing relationship with them no matter how fraught and constrained, no matter my grief at air travel (that is so destructive to the planet) is part of the pedagogy. For now, I choose my poison, not knowing how much longer this body (and this planet!) can abide such means of mobility that alone, in my current exilic condition, makes possible the bodily tutelage to this other way of being.

But for now, I'm grateful there is yet a bit of that other organic life right outside my window (here in Wawiiatanong, the post-industrial city of Detroit)—the generous world of soil, air, trees, rocks, squirrels, birds, bushes and other growing beings—requiring just as much *pamati* (deep listening) to feed and tutor my soul's natural being. I know in my bones that the time is coming when we shall all realize that the future is Indigenous, as our Jesuit scholar-friend, Fr. Albert Alejo, likes to say. For as long as the Wild remains and we have ears to hear and eyes to see, we, too, may yet experience the summons of that other world calling us to "offer ourselves up" for the work of witnessing to its reality, once the emergency of our times has finally been "made articulate" and appallingly apparent to us by this other way of seeing.

Endnotes

1. Shaw, M. (Nov. 30, 2016).
2. A Philippine grassroots organization committed to cultural regeneration and revitalization of local ancestral and traditional knowledges and practices in the Philippines and primary host of the planned gathering.
3. A movement for decolonization and indigenization among diasporic Filipinos on Turtle Island (US and Canada)
4. Here, I will occasionally refer to what modernity labels "objects" as personal beings who are alive, to honor the worldview of the hosts themselves as well as serve notice to "rational objectivity" that such is a cultural construct betraying capitalist bias, not an actual "truth" about such realities.
5. And is a Tao Foundation trustee.
6. A town east of Manila.
7. Namely, the Center for Babaylan Studies (CfBS), GINHAWA, Institute for Spirituality Asia, and the Carl Jung Circle.
8. I.e., without honoring and without asking permission from the living beings now reduced into mere "resource" or "raw materials."
9. Witnessed at the first 2015 Pamati.

References

Chalambert, V. d. (2016). Kali takes America: I'm with her. *Rebelle Society*. Last accessed 12/06/2020 http://www.rebellesociety.com/2016/11/18/veradechalambert-kali/

Gibbens, S. (February 2, 2021). The world's wetlands are slipping away. This vibrant sanctuary underscores the stakes. National geographic. Last accessed 2/14/2021. https://www.nationalgeographic.com/environment/2021/02/world-wetlands-are-slipping-away-agusan-marsh-underscores-stakes/

Kremer, J. W. & Jackson-Paton, R. (2013). *Ethnoautobiography: Stories and Practices for Unlearning Whiteness, Decolonization, Uncovering Ethnicities*. Sebastopol, CA: Re-Vision Publishing.

Nelson, S. (1997). Shamanic ritual—the real thing. *Independent*. Last accessed 12/06/2020 https://www.independent.co.uk/arts-entertainment/shamanic-ritual-the-real-thing-1243668.html

Prechtel, M. (2012). *The unlikely peace at Cuchumaquic: The parallel lives of people as plants: Keeping the seeds alive*. Berkeley, CA: North Atlantic Books.

Shaw, M. (Nov. 30, 2016). Trailing the Gods back home: An interview with Dr. Martin Shaw. https://www.youtube.com/watch?v=g28G7GOym_I . Last accessed 2/7/2021.

SOTA [Shift of the Ages] (2013). *Indigenous leaders share the reunion prophecy of the Condor and Eagle*. Last accessed 12/06/2020 https://www.youtube.com/watch?v=JHMXHoO8f4s&feature=emb_title

Wolloch, N. (2013). The liberal origins of the modern view of nature. The Tocqueville Review/La Revue Tocqueville, XXXIV (2), 107-131.

Fear, Hope, and Love in Covid Times

Glenn Aparicio Parry

Love in the water.

I was blessed to know and work closely with Grandfather Leon Secatero, the late Headman of the Canoncito Band of Navajo, whose reservation is located thirty miles west of Albuquerque, New Mexico, where I make my home. Leon was the kindest and sweetest soul I ever met, a man of great love, wisdom and patience. Like many Indigenous people, he was thankful for the gift of life and offered prayers each morning to the light, air, water, and earth that we are made of (he considered the elements to be the creators). But of the many lessons he taught, perhaps the one that had the greatest impact upon me was a prayer he regularly made to the west direction each day. He prayed to the ancestors, *thanking them for everything that has happened to bring him (us) to this moment in time.* I found this prayer so powerful because it taught how to accept all of life experience, without exception, to be a blessing.

This was not only a prayer Leon made, but the way he lived. He never complained or held grudges. His own children told me he never got angry with them. The fact that a Navajo elder could do this—whose ancestors had been rounded up at Canyon de Chelley in present day Arizona and forcibly removed to Fort Sumner, New Mexico on a deadly 300-plus mile journey known as The Long Walk—was remarkable. Here was a man who had every right to be suffering from historical trauma, but

Glenn Aparicio Parry, PhD is the author of Original Politics: Making America Sacred Again (SelectBooks, 2020) and the Nautilus award-winning Original Thinking: A Radical Revisioning of Time, Humanity, and Nature (North Atlantic Press, 2015) and the forthcoming Original Love, of which this essay is partially excerpted from. Parry is an educator, ecopsychologist, and political philosopher whose passion is to reform thinking, education, and society into a coherent, cohesive whole. The founder and past president of the SEED Institute, Parry is currently the president of the think tank: Circle for Original Thinking www.originalthinking.us and the host of the Circle for Original Thinking podcast.

instead had moved beyond it. Leon held in his heart a prayer for all humans (five-fingered ones) to unite and walk together in beauty. I think of Leon every day, and especially during these challenging times we are living in.

Clearly, during a pandemic, it is extremely difficult to accept everything that happens as a blessing. Fear predominates, and many of the things we ordinarily hope for seem remote and unattainable. The same is true for love. It feels out of reach. We are not even supposed to touch, hug, or share in-person time with friends and loved ones outside our home. Anxiety, isolation, and despair have become more widespread than the virus itself. The public suffers, both healthwise and economically, while the media cashes in on the sensationalism. The economy can never rebound if the virus is not brought under control—something the previous administration did not seem to grasp. A vaccine and a new administration bring hope. But things are never as simple as they appear.

The Biden administration brings hope to those that were afraid of the direction the country was going during the Trump administration. Our new president represents a return to a semblance of normalcy. The majority of Americans remember the Obama-Biden administration as Hope and Change; many of those same people saw Trump as representing *Fear of Change*. Many, but not all. Some of the people who feel most hopeless in America—people living in rural America where the system is no longer working for them—voted for Obama twice, then turned around and voted for Trump. How could that be?

One possible explanation is that the relationship between hope and fear is reciprocal. *Our hope is our fear unmasked—and our fear is our hope unmasked.* We hope that the pandemic will end soon; we fear that we or our loved ones become ill or die. We are either hoping for a better situation or fearing that things will get worse. In both cases, the present is somehow unacceptable. The way to break this impasse is to accept what is happening right now as it is—as a blessing. Accept our hopes and fears as they are—as a

Raven fear.

measure of how you feel now, without trying to change anything. All our experience is grist for the mill, something to learn from and grow. It is in this sense that fear is the beginning of wisdom. If we recognize that fear and hope are both ways to psychologically escape our current situation, this is what

> Our hope is our fear unmasked—
> and our fear is our hope unmasked.

enables us to transform discontent over what we do not have (or what could go wrong) into seeing what we do have as a blessing (such as our health, home, food, and loved ones).

This is not to say that the pandemic presents unfounded fears of loss of job, income, home, or lack of healthcare in case of emergency. With whole sectors of the economy being shut down, these anxieties have a basis in reality. Other primal fears are stored in our reptilian brain—such as being chased by a mountain lion or bear. These kinds of fright and flight responses are necessary and real. However, most fears in modern life are quite different than this. They have complex, psychological roots: fear of failure, fear of being unloved or uncared for, fear of losing one's status in life. Most modern anxiety concerns being hurt not physically, but emotionally.

These fears are defense mechanisms that buffer us from life's harsher intrusions. They are typically rooted in unresolved, unseen parts of our personality. Instead of accepting the unseen parts of ourselves, we typically project them (see the unrealized trait in others). If we were to confront our fears, particularly the unresolved, unrecognized shadow aspects of our personality, we would become more whole. This is why Jung purportedly said, "I would rather be whole than good," a recognition of the importance of self-awareness through integration of opposites. If we unify and accept opposites within ourselves, we are likely to become kinder and more compassionate toward others. We also become more accepting of ourselves and our present circumstances. We would not fall back upon hope of change so much.

This is not to say that hope, like fear, is all illusion. Hope also has a biological purpose. Without hope, we can sink into depression, wither and die, like flowers without water. We sometimes need hope to keep us going. Hope also has a relationship with inspiration. When there is hope, there is openness to spirit, insight, and vision. A hopeful spirit is an optimistic one. There is no great vision that did not begin without opening to something larger than oneself.

Love: The Greatest Transformative Force

A love that is based in acceptance, not circumstance, is unconditional. With this form of love for life, all things are capable of being transformed, including our fears and hopes. Unconditional love for life itself is the greatest transformative force; however, it is much easier to speak of than do, especially during a pandemic. But this is when it is needed most.

Of course, love can also be wrapped up in hope and fear, particularly when our understanding of love is limited to a personal level of feeling secure and protected. If love is treated as a personal protector or savior, it will be reduced to wishful thinking and romantic daydreaming. I'm speaking instead of a love that extends beyond the interpersonal human context, and originates in nature.

A key to understanding the depths of love is to understand it is an original energy in nature. Without love—the unseen force that binds things together—the solar system, our galaxy, and, for that matter, all galaxies, would simply break apart. Nothing would work. Instead, everything holds together. Scientists call this force of attraction gravity. But gravity is not something that has ever been understood—not by Newton, or by anyone since. All we know of gravity is that it exists. What is the force that makes the moon want to be with the Earth, and the Earth want to be with the Sun? You could call it gravity, but that is such a grave term for allurement. We might as well call it Love.

Speaking to the beloved in all of creation is the highest expression of love. "Love is the water of Life; jump into this water," implores Rumi. Water is an excellent metaphor for love. When the underground rivers are thirsty, they cry out to the Cloud People, calling for the rains to come down. It is the love between the Groundwater and the Sky Water that brings the rains. We humans cannot go without love any more than we can go without water. If we hold back expressing our love,

Love in nature.

eros will wash over and drown us, like a tidal wave engulfs the shore. Love is an unstoppable force as powerful as the moon and tides.

ReVisioning Fear, Hope, and Love

It might seem counterintuitive, but these times of uncertainty and heartache offer us the greatest opportunity to reimagine fear, hope, and love. The crack in our routine allows in new light. An alternative way of thinking is emerging. For the way we were living—our so-called normal—was untenable. It was not only the political, economic, and healthcare systems that were not working. Our personal relationship with the living Earth was dysfunctional. We were destroying life.

When a global pandemic threw everything into disarray, the incessant activity of human industry ground to a halt in an effort to save lives. Then, a police officer kept his foot on George Floyd's neck, causing him to die, but giving birth to a renewed social justice movement. This was a metaphor for what humanity had been doing to the Earth. We had been keeping our foot on her neck, paving over the natural world to pursue our short-sighted economic interests. It was Mother Earth that could not breathe. If we did not change, much of the natural world would die.

It is always a challenge to fully grasp the moment we are living in. "Life can only be understood backwards, but must be lived forwards," according to Kierkegaard. We have never lived through a time exactly like this. But we have lived through crises before. We know from experience that every crisis presents both danger and opportunity. The opportunity now seems clear.

Sounding the alarm about climate change has not worked; but the people will protect what they love. This is the moment to rekindle love for each other and for Mother Earth. There is no time to waste. The ancestors and spirits of this land are aware of the urgency. This is why they whisper messages to us or our loved ones: "do this now: save this lake, river, old growth forest, frog, or bird—rebuild the soil, plant this garden, buy this farm, write this book." It is up to all of us to listen and do our own part.

Love is what we need when the universe feels hopelessly complicated, chaotic and random. Complexity need not be scary. To be complex is to be surrounded, encircled, embraced, and braided together. All of creation is woven together with love, in a myriad of patterns of interconnections and feedback loops that self-organize and organically replicate in countless fractals of repetition.

The natural world is composed of relationships upon relationships upon relationships. Some of these are predator and prey relationships, and involve aggression and fear. But if you ever watched the dance of predator and prey, you will observe the moment when the prey submits to their fate. They seem to give themselves up in an act of sacrifice. It is that sacrifice that makes the predator-prey relationship sacred, even loving.

Spider fear.

In most activities in nature, it is not fear that predominates. The preponderance of interactions are based in a profound degree of cooperation and respect, what could be called love. Is it love when a fruit tree senses a bee approaching, and increases her attractiveness, secreting a burst of sugar into her nectar? If it is not love, it is at least seduction or courtship, because it works. The bee is attracted.

The ultimate symbol of love in nature may be what the Keres-speaking Laguna people of New Mexico call their original being: *Tse Che No*, or "Spider Woman." It is from the belly of Spider Woman that all the world was created. During these times of separation and social distancing, I find the image of Spider Woman viscerally appealing. I can feel Spider Woman in my own gut. I too was once attached by a similar thread, which we refer to as an umbilical cord. Imagining this form of creation is pleasing—not a violent explosion like the Big Bang, but a gentle weaving. The silky thread that Spider Woman spins is flexible, yet strong. It creates all things while maintaining a connection to its mother. Life that comes from life and is connected to all things feels whole, beautiful, and loving. My hopes and fears dissipate. There is just oneness, undivided oneness. All is connected. All is whole. All is love.

All images courtesy Pixabay

When the Ancestors Call, How Do We Answer?

Princess Bari, a Heroine's Journey

Helena Soholm, PhD

During the early part of last year, I woke up after a strange dream of the fictional film character, King Kong. I was trying to contain King Kong in a small room and stood at the doorway knowing I could not hold him in this room for very long. Moments later, I ran out of the house realizing he would be unleashed into the world to cause complete destruction. The pandemic has been like this King Kong, taking away the world we know and our collective sense of security and predictability. 2020 has been an intense year of rapid change and uncertainty. We have been grieving the loss of loved ones as well as reflecting on the things we have taken for granted before the arrival of the COVID-19 virus. The damage caused by the pandemic will leave a lasting scar, but the death of outdated patterns will force us to face

Helena is wearing the iconic cone hat and costume for the "Bulsa" Grandmother spirit, who is a deity associated with Buddhist practices. She is a spirit of compassion and heals the hearts of suffering people. (Photo by Jordan Nicholson)

Helena Soholm, PhD is a transpersonal psychologist and a Korean shaman (Mudang). Helena holds a PhD in clinical psychology from Saybrook University and a master's degree in theological studies from Harvard Divinity School. Her research interests are in the areas of contemporary forms of shamanism and the arts. As a practitioner and scholar of shamanism, Helena's work focuses on spiritual development and identity, including both the clearing and honoring of ancestral energy.

a novel and unknown world. Physical lockdown and restrictions on our movement offered a unique opportunity for all of us to travel inwards and sit with ourselves. The external limitations also offered an opportunity to work on healing and renew our vision for a better future. Perhaps you were one of the lucky individuals who received inspiration for a different kind of world, where kindness and compassion are priorities.

The lockdown offered a time to focus on the themes of personal and collective ancestral healing. The messages of my ancestors have been focused on building a world that honors the interconnectedness of life and to create sustainable structures for future generations. As a recent initiate of Korean shamanism, I am learning the indigenous spiritual practices of Korea. I am a first-generation immigrant from South Korea, and I grew up in a Protestant Christian household, which meant my family and I were cut off from the traditional spirituality of our ancestors. However, the power of the ancestral call cleared a path for me to step into recovering the traditional religion of my native country. I am also a psychotherapist who has been trained in Western psychological theories to assist people in healing past trauma and early life wounds. My work is situated between traditional Korean shamanism and neoshamanism as well as indigenous Korean cosmology and Western psychological perspectives.

Many people have also been listening

> All humans walking the planet today hold ancestral trauma.

for the messages of their guides but they are feeling a bit lost on how they can act towards personal and collective healing. So we ask, "When the ancestors call, how do we answer?" Let me share the different ways that the ancestors have spoken to me this year as illustrated by the Korean folktale of Princess Bari, who is considered to be the first Mudang or shaman and patron deity of all shamans. Old stories, myths, can offer fresh perspectives and guidance for troubled times.

Gut Ceremony Altar with offerings and tools representing the deities of Korean shamanism. (Photo by Jordan Nicholson)

Bari, the Abandoned Princess

In a faraway kingdom under the heavens, a king and a queen are preparing for their wedding and receive counsel from an important royal advisor in the palace. The advisor tells the king and the queen not to rush their wedding since there will be great misfortune of having seven daughters and no sons if they were to get married in haste. However, the king and queen move forward with their wedding plans and are wed soon after. Just as the advisor had foretold, the king and queen end up having six daughters. In contemplating another child in hopes of having a son, the queen dreams of a dragon, which is an auspicious sign of a male heir. The king and queen are assured of the arrival of a son due to this dream, and the royal couple have another child, their seventh daughter. The couple cannot accept another daughter and abandons their seventh child. The princess acquires the name, "Bari Gongju," which means "Abandoned Princess." Shortly after, the abandoned baby is found by an elderly couple and raised by them as their adoptive daughter.

After some time has passed, another great misfortune falls on the king and queen. They fall gravely ill and are told the only cure is a rare potion and flowers from the far western territories procured by one of their children. None of the king and queen's six daughters are willing to travel to the far west to find the medicine their parents needed to survive. So, the royal couple had no choice but to seek out their seventh daughter, Bari, whom they abandoned at birth. Although, her parents abandoned her, Bari does not act with resentment and anger but is happy to reunite with her family and agrees to travel to the far west to bring back the cure her parents need to survive the illness.

The Princess disguises herself as a man for safety and travels to the far western territories. On the way, she enters a dangerous underworld where she takes the time to save the suffering souls by using magical spells and a rattle. In the underworld, she encounters the guardian of the underworld who discovers she is not a man and requires Bari to marry him and give him children. During this time, Bari learns which flowers and potions can save her parents. After serving the guardian of the underworld for many years, she finally returns to her parent's kingdom with the potion and flowers, along with her husband and children. However, upon arrival at the kingdom, she learns of the death of the king and queen. The royal funeral was already taking place. Princess Bari quickly opens the king and queen's caskets and administers the medicine and flowers, reviving her parents from death.

After years of toil and suffering, she completes her mission of saving her parents, returning as a powerful healer. For this accomplishment and dedication, she and her family are given sacred titles in her parent's kingdom. She is considered to be the first Mudang or shaman and is worshipped as the patron goddess of shamans.[1]

The myth of Princess Bari is sung during Gut[2] ceremonies held for the deceased. In the Korean shamanic tradition, the Mudang plays the role of a medium who channels and guides the spirits that are stuck or at unrest and unable to peacefully move into the realm of the dead. The Mudang also plays the role of the priestess in offering ritualized ceremonies where she wears different costumes to possess the various deities that play specific roles in the Gut ceremony. The shaman enters trance states through dance and music.

Princess Bari is a goddess closely associated with funeral rites. While on a mission to save her own parents, she took the time to assist the souls of the dead safely transition to the underworld.[3] In Korean mythology, she is a significant figure for the above reasons but also due to the storyline of the heroine's path, which tackles the theme of gender and power within a highly patriarchal and Confucian society. As a woman and an abandoned daughter, she later gains a high status by her willingness to enter the feared world of the dead and bringing her parents back to life.

Princess Bari's tale follows the path of "The Hero's Journey,"[4] a term popularized by Joseph Campbell. According to Campbell, the mythological adventure of the hero includes the components of Separation, Initiation, and Return, which is clearly demonstrated in Bari's narrative.[5] Besides the obvious acts of courage and strength within this heroine's journey, the tale of Princess Bari has a special meaning in our current situation. At its root, the tale of Bari is a story of healing, where the princess steps into her power to serve in the most meaningful and compassionate way. By healing from one's personal trauma of abandonment and helping those who have caused her pain, Bari demonstrates the ultimate love of a true healer. Her life story illustrates the beauty of a healing arc which begins with the focus on the individual but ends in addressing the needs of the group. In honoring her intuition and stepping fully into the heroine's path, Bari gave us a blueprint for how we can answer the call of our ancestors in a time of uncertainty and crisis.

Ancestral and Generational Trauma

In my work as a psychotherapist and Mudang, I witness trauma as the source of most human suffering and malady. We all suffer in one way or another, and the act of healing is not just for the select few but for all of us. All humans walking the planet today hold ancestral trauma. Life has not been easy for our ancestors and they suffered physical hardship from their environment, war and political turmoil, famine and hunger, social disparities, and individual family dysfunction. Modern science has given us the tools to speak about ancestral and generational trauma seen in concepts such as epigenetics, which explains how the legacy of traumatic events can sometimes be passed down through multiple generations at the genetic level.[6] Ancestral trauma affects us unknowingly, causing us to react in ways that are inconsistent with our own life experiences. The devastation of the Korean War touched the lives of my immediate family members. My grandparents experienced the trauma of loss of home, livelihood, and loved ones, which negatively affected their children's sense of safety and security even if they did not directly live through the devastation of war. Without awareness, many people can be affected by their ancestral trauma, which can compound the effects of daily stressors, leading to the mental health epidemic seen in modern societies today.

Living in technologically advanced societies, where healing and connection to self are not always prioritized, consciously working towards self-healing becomes an act of political and social resistance. With the arrival of COVID-19, many people have been forced to take the inward journey. Our culture has an abundance of tools which keep

The yellow costume is for the ancestral grandmother spirit called, "Daeshin Halmoni." This grandmother spirit is an ancestral spirit who helps people get in touch with their own ancestors. She is often accompanied by children spirits called, "Dongja" (little boy) and "Dongyeo" (little girl). (Photo by Jordan Nicholson)

us distracted from our soul's calling, as indigenous traditions understand it. The pandemic has made it more difficult to continue engaging in these distractions and forced us to listen to our deeper calling as our ancestors did through initiations and ceremonies.

One of the themes that emerged from my work with clients during the pandemic is fear and anxiety derived from modern living inundated with toxic messages. Daily life as it is lived in modern societies is one of distraction, disconnection, and dissociation.

- Distraction: We keep ourselves busy to the detriment of our health (mind and body) so that we can feel good about being productive and therefore having worth.
- Disconnection: Work, entertainment, and leisure activities are designed to keep us further away from our authentic selves instead of connecting us to our purpose and to others in a meaningful way.
- Dissociation: We engage in numbing ourselves through food, sex, alcohol, drugs, and technology to disengage from the experience of living in the moment. Mindless activities fill our days leaving us feeling empty and alone.

So, it makes sense that when many of the activities of distraction have been taken away from us that we start experiencing acute surges of anxiety and angst. This crisis is an opening and an opportunity to face our fears in order to permanently end the cycle of distraction, disconnection, and dissociation. The shifting life goals can be towards one of meaning and purpose.

Princess Bari lived a life of radical self-healing. Having suffered the generational trauma of sexism in a culture that did not value the life of a girl as much as a boy, she endured a personal trauma of being abandoned by her own parents. In modern psychological conceptualization, Princess Bari may have suffered from attachment and self-worth issues due to the trauma of abandonment. One can also conjecture that her adoptive parents were loving enough to have provided a stable environment where she grew strong each day, preparing for her fate as Bari, the warrior shaman who saved the souls of the dead and brought healing to those who were desperately in need of her gifts. Unbeknownst to her, she followed the call of the ancestors to fulfill her destiny. So, the act of healing oneself is no longer just a luxury. It is an imperative act not only to have a good life but to ignite a movement of healing the collective human consciousness.

Moving from the Individual to the Collective

Once we have achieved sufficient healing, we become aware of the "other" rather than being focused only on the self. Princess Bari beautifully demonstrates the healed soul who can act towards the collective good rather than being stuck in one's woundedness. This is not an easy act, to care for others when one is also hurting, especially if the other is the very person who has caused one's personal suffering. When the parents of Bari fell ill, the six older sisters who had the privilege of being raised in their biological family in the luxury of palace life, do not answer the call of awakening their souls. They choose to stay distracted, disconnected, and dissociated in a state of trauma from the generational and dysfunctional patterns of their family. However, the outsider, the one who lives in liminal space, answers that call. A true shaman holds the wisdom of awareness of trauma and pain at the collective level and acts to alleviate the suffering of others.

If Princess Bari had not spent the energy and time to heal herself, she would not have been able to answer the call of the ancestors. The healing allowed her to gain discernment in knowing that the call to help her parents was not only personal but a collective call for action. The time has come for all of us to answer the call of the ancestors even if we do not feel ready. Heroes are created during the journey. Bari likely felt feelings of resentment and anger towards her parents as well as fear of the unknown journey to the far western

The altar is where the shamans host the spirits during the ceremony. Helena has developed her own unique style of ceremony from the traditional ceremonial practices of Korean shamanism. This altar is a small version of the grand ceremonial altars that mudang would set up to do "Gut" ceremonies. In this photo, Helena is purifying the five-colored fabric used for purification. (Photo by Jordan Nicholson)

territories. However, the heroine is created in the act of answering the call and stepping forward even when fear is present. The wisdom lies in knowing that by answering "Yes" to the ancestors, one is also answering for all who have been entangled in the trauma of collective life on the planet. It is indeed a time for all of us to reassess if we have been too engaged in the selfishness of thinking that our healing was only for ourselves. Our personal healing journeys have been a training ground for the next level of development, attending to the other.

Answering the Call of the Ancestors

This year, many people heard the call of the ancestors to heal themselves and to rise to the occasion of assisting our neighbors in need. To hear the call is a blessing but so many of us struggled and continue to struggle with knowing the concrete ways that we can live our purpose. In the folktale, Princess Bari had the wisdom to know what to do. As a human person, she had fears, doubts, and insecurities that could have hindered her ability to act. An important aspect of her actions is that she did not set out to gain power or status as the first shaman and become the patron deity of shamans to come. Instead, she simply answered a call to help her family. It is in the realm of relationships that Bari fulfilled her purpose. This young woman did not know how her story would end while she traveled to the far western territories and to the underworld, becoming the wife of the guardian of the underworld and raising a family, so that she could save her parents. In the darkest night of her soul, Bari maintained her conviction and completed her mission. For some of us, the pandemic has been the dark night of our soul. How can we receive divine inspiration from the story of Bari and move forward with the courage of a warrior shaman?

From Helena's initiation, "Naerim Gut" May 2018. (Photo by Stephen Wunrow)

People seek my help as a psychotherapist and Mudang to live happier lives. But I see myself guiding people to live meaningful and purposeful lives. Sometimes, a meaningful and purposeful life is not necessarily happy or joyful on a day-to-day basis. Our society lacks the wisdom of elders. Most of my clients are intelligent, often gifted, young people who have spectacular material lives without much soul. Many are graduates of prestigious institutions and they work at the top levels of society, but they are lost to themselves and to their purpose. I keep reminding them that if they were to have been raised in traditional or indigenous cultures, wise elders could have seen them for who they are and guided them on their path based on their soul's purpose. They would have gone through initiatory rites to give them confidence to authentically enter their adult lives. Instead, these young people feel that they have followed and complied with our society's expectations only to find themselves disappointed and wanting. They are working for successful companies, making lots of money but they are not fulfilled.

During the pandemic, divine opportunity to live a fulfilled life has been offered to us. We learned that a society built on competition and greed does not ultimately serve us. No matter how comfortable it may have been before the pandemic, the soul starved behind the lure of capitalism and materialism. With the deprivation of toxic food of pre-COVID life, we can finally take in the nutrition we need to feed our souls.

So, how do we start the journey? Like Bari, we take the steps that are immediately before us. First, work diligently towards your personal healing because all endeavors within the personal healing

> The great heroic journey is your life as it appears to you right now.

space is never selfish. A single person working towards healing is an act of love for oneself but more importantly for the whole planet. Your healing efforts are never in vain. Healing can take place through diverse avenues of going to therapy, receiving coaching, working with indigenous healers and elders, or creating art. We live in a time where healing technologies and methods exist in abundance. One must take the initiative and take an active approach to healing.

Second, we need a community of supportive elders and friends who can guide us in realizing our gifts and purpose. The story of Bari demonstrates the princess's initiation into her calling as the first shaman, but not everybody is meant to take this path. We need people in all sectors of society to work towards building a kind and compassionate future. Again, it is in relationships that we can realize what is being asked of us. The heroic journey does not exist far away in lofty kingdoms or foreign lands. The great heroic journey is your life as it appears to you right now. What is being asked of you at this moment from those closest to you? Or, what is being dreamed within you that you are afraid to birth and manifest? Listen carefully and pay attention to the ordinary call of the ancestors to attend to your life as it stands. The call of the ancestors is not always glamorous or attractive. Bari was asked to help the very people who caused her early life wounds. In that moment, she did not reject but she fully stepped into her calling no matter how unpleasant it was. Healing entails turning towards and transforming one's wounds as a gift for others.

Lastly, an important aspect of the tale of Bari is the central theme of feminine power. During the pandemic, the structures which have been built under colonization and patriarchy have come into question. Sociopolitical acts of oppression and subjugation of groups of people as well as the destruction of the natural environment have finally caught up to us, forcing us to face the consequences of our actions over the span of our species' existence.

With the arrival of COVID-19, we began to see the toxic ways in which we chase and energetically invest in greed and power. In the ways that the king and queen in the folktale continued to desire a son, perpetuating the patriarchal practices, our world also did not listen to the wise voice of the elders and ancestors. The queen's dream of the dragon was fulfilled but not as the queen expected. The ancestors sent a gift of life through Bari, but the king and queen refused to hear the new narrative. The royal couple was taught a critical lesson via the unconditional love of their daughter, representing the compassion seen in feminine deities such as Kuan Yin.[7]

A common analysis of this Korean folktale is the demonstration of Confucian ethic of filial duty. However, at a deeper level, the story of Princess Bari is a universal tale of the hero's journey through the exaltation of feminine values in honoring the interconnectedness of life. The wise princess knew that the rejection of her own parents would become the rejection of herself. She also realized that her healing could not be complete without the acceptance of her relations.

As the ancestors call, I hope we can answer with confidence even when we are not sure of our paths because the path will become illuminated as we simply take the first step towards our great adventure.

Endnotes

1. "Abandoned Princess Bari," Encyclopedia of Korean Folk Culture, https://folkency.nfm.go.kr/en/topic/detail/5353 (accessed 9 December 2020).
2. Traditional Korean shamanic ceremony.
3. "Korean Mythology," Wikipedia, https://en.wikipedia.org/wiki/Korean_mythology#Princess Bari (accessed 9 December 2020).
4. Joseph Campbell, *The Hero with a Thousand Faces* (Novato, CA: New World Library, 2008).
5. Campbell, *The Hero with a Thousand Faces*.
6. Natan Kellermann, "Epigenetic Transmission of Holocaust Trauma: Can Nightmares Be Inherited?" *The Israel Journal of Psychiatry and Related Sciences* 50, no. 1 (2013): 33-39; "Genetics and Epigenetics in the Psychology Classroom," American Psychological Association, February 2019 https://www.apa.org/ed/precollege/ptn/2013/02/genetics.
7. Buddhist Bodhisattva or Goddess of compassion.

Photo by Jürgen Werner Kremer

Strumming the Strings of Hope

Michael Gray

What are the images of hope that flit and dance through our psyches? For me, hopes often feel like the children's party game--pin the tail on the donkey—where groping in the dark, the tail is our frustration, our loneliness, and our dreams of a tolerable future, and the elusive donkey is the future.

It is the past that keeps stirring up those hopes, because petitions for a better future are woven from past experience. But, as if abiding in another universe, the future has no tail, missing or otherwise. It is always arriving, but never arrives. It is the living face of infinite possibility, which we can never actually manage to see, let alone capture. There is only the eternal present.

Michael Gray has published three books: The Flying Caterpillar (a memoir), the novels Asleep at the Wheel of Time and Falling on the Bright Side, and he is seeking a publisher for his spiritual memoir, Winter Came Early, in which he tries to find meaning in the death of his son two years ago. A regular contributor to various journals, most recently to Kosmos, Gesar, and T.J. Eckleburg Review, Gray writes a weekly blog on www.michaelgrayauthor.com. He co-founded Friends in Time (a non-profit providing services to people whith MS and ALS); and was Board president of The New Mexico Parkinson's Coalition and Pathways Academy (a school for kids with autism and other learning issues).

Tower, by Ann Hamilton, Oliver Ranch, Sonoma County. (Photo by Gary Newman)

Thank goodness for that. Thank heavens that we can't grab hold of the future and put it in the pen where we keep our dreams and our hopes. Even when we include the needs and wellbeing of others in our hopes and prayers, the future doesn't show up, should those prayers be answered. Only the present can receive the gifts of time: whether we are hoping that a gleaming red bicycle will be standing beside the illuminated tree on Christmas morning or hoping that peace and fairness will appear in the stockings of all the sad beings with whom we share this beautiful planet. The future, and the hopes we charge it with fulfilling, can never be confined within the lives we have been given to live. As we sail along on the ocean of time, through the vast reaches of the space that shows up wherever we look, it is not given us to ever reach home port and settle in there for good.

Hope must be born afresh in each human heart.

Even if it was ever the nature of life in this world, we cannot now sit back and say, "Make that a double and pour one for everyone." Such a juncture of well-being cannot be found in the sands of time, where the future of our world may or may not be written.

So where do we place our hopes that a kinder and gentler life may be restored for all those beings who are separated from their families, who are forced to spend their short lives standing in their own feces in crowded pens, or for the whales running aground, desperate to escape the lightning strikes of sonic agony in their majestic heads?

Whither has flown the Master's care for the swallows of the air and the lilies of the field? Whither the sparkling streams and burgeoning harvests flowing in harmony with the natural world?

Lamenting the damage that has already been inflicted cannot be our song of hope, though coming to terms with failed hopes and dreams can start us on new paths, with new lessons learned. We are the corporate farms devoted to mono-agriculture, the distribution systems that ladle off the cream for those who control them, the legislatures and administrations whose office holders—as soon as they have unpacked their bags—quickly close the curtains on all who wander in pain on the sidewalks below. What will penetrate the walls around our dormant hearts?

For those in the middle and upper classes, ours cannot be to hope for a bigger share [yet for some who lack enough for basic survival, this might be their hope—to have enough to survive]; not unless we can trust ourselves to devote our accumulations to those we love and also to those we do not love. Even then, heeding the siren call of Scrooge McDuck diving into vats of shining gold coins; the rich and comfortable so easily forget what it was like, as a child, to dive off a floating raft moored out from shore above a sandy bottom, where the water was so clear that it was as if the future was swimming alongside us. Well, that was my experience at least, growing up on the West end of Montreal Island, swimming in the waters of the Saint Lawrence River before lamprey eels and clouds of algae made chlorinated pools the only option.

Perhaps hope is not about calling out into the night for Lassie to come back so we can get some sleep. Perhaps hope is not even that sheep who have gone astray can find their way back to the protection of a shepherd who cares for them? What if we are that shepherd and have forgotten our promise to be good stewards? Once depression, exhaustion and demoralization have taken over our mind and hearts, who's to say what we will still remember?

Perhaps hope is like the gentle rain falling on the meadows beneath. Perhaps we never really know what we are hoping for until we find it; and only then can we see our true reflection in the pools of water left behind.

Hope was not the quality celebrated in the *Merchant of Venice*. It was *mercy (falling like gentle rain upon the place beneath)*, whose praises Portia sings. As

We will always have one another, if we let ourselves lean on the innate generosity of the human spirit.

I remember it, hope doesn't play much of a role in Shakespeare's play. Portia seems to have a vision of what it means to become a better person, but her victory is to outwit, not redeem, the coiled serpent of vengeance.

Our society is extracting its pound of flesh from countless beings whose lives are already miserable. There is no Portia in the wings to argue that the contract between human stewards and the animals whose lives we have been given to protect, permits not one drop of blood to be shed. Abuse of animals is so embedded in our way of life that it takes a Temple Grandin to even improve the conditions in which we wield our knives.

If we do manage to feel a little hope wafting into the secret chambers of our hearts, can we spare a little for these beings who cannot speak for themselves? Even in this time of darkness, in which individuals feel so helpless, can we spare a dream or two for the lambs who have never gamboled through fields of waving grasses, and for the fathers who do not know how to ease the pain of their children, many of whom are silently suffering in deep unhappiness?

I am safe at home with plenty to eat and central heating at the touch of a thermostat. But I too am one of those fathers who has been separated from his child. My son, Jon, took his own life on Easter weekend of 2019, at the age of 27. And to this day, I don't know how I could have helped him want to live.

Personal responsibility, even guilt, continues to lap against the shores of my being. But, like all of us, my son and I were citizens of this world. Our chief difference was that I was able to find hope for the future in friendship, and in ancient traditions that have fathomed the nature of what it means to be born a human being. I tried to share some of that understanding, which I personally find so nourishing, with him. But he told me that it didn't have anything to do with the world in which he had to find a place. In fact, he said it made it worse.

Hope is deeply personal and radically situational. Hope must be born afresh in each human heart. So how can we create a world where that is possible? It seems that those who access hope in their own hearts are also doing what they can to create conditions that inspire hope in others. Even those of us who are not natural leaders can let their personal losses be a window into the pain that afflicts so many all around us. I can no longer change what has happened but I can refuse to be broken by the terrible "what if's" that visit all survivors—whether it is the death of someone we loved and for whom we were responsible, or as stewards of our beautiful world. I believe that in our private losses we can find the forgiveness, self-respect and courage we need if we are to accept the truth of the impermanence that shadows us from birth to death. In this understanding we learn to care what happens to ourselves, to others and to our planet.

I am beginning to see that there are very few places where the young can find joy, hope, confidence, or witness fairness being given its rightful place in the public sphere.

Emily Dickinson's famously pronounced that "Hope, is the thing with feathers". And we can certainly find a spirit of freedom, balance, and hope for our lives in the image of a bird.

In Buddhism—whose hopeful vision my son said just made his life more impossible, creating expectations that he could not realize and which did not support him in his own challenges—there is the image of a bird having two wings: *compassion* and *wisdom*. It is not hard to see that with either wisdom or compassion alone we will be unable to fly. But it took me years to realize that it is not just the absence of either understanding (wisdom) or caring (compassion) that can prevent the bird from flying. There must also be a bird that wants to fly.

I wish my son had wanted to fly. For that, he would have needed to find someone—other than me—to teach him how to fly and to inspire him with confidence that he could open the window and see a world out there that was worth flying into.

In Buddhism, we hear that we are living in a time of increasing darkness, called the Kaliyuga. Since the historical Buddha spoke of this time, it must have already been visible 2,500 years ago. Or at least its footfall was already sounding outside the door of time.

But now, the Kaliyuga is not just a philosophical theory about the rise and fall of civilizations, not just a message about the erosion of the capacity for hope in human societies. The jackboots are marching outside our doors, carrying the darkness of the past to the very threshold of the future. And those of us who are unwilling to join that march, just don't know what to do.

Tower, by Ann Hamilton, Oliver Ranch, Sonoma County. (Photo by Gary Newman)

Do we turn inward, meditating and chanting our way to ease and inner peace? Do we turn outwards and feed the homeless, care for the sick? Can hope be found in a grateful heart and quiet mind; in a life of service? Can we allow ourselves to hear the cries for help without being deafened by them; can we allow ourselves to feel all that pain when we don't know how to heal it?

One thing seems clear: we need to restore balance between our minds and hearts. I think that's the deep meaning in the phrase: "Wisdom and compassion are like the two wings of a bird." With wisdom that sees the emptiness (the dream-like nature) of everything we call "real," we will not be able to act as if it matters what we do. With compassion for all the pain that we can never ultimately heal, our hearts will be so exhausted that they will eventually shut down. But together, understanding and caring can support one another; and on a good day we will find ourselves rising above the meadows and hills with our hearts full of hope.

We will always have one another, if we let ourselves lean on the innate generosity of the human spirit. More than we can realize, when we are in the crocodile jaws of depression, when we are hypnotized by the conflicting choruses of dueling certainties, we can remember that nothing is ever solved using the same tools that created our problems. This is not just a mathematical proposition—even though it was the mathematicians Einstein and Gödel who made this a catch phrase for our time. It is the glad news that carries the warm breath of hope. Nothing prevents us from looking with fresh eyes at the abiding beauty of this world.

The eternal lapping on the shores of this present moment, whispering that we are free to change our path, is the starting point and touchstone of our lives. When we greet the future with an open heart, we can feel the breath of hope arriving across the threshold into this living present. Then we may remember that the future is the infinite realm in which resides all that is and all that ever can be.

gift

like endorphin down the column
like anointing
like messiah
like jazz
all on the hand
round the thigh
raising toe
creating mind
pumping blood
up bone like the
millennium
each milli-second
the flash of retinal release
the eye orgasm of hope
the shrine of lip on bread
the beat of heart storm
lightening on ocean
tornado on plain
corona of enlightenment heat
a single gift
a single gift
a single gift
of hand on hand on head
on god.

your hand on godhead
your bean in the mouth of being
your tongue stammering eternity
your knee the ground-wire of deity
your foot-soul the only depth of infinity
you are the message
you are the grammar
you are the silence between
you are what could be
you
are the only gift
there ever has been
given
like wind
through the tiny void
of charged attraction
that is your own unique molecule
and do you really think
you will disappear into the vast everything
like a drop of rain dying into the sea
or will your own broken open surface now
finally fill
with the entire ocean of what is?

—jim perkinson

Archiving Hope

Leny Mendoza Strobel

What about yourself cannot be tracked? Is illegible? Can't be archived?

—Bayo Akomolafe

Krishnamacharya, the father of modern Yoga, towards the end of his life preferred not to talk about his personal history. What was important to him is the distillation of the teachings of Yoga as a path to reduce suffering and to experience unity within the body, mind, and spirit. In this tradition, Memory, as one of the activities of the mind, can be considered an obstacle to clarity if those memories are not purified of their shadows. I think of this now as a student of Patanjali's sutras while contemplating about Hope and how an archive of Memory can be useful (or not).

Leny Mendoza Strobel is Kapampangan from the Philippines and presently a settler on Pomo and Coast Miwok lands. She is Professor Emeritus of American Multicultural Studies at Sonoma State University. She doodles when she tries to quiet her Mind.

Many years ago, as a tourist in a small village in Languedoc in the South of France, I was impressed by the historical markers everywhere. It made me wonder about my "third world" homeland and my lack of adequate historical knowledge due to the lack of visible markers of important places, events and people in history that would have made me proud to be Filipina. Where are our archives and why hasn't our educational system done a good job of turning me into a nationalist by making sure our historical archives got integrated into our canon?

In another site, the Chicago Field Museum is holding thousands of Philippine archived ethnographic materials in the basement; no longer on display because the U.S.'s interest in the Philippines is not like what it was in the late 19th century when the U.S. needed to formally flex its power on the global stage by colonizing the Philippines in 1898. So the cultural artifacts gathered by the anthropologists of that era are now gathering dust in the basement of the museum. I wondered why the Philippines doesn't have its own version of NAGPRA (Native American Graves Protection and Repatriation Act) and a museum curator in the Philippines told me that the country doesn't have the infrastructure and resources to bring home these archived materials.

I also do not know what to do with the research materials that have piled up during my academic career. They are languishing in file cabinets in the garage and storage boxes. At least most of the books have found their home in two institutions but not my personal files. I suppose I can do research and see where these might go and who would want them in their library. Or I could wish that some Filipino American graduate students would be interested in my work. But I've not put in the time and energy needed to archive my materials.

All of the above arouse feelings of inadequacy and inferiority because I hear the script of cultural conditioning around "legacy" and "heritage"—the importance of keeping records of the milestones that crown our lives. After all, don't we all need and want to be remembered for our achievements and believe that we have done something good in our lifetime to make the world a better place? Ah, but these feelings are fleeting. A part of me doesn't really care about the tradition of archiving.

Confessing this is ... unsettling. Let me pass on a story.

Bayo Akomolafe tells the story of the Dibia, the Rainmaker, among his Igbo people in Nigeria. This Dibia has an apprentice who is overeager to practice his powers to bring on the rain. The apprentice listens surreptitiously to the Dibia and tries to memorize the spell that is cast by the Dibia when he makes the rains come. One day the Dibia had to go away to visit another village and at the same time, the apprentice was summoned by a different village to make the rains come. The apprentice thought this was his chance to be his own rainmaker. He recited the spell and no rains came; repeatedly with each spell, no rains came. He felt like an utter failure and became despondent. When the Dibia returned and heard the news, he took the apprentice aside and told him that it isn't the spell that makes the rains come, it is the Gathering—of the winds, the birds, trees, guardian spirits, the village people, the stars and the sun—and those gathered talk amongst themselves and decide together to bring on the rain.

I love this story! It points to what's illegible about myself, what hasn't been tracked and archived—the gatherings in my village in Northern California where we summoned the Spirits: of inquiry, generosity, hospitality, kindness and over a couple of decades have become a cultural movement of decolonization and re-indigenization in the diaspora among Filipino Americans. The movement has grown mycelia-like and I can't tell where the archival sites of this movement's important achievements are located or who the "rainmakers" are. I am content to know that the movement (of resistance, of beauty-making, of meaning-making) is alive and well and continues to flow through the river of Time.

In the absence of archives, what we do have in abundance are the imprints in our hearts, psyche, and our soul where our arms have held each other, when we've cooked and fed each other, when we've sung and prayed together, and cried together. This is *Kapwa*—the Self-is-in-the-Other—remembered and embodied every day in the ordinariness of our lives. Recorded in the hearts and minds of our shared Self, we turn to each other through the thick and thin of living in the belly of the beast. Those who witness this from the outside remark that we are the kindest, most generous, happiest, and most resilient people.

Yes, of course, we have the written word, too, and we have been "educated", but according to a recent "reading literacy assessment" conducted by the *Organization for Economic Co-operation and Development (OECD)*[1] the Philippines is *kulelat* or at the bottom of the list. The test was given (in English) to over 600,000 15-year-old students around the world. This test was administered in mostly non-OECD countries and now also includes Cambodia, Laos, Myanmar, Vietnam and other "developing countries." The Philippines is also *kulelat* and second to the last in math and science (last is Dominican Republic).[2] Is this because we have failed at archiving?

In David Abram's *Spell of the Sensuous and Becoming Animal,* I feel I'm being asked to remember the time when we weren't an archiving species yet. I'm being asked to return to the time when there was no written word; when the quality of presence mattered most because sound (aural/oral) is the only mnemonic device. No vowels and consonants and no printing presses to record selective information deemed precious enough (by whom?) to be recorded and saved for future generations. To communicate, ancient folks had to turn their faces to each other, lean towards each other's ears to listen and to remember. My people even had the tradition of *ungngo*—of exchanging Breath with the other—the ultimate gesture of connection. In this form of communicating without the written word we understood our connection beyond the gross body and intimately knew that our subtle body is connected energetically with the unseen realms. Although we have been colonized and educated and inducted into the modern era, this subterranean self has remained untracked, illegible and unarchived. And I am grateful.

Abram writes about the recuperation of this oral/aural presence through the written word. Perhaps this is what I am doing by writing this. I am following the tracks made by indigenous writers like Linda Hogan, Robin Wall Kimmerer, Martin Prechtel, Bayo Akomolafe, Martin Shaw, Rowen White, Greg Sarris and many others. They are the ones who are archiving Hope for me today because I am hearing the voices of the ancestors in their writing. I am learning the Original Instructions from their poetry, mythic storytelling, short stories. My heart comes alive when I read them and my mind quietly abides with a recognition of the seeds that are being sown. There is a tacit knowing that lives in my cultural genes that gets awakened when I am on this road.

What about yourself cannot be tracked, is illegible, and cannot be archived?

How to answer this question when, clearly, I am making self legible by writing which could lead to being archived somewhere someday. Would all the pieces of writing I've published over two decades when tracked, catalogued, and stored on iCloud be considered an archive of Leny Strobel's life work?

I don't think so. What about the deepest thoughts that I couldn't write in English because it is not my native tongue? What about the memories that I have kept secret? What about the silences and absences of history that didn't make it in my writings? What about the dreams I never mention in my writings?

What about Hope?

In my diasporic community, some writers lament the state of our "illiteracy;" that we do not sell enough books because supposedly our people don't read; that our scholars are not writing and publishing enough. Young folks don't read anything anymore that's longer than a meme or a headline. In other words, we are *kulelat* again.

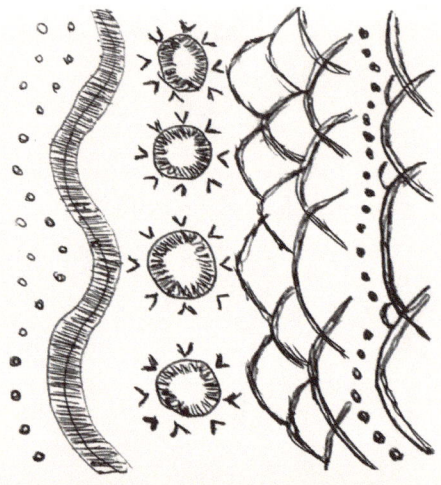

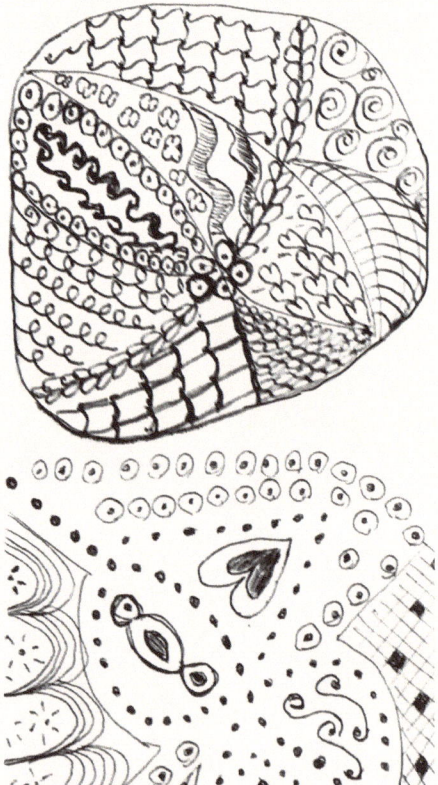

I will be subversive and say that this *kulelat* syndrome is negative only in the context of a globalized idea of what it means to be modern and civilized. Only in the context of a schooling system where English and the Western canon is globalized and privileged over the immense diversity of languages and cultures around the planet. Only in the context of the flawed assumptions of a modern worldview that values the written word and sacred texts first and foremost.

Datu Vic Saway, tribal chief of the Talaandig tribe in the southern Philippines, once said: *They (outsiders) say that we are primitive and uncivilized because we do not have a sacred text. But we do have sacred texts—we have the Mountain, Forest, Rivers, Sun, Stars, Moon, Animals—we have the biggest sacred text of Nature! Why do we let them make us feel inferior? We know how to read the Wind, we know how to read the Sky.*

Whenever I hear this voice in my heart, it enlivens me. It gives me Hope. It makes me want to get to know the redwood tree in my backyard and the creek around the bend and the wildweeds in the cracks of the pavement around my tract home in the suburb. Theirs is a language I want to learn and a language I need to hear.

I am content to slow down and linger among the non-human beings in this place where I am a settler. If I am to have Hope, I wish for this kind of slowness and smallness. I wish to step away from my gadgets more often. I wish to dance and sing more. I wish to be consistent with my yoga and *qi gong* practice. I wish to look at the sky and make gazing my source of sustainable joy. I wish to meditate with my gaze cast downward at my heart and imagine her spaciousness and her capacity to hold the universe with awe and tenderness. And then in this smallness and slowness, I could tend to the garden and the circles of belonging in this Place.

In this way, this modern self will begin to unwrite itself and become illegible, untrackable, and there will be no archive. But there will be something else.

And maybe this is the gift of the virus, the California fires, the craziness of politics, and the climate crisis. In the place where I live I see more and more people who are turning inward trying to make sense of it all, looking for Hope. I am currently tending a small cohort of local folks who all responded to the invitation to meditate on these questions: *What does being a settler in this county mean to you? When did you or your ancestors come to settle here? How does the history of Native genocide impact your sense of place and identity?* Before convening this gathering, I called on local Indigenous elders and leaders to ask for permission and guidance to do this work. I mentioned that we hope, someday, after we have done our inner work of decolonization, that we could co-create a ceremony of apology and forgiveness so that we may heal together from historical trauma.

As we do this work we are not recording and posting any aspect of it on social media. We are focusing on building relationships with each other towards a sense of community; towards a deeper connection with the Land; and learning to understand how our recent presence in these Indigenous lands constitute a shadow that needs to be acknowledged for its damaging effects and consequences over millennia and which our generation is finally accounting for. Often it is also a test of how we bridge across differences; this is the path that is always fraught with traps from the conditioning of cultural identities, the blind alleys of supremacist beliefs, and the reptilian brain kicking into its fight or flight mode.

Many indigenous scholars have been calling attention to the erasure of native genocide as the "first sin" at the foundation of the U.S. No apologies. No reparations. So we remain a broken nation. Hope then, for me, lies in these small acts of connection and accounting that make historical shadows visible and rippling out to join the larger arcs of transformation elsewhere.

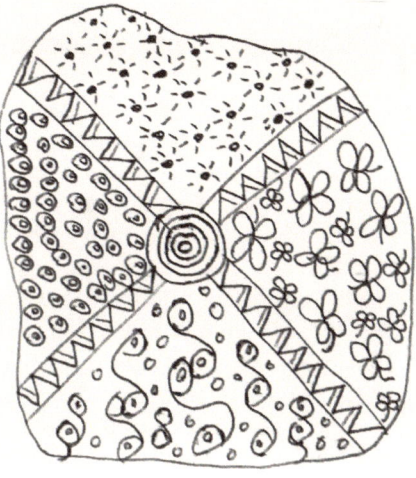

What about yourself will not be tracked? Is illegible? Cannot be archived?

In spite of these written reflections, something else escapes the pen. *Something else* is a refusal to be fixed on the page that would tempt essentialists to see me only in the dimension of what is written. *Something else* is what has been left behind and is no longer a sharp pain in the heart when remembered. *Something else* is the beautiful silence of the Mind when all the questions of angst and existential meaning find their angle of repose. *Something else* is a scent from the jasmine that evokes ancestral connection to my Apu Sinang. *Something else* are all the footprints of those who have walked in and out of my life leaving no residue, only the spirit of gratitude that we had passed each other on the road. *Something else* is the trust I hold in the wisdom of the youth who are out in the streets marching for the right to live with sustainable joy.

Something else is what the modern mind, so bounded by hardened categories, is incapable of imagining at this time while waving the empty banner of Hope to keep a dying civilization alive. *Something else* is the budding of new visions, emerging in mostly liminal spaces, breaking through the cracks to let the Sun through the broken planks of what is perceived as real. *Something else* is the not-yet-visible but palpable, an ineffable movement towards righting the wrongs of the past, seeking reparations and repair.

Ultimately, Hope will always be that *something else*.

Something else is what will remain unsaid in this quiet afternoon of writing these meditations about Hope.

Endnotes

1 https://medium.com/@lenystrobel/kulelat-15e4e1a60b53

2 https://www.oecd.org/pisa/Combined_Executive_Summaries_PISA_2018.pdf

Graphics by Leny Strobel

Ecomorphic Eudaimonia

Three Principles Toward a World-Worth-Hoping-For

Layman Pascal

Wavefield, by Maya Lin, Storm King Art Center, New York (Photo by Gary Newman)

This personal essay is not a linear argument but is perhaps more like a mood or a landscape in which I will try to approach, from various angles, three of the principles in which my own sense of hope is nested. These forays, taken collectively, might be able to give you a sense of the way in which I feel confident about the future of life on this planet and beyond. It reflects my summary responses to our current situation without trying to document all sources that have inspired my stance.

My first principle is that of *leaning into a voluntary hopefulness*. This does not mean to ignore doubt, worry and real limitations but rather to acknowledge, enfold and gesture beyond them as a free choice. We are not always in position to make a choice of that kind but it may be important to try when we can. Secondly, I will describe the direction of my hopefulness via the principle of *ecomorphism*—which is the possibility of a more benevolent creative participation between culture and nature. I believe that what human beings call "naturalness" could be usefully thought about as a set of patterning styles that are co-produced by nature and human systems in the degree to which the latter embodies the former in multiple domains and formats. That means that a world worth hoping for is neither a biosphere devoid of human thriving nor a human civilization blind to the facts and needs of the environment and other types of beings. I will argue that the deep recognition of the interdependence and mutual identity of culture and nature must inform our minds, hearts, actions, tools and social procedures if we are to steer ourselves toward worthwhile futures. And finally I will sketch the broad outlines of what we might call *a new shamanism*—trying to catch the flavor of the type of human being that may be required in order to cultivate and populate what I consider to be a "better world" that does not fall prey to the dystopian results of most utopian attempts.

I will try to keep this very personal but when I do happen to say "we" it should be understood that I mean three things simultaneously: the human species generally, those members of the human

---

Layman Pascal is a philosopher, author and public speaker concerned with postmetaphysical spirituality, meta-progressive politics, nondualism, developmental theory, collective intelligence and sacred naturalism. He is known for his work on the Metaphysics of Adjacency and the "integration-surplus" model of religion and spirituality – as well as his diplomatic work bridging overlapping communities engaged with metatheory, developmentalism and the cultivation of a planetary wisdom-civilization. Co-chair of the Foundation for Integral Religion and Spirituality, he also hosted the Integral Stage podcast series since 2019. Layman Pascal currently lives on the north shore of Lake Superior in Ontario, Canada.

species who specifically find themselves concerned about the future wellbeing of life on this planet and, finally, the possibility of a shared spirit of hope. The processes by which people grow together into an intersubjective identity are not well studied, but I would like to at least hold out the possibility that you, the reader, and I could purposefully practice sharing a mutual desire to move civilization toward a more nature-enriching and naturally enriched way of existing on this planet.

This essay is unapologetically futurist, pro-science and pro-human, but I hope you will slowly come to realize that the way I think of these things is deeply involved in embodiment, plurality, ecology and a veneration of a holism that was not foreign to our ancestors.

1. Leaning into Voluntary Hopefulness

People who ask me "How are you?" are often surprised and delighted when I respond that I am "probably better than anyone has ever been." This is rapidly becoming my standard reply in regular social communication among my circle of far-out thinkers who are yearning for a real upgrade to civilization and ourselves. Why do they like it? I suspect that it reminds them that, despite our deep insight into the world's problems, there is something liberating about simply volunteering for confidence. Within certain limits, human beings can give themselves permission to have a truly great answer about how we are doing and freely-chosen hopefulness about the future of our societies and our planet. It is an option that I am trying always to teach myself because I know that at some level I am responsible for my attitudes about the world.

Dabbling in the art of intentional emotion might seem like a luxury. I am in a relatively privileged position as a fairly well-liked, tolerably-educated (and luckily not starving or bleeding to death... at the moment) adult Canadian male of mostly northern European descent. However faith and choice are very basic and widespread human tools. Practices for the intentional selection of feeling-states are found across most cultures and religious traditions. It is common to find socially-encouraged injunctions to, say, willfully believe legendary tales or to feel gratitude on purpose, or to try to be socially convivial rather than prone to angry outbursts. The inner practice of deliberate feelings is widespread across many types of human communities and so it is not particularly strange to suggest that we might want, if it is possible, to choose hopefulness. In fact this may already be common. There is certain privilege and luxury involved in being able to sit back and cringe about the uncertain and dark trends of the world while, conversely, in communities that face immediate suffering, alienation and deprivation people can often be acutely aware of the need for a pragmatic optimism that helps them get through the day.

Perhaps it is even our moral duty to

> I believe that what human beings call "naturalness" could be usefully thought about as a set of patterning styles that are co-produced by nature and human systems

hope? I wonder about this possibility. It could be that I am letting my friends and loved one down when I fail to *decide* that positive outcomes are possible. But, even supposing that it were my duty—would it be true?

Is it honest?

It is certainly debatable whether my standard superlative responses and my cultivated expression of hopefulness indicate an actual objective truth. However, I am pretty damned sure it is at least as *true* as the depressingly ordinary answer: "Fine." We should not overlook the fact that many of our negative, uncertain or moderate responses are also habitual, cultivated and not necessarily based on objective facts. Each of us has a shifting degree of freedom when it comes to setting our default tone and communication habits. And the degree to which we recognize that freedom may cause it to mutate into a responsibility.

Permission to Hope

We are all vulnerable to a certain attitudinal passivity in which, for example, we might find ourselves waiting for some new fact, theory, event or tweet to tell us whether or not to feel hopeful under the looming, uncertain shadow of the massive, multifarious metacrisis that plays out on the nightly news. "Metacrisis" is a term used in metamodernist philosophy to refer to the simultaneity of large-scale problems such as climate instability, political polarization, educational crises, the insufficiency of our collective meaning-making practices, the accumulating side-effects of the global economy, including vast inequalities among the human family, and the uncertain dangers of radical new technologies. It is the crisis of all these crises. A metacrisis.

It is very understandable that informed and sensitive people are anxious and uncertain when contemplating the convergence of so many potential (and already occurring!) disastrous trends that seem so deeply entrenched in the political, economic and technological systems upon which we rely. Very naturally, I

> I know that at some level I am responsible for my attitudes about the world.

think, our hearts cry out for some proven idea or external fact that would give us the emotional *permission* to shift into a hopeful mode of neurochemistry. I certainly feel this way. I would love to be able to point at some convincing objective fact that would confirm the wisdom of pouring my energy and efforts toward deeper, healthier and more integrative futures for this planet. How wonderful it would be for anyone of us to hear an idea that strikes with the force of revelation and makes us feel like we really could succeed at shaping our personal lives and our shared civilization into a more satisfying and sustainable form.

Unfortunately, I do not know exactly what that idea is. I am not sure what a better world might mean or how it would have to look. And, even if I did, I would still be vulnerable to doubt and uncertainty. This is a problem. Why? Because I do not seem to accomplish my most productive work when I am doubtful, anxious and psychologically recoiled from a world that does not seem to justify my efforts. A vicious circle where the word and my feelings either hold each other down or, perhaps, learn to lift each other up.

The need for confirmation of hopefulness is a very broad principle. The cells in our bodies kill themselves (called "apoptosis") if they do not get validation signals from their neighboring cells. Our dearest friends can slip into despair and self-destruction if there is no one to confirm and reinforce the feeling that their lives are *worth the effort*. This tendency has analogs as many scales. Yet although we human beings may need this experience of hopeful confirmation, we cannot simply rely upon the volatile facts of the world to provide it for us. So what is the alternative? Famous teachers from Buddha to Christ, from Confucius to Kierkegaard, have made some version of the argument that each human being has a certain amount of inner leeway to practice highly valuable feelings like meaningfulness, trust, gratitude and hopefulness. It is a useful art that requires certain prerequisites. Obviously a person must have the opportunity and capacity for introspection along with many other supportive factors. These factors might come in many forms. A poor farmer may end up having much more time for contemplation than a wealthy industrialist. However if you have some opportunity and capacity, then you still have to make an inner decision and take a risk that might not be justified by the world.

My pal Jim Rutt, complexity theorist, godfather of the GameB movement

> Famous teachers from Buddha to Christ, from Confucius to Kierkegaard, have made some version of the argument that each human being has a certain amount of inner leeway to practice highly valuable feelings like meaningfulness, trust, gratitude and hopefulness.

(Rutt, 2020) for civilization upgrade, tells people that basic healthiness requires us to get outside for at least an hour a day—regardless of the weather. That means making a practical decision, for your own well-being, in a way that is relatively indifferent to external facts. To follow Jim's advice, I have to give up "waiting to see whether the weather is good or bad." I live on the north shore of Lake Superior so we get several months of deep freeze every year. It can be difficult to decide that you are going to be happily engaged with your environment no matter how it shows up. Yet I have found this practice to indeed make me happier, healthier and more involved in the world.

It seems worth considering that, at some point, if we want better outcomes in our lives or better outcomes for humanity and the Earth generally, then we may

> Naively solipsistic positive-thinking turns a deaf ear to the world and can lead people into disaster.

have to stop waiting to see if there is an outside reason that will make us hopeful and start practicing hopefulness.

This is a matter for *serious play*.

I am reminded of a classic Radiohead song (Greenwood, 1994) that says, "*You do it to yourself, you do... and that's what really hurts...*"

Integrating Pessimism

However, despite the charming encouragement presented in the paragraphs above, I am not an optimist. Instead (rather pompously) I imagine that I am a *trans-pessimist*. That is a word I made up to remind myself that human beings, if they are lucky, have an emotional capacity to accept all the dispiriting facts of the world while also feeling beyond them. In my reading of "The Birth of Tragedy" (Nietzsche, 1872) he seems to gush with praise for the trans-pessimism of the pre-Socratic Greeks. He discusses their open embrace of tragic folly and the doomed heroes scattered throughout their epic plays and poems. He recounts the ancient Mediterranean legend of the wise satyr Silenus, intimate companion of the god Dionysus, who was asked by King Midas to explain the best thing in the world. What was the answer? The best thing is never to have been born. The second best thing is... to die early. Bleak!

However this cultural celebration of bleakness does not seem to have slowed down Greek culture. From Pythagoras to Archimedes, from Socrates to Solon, from Thales to Aristotle, multitudes of scholars have honored the scientific, mathematical, philosophical and political innovations that occurred in that bleakness-obsessed little corner of historical time and space. They were not naive optimists, but somehow they nonetheless were trans-pessimistic. I do not think this principle is limited to the peoples of the ancient Mediterranean. One need not search very hard to discover that many great civilization-building cultures around the world, from Egypt to Mesoamerica, from Persia to China, (at least if we take their ancient art and stories seriously) were prone to contemplate inevitable and vivid apocalypses, bewildering tragedies, sadistic torture rituals, confusing and capricious deities, etc. This powerful focus on tragic and disturbing outcomes did not make them unproductive in their attempt to solve the problems of their day. They did not always get the solutions right, of course, but they were creative and energetic in mobilizing in attempt solutions. Whoever hopes today for a significant, large-scale upgrade of collective human behavior on this planet certainly does not want to recreate the brutality and unfairness of the so-called Great Civilizations of the past, but we do, I think, wish to match or exceed their level of energy, innovation and shared spirit. And perhaps that is related to the way in which they appreciated and enfolded troubling images, omens and situations?

A future-worth-hoping-for, whatever that means for each of us (see the next section to sample what that means for me), will not likely come about from a blinkered avoidance of negative sentiments and depressing facts. Naively solipsistic positive-thinking turns a deaf ear to the world and can lead people into disaster. Human beings need to be grounded, clear-eyed and antifragile (Taleb, 2020)—Nassim Taleb's name for the property of benefiting from stress, surprises and offensive encounters—if we are going to rouse ourselves into productive efforts in conjunction with the real world. How can any of us change things with which we have no visceral contact? One must be willing to get dirty, so to speak, if one wishes to clean the house.

We must acknowledge that the Earth's forests are burning, fascists are winning elections, global business is perversely incentivized, distrust is rampant, people are starving and sick, biodiversity is collapsing, algorithms are hacking our brains, and many people claim not to know what to believe in anymore. These are real things, but that does not mean they are the final word on our situation. My hope is to make a deeper connection with these apparent aspects of contemporary life, to integrate them, but not to be defined by them. Making authentic contact with whatever you believe are the problematic aspects of life is essential if our voluntary hopefulness is going to be sane and grounded.

Perhaps we have misinterpreted many dark and futile feelings as a threat when they are actually only the watchful gargoyles at the entrance to a new and fertile kingdom? We know that something like this is true at least at the individual level. The principles of acknowledgment, acceptance and authenticity are important elements of personal psychological transformation. We should consider that they might also be important collectively, both within distinct cultures and in the inter-cultural and meta-cultural framing of an emerging planetary civilization. Pessimism may be a good ally at many scales. Contemporary cognitive science has suggested that pessimism usefully inhibits some of our inherited cognitive biases toward hasty, self-satisfied thinking and encourages human brains to make more accurate evaluations and predictions. Pessimistic automobile drivers are more likely to stay alert and follow safety-oriented precautionary rules than are cavalier, overly-confident drivers. A dash of skepticism and worry can be a good thing. You see—I'm even optimistic about pessimism! If pessimism can be a reason for optimism, and accepting your negative feelings can be a way of encouraging positive psychological transformation, then might it not be possible that hopelessness could be a cause for hope?

In episode #164 of the Lex Fridman podcast, neuroscientist Andrew Huberman describes the role that deliberate positive attitudes may play in allowing the reward chemical dopamine to modulate testosterone production. Cholesterol can be converted either into the stress hormone cortisol or into testosterone which, as Huberman explains, "makes effort feel good" (Huberman, 2021). Human nervous systems have a certain amount of wiggle room in terms of using intentional good feeling to predispose our neurochemistry toward productive efforts. The amount of influence you can have in this fashion is uncertain, and testosterone increases are not a magical pill with only positive effects; however, there is a general idea being elaborated here. It is that, within certain limits, our mind can use intentional affirmative gestures to skew the cultivation of our biochemistry in ways that make us *more capable of the labors needed to rearrange our environment.* Voluntary hopefulness—mixed with frustrations—may help to catalyze and fuel the activity of trying to improve our lives and our planet. I have a theory about what kind of activity that is, but that is for the following sections of this essay.

There are unique challenges in this historical moment (dying, plastic-choked oceans and autonomous flying robots armed with bombs were not anything our ancestors had to deal with), but human cultures must still retain connection with those basic human mechanisms and skills that have evolved to help us

> The principles of acknowledgment, acceptance and authenticity are important elements of personal psychological transformation. We should consider that they might also be important collectively...

in problem-solving efforts of all kinds. Choosing hope in the face of huge challenges reflects a circumstance that has confronted living organisms for a very long time. Every rhizomatic root-system under the soil faces a world that is dark, massive, uncertain and full of threats. Yet they give themselves and each other a signal that triggers them to reach into that darkness in hopes of creating appropriate organization and fertility.

In some ways the most basic thing we inherit from evolutionary dynamics is a deep drive to confront stagnant, confusing and dangerous environments and struggle to convert them into more balanced, vitalizing, meaningful, and synergistically beautiful living conditions. Adequate life-worlds have never been a free gift. They are the result of labor.

Orienting Ourselves Toward Value

The fact that we *can* hope, that it comes pre-installed in human beings, gives me hope. That hope deepens when

I consider that hopefulness is very useful to make activity happen. And it deepens further when I imagine myself standing in the lineage of my countless human and nonhuman ancestors who all faced confusing, dangerous worlds that needed to be improved. The question is—improved in what way?

Individuals and groups rarely have a robust, shining vision of how we would like things to turn out. Even when we do have an inspiring goal, its compelling hopefulness fluctuates in our hearts and it may turn out to be naive, unrealistic or secretly flawed. The great genocides of the 20th century often started out with hopeful dreams of a specific better world. So we need to strike a better balance in how we handle these things. We need, on the one hand, an inspiring directionality that we can link to our hopefulness—a future trajectory that suggests the type of changes we can endorse and which can be clarified over time—and on the other hand we cannot slip into the dangerous trap of holding a fixed image of a utopia for which other values and other lives need to be sacrificed in great numbers.

In the next section of this essay, I will begin to suggest the open-ended set of trends which, if they are helped to continue and converge, would begin to describe a world that resonates with my decision to be hopeful. Yet there is one more thing I would like to touch on here while I am discussing the subjectivity—issues of faith, choice, intentionality, neurochemistry, etc.—of hopefulness. It concerns this question of clarifying the direction of improvement, and it basically repeats the point that I made earlier about the need to enfolded negativity into our optimism (sanely and to the best of our ability in our circumstances). What does it mean to think about improvement? How do human beings orient toward feelings that might be interpreted overall as a better direction of outcomes and actions?

A lot of basic learning about improvement involves the experience of pain and frustration. The classic example of a child jerking its hand away from a hot surface is an instance of quick, high-intensity, value-clarifying, experiential education. I may not know exactly where is the perfect spot for my hand to be located at this moment, but I definitely do not want it to be *there!* The set of

> The scale of the problems facing the world requires that human beings grow, to whatever degree they can, beyond the limitation of simply "waiting to hear if the world justifies our hopefulness."

possible hand locations corresponding to my implicit value structure has suddenly narrowed. In other words, there is an increase in the precision of my definition of benign outcomes. That is so simple and obvious that it hardly needs to be mentioned. What does it suggest to my way of thinking? Should people be sitting down, personally and in groups, to list the things we hate the most, that hurt the most, and then listing whatever we decide is a plausible opposite or alternative to that? And then working on those while also grouping them together to see if they have commonalities that could describe a general direction of changes-we-can-endorse and to which we can commit ourselves with hope?

Yes, of course.

However my point in this section is a little more abstract and internal. It is about using negative evaluations very directly to make phenomenological contact with the "energy or quality" of value inside each of us. When thermometers register coldness they are actually still registering a quantity of heat in which they are in immediate contact. When you discover that you are facing South then you also immediately know where the North Pole is located. Or at least that knowledge becomes possible if you can zero in on the contextual comparison implied by your feelings. Frustrating situations provide an option, if we are free to take advantage of it, to enhance phenomenological contact with that part of ourselves that can emotionally confirm our existence and our efforts. For me, this is summarized in typically provocative aphorism (Nietzsche, 1886): "He who despises himself still honors himself as one who despises." That suggests that a negative valuation indicates the presence of our evaluative capacity which either generates or is directly engaged with our experience of value. Human hearts are metaphorically touching their values in order to gauge how well they are related to the given circumstance. Remembering this odd idea, trying to remember and enact it whenever possible, is a metacognitive skill that I believe helps people to become better agents of hopefulness.

To say it again in a very non-Nietzschean way, virtuous people are those who remember and embody their values during frustrating, painful and obstructing situations. They remain oriented toward "the north pole" even when they are facing south. They are able to leverage the immediate experience of unsatisfying situations in order to align more purposefully with their unfolding understanding of what positive changes would look like. Clearly we cannot all do this strange inner movement all the time. Just as clearly my frustration at the mass slaughter of sharks by industrial Chinese fish boats is different from a Syrian mother who just saw a bomb dropped on her family home. And yet we do all have some degree of internal leeway. In his book *Man's Search For Meaning* (Frankl, 1946), Victor Frankl describes the significant difference in health and survival rates among Nazi concentration camp prisoners who did or did not have a strong inner connection to value and hope.

Most cultures have some idea of a saint. An idea about extraordinary individuals who are able to enact and embody personal or cultural values with some indifference to their circumstances. I am not a saint. I cannot resolutely connect to positive value through encounters that I evaluate negatively. However I can aspire to be better at remembering, refining and re-finding that subjective inner sense that makes me feel as though I know what direction of action corresponds to "better."

I will suggest in the third section of

this essay that we all need to be, in some degree, shamans. Instead I could have said that the citizens of a better world need to be partial saints or boddhisattvas. Either way, unless we can get better at connecting with and feeling into our private experience of *worthwhileness,* then we probably lack the motivation, self-confirmation and directionality needed to make efforts at improving all life on this planet.

Hope and hopelessness are intimately related with and defined by each other. We must start thinking about how to use them as a team. The presence of the latter must become, in part, the justification of the former. I know this might sound both abstract and moralizing, but I would like anyone reading this to consider that the scale of the problems facing the world requires that human beings grow, to whatever degree they can, beyond the limitation of simply "waiting to hear if the world justifies our hopefulness." There is a need for all kinds of people to be involved in serious conversations about the kind of lives and the kind of planet that is important, worthwhile and worth struggling toward—but there is also another conversation. In this other conversation the reason for hope is, sometimes, just because you decided to be hopeful.

II. Worlds Worth Hoping For

The ancient Romans imagined their imperial city as a deity. This suggests that they contemplated their form of life as though it were an awe-inspiring power—a transhistorical glory that reflected their culture back to them with an excessive quality that approximated the way in which they imagined the realm of gods, goddesses and other supernal potencies. Society as *peak experience*. That is to say, a shared artifact (the city) imaginatively transfigured by a social style that seemed to call the citizens beyond themselves, asking them to experientially recall and embody the fact that they are part of a greatness that transcends them.

In the first section of this essay my concern was to explore the possibilities of voluntarily deepening our connection to a sense of valuable hopefulness within the personal experience of individuals. Now I will consider the issue of hope more broadly. What is a good society? Apart from the retrospective historical analysis of a society's decency and its effects upon the ecosystem, the basic implicit test might be whether large numbers of people living in that fashion are feeling a strong, shared background appreciation of their collected social habits. They may not be able to define it very well, they may anchor it in mythology, but a functioning society, by my definition, gives people a reason to get out of bed (if they have beds) in the morning. There must be a *broadly distributed experience of amplified meaningfulness* that unites disparate types of people in a shared willingness to work toward sustainable improvements—according to their understanding of what that might mean. The Romans were able to accomplish this, to some degree, despite their ethnocentric aggression and their disturbing tolerance for cruelty and slavery. Many tribal societies seem to have accomplished this despite their low-tech, highly regional grasp of the world. For me this sort of shared vivifying spirit is the minimum that we should expect. It is the first sign of a society that is worth hoping for and therefore worth struggling to achieve. However, clearly, that can come in many different forms...

When I contemplate hopeful futures—as I did for Bruce Alderman's Eutopia series on The Integral Stage podcast (Pascal, 2019)—I have in mind a "city" that is significantly more worthy, in my opinion, than old, noble, slave-hoarding and blood-stained Rome. I am envisioning a similar apotheosis, an equal or greater sense of feeling impressed and engaged by human culture at the worldcentric or cosmocentric scale that frames the current educated human conservation. ? do you mean "conversation"? unclear what this last phrase refers to. Despite the fact that many people still passionately identify with subcultures, nations and tribe-like factions, the majority of human beings also implicitly understand that phones, computers and electricity are connecting the entire planet. We are (at least tentatively) a spacefaring species. Whether we are politically motivated to assert or denounce global climate change, we do so either way in a conversation that is formally framed by the concept of the whole planet. This is the hill upon which our city will have to be built. Such a society should be conceived in a way that (a) inspires us to build it and which (b) provides, as it emerges, a shared sense of being unambiguously worth the efforts necessary to protect and enhance it. That is my notion of the minimum requirement but it is certainly not enough. Intelligibility and benevolence are also required. What is a better world that both "makes sense" and "is good?"

That's hard to envision but I am going to at least try.

The Ecology of Hope

A civilization of which I would be honored to be a citizen cannot be one in which the basic conditions of life are sabotaged. I think this is a general human concern. We will all need clean air, clean water, diverse forests, thriving oceans, living landscapes, beautiful environments and healthy bodies. We all need a vast, flexible and interacting balance of innumerable kinds of organisms.

> There must be a broadly distributed experience of amplified meaningfulness that unites disparate types of people in a shared willingness to work toward sustainable improvements.

Despite many diverse cultural attitudes on this planet, I think we all want a situation in which we are not drowning, burning, being torn apart by storms, or made subject to coercive social systems that ignore the multifarious needs built into our bodies, hearts and minds.

From my way of thinking, all this stuff has something in common.

This sample of conditions necessary for a desirable human civilization all involve knowing about, appreciating, adapting to, and contributing to the natural systems of the world. Either we relate well to the organismic (including our own human bodies, organs and bacterial communities), ecological and climatological realities—or we don't.

> We all need a vast, flexible and interacting balance of innumerable kinds of organisms.

This is such a hugely important and obvious factor for evaluating possible futures that I would like to spend a moment unpacking what "relate well" means. Relating well is a concept of *dynamic coordination* that produces outcomes that are adequately pleasurable and sustainable. To be coordinated means that you responsively acknowledge the Other in ways that reflect both its needs and your needs. The understanding of "needs" presupposes an understanding of structures. I simply cannot help you get out of a pit if I do not see, hear or know that you have fallen into it and that the form of your body does not enable you to leap out of deep holes in the ground. I cannot viscerally cognize the moral need if I am blind to the structures.

If I am blind to the patterns of the climate, the ecosystem or my own organism, then I will not behave in ways that coordinate with their needs. We will not be relating well. So the first thing is awareness. I have to perceive you in some way. And there are many ways: I can perceive you consciously or subconsciously. I can perceive you intellectually or emotionally or aesthetically. Etc.

Imagine that I go deep into the forest and touch a huge, beautiful cedar tree. Then I smell it. Maybe I spend time *feeling* about it (and with it). Perhaps I have paid attention to diagrams of tree anatomy and also heard new findings about the interdependence of its roots system on other organisms. These are all complementary ways of increasing my "mapping" of the tree. I am perceiving it more richly and, hopefully, more accurately. I register it more completely and in a manner that more closely resembles the mystery of its actual complex, multidimensional structure. Although this process is never perfect, I am now in a position to understand its needs better and therefore to coordinate with it in greater mutual fidelity.

The inner networks that comprise my personal psychology now include patterns that more closely resemble the networks that comprise the Western red cedar tree in question. This is essential for increased coordination. Likewise if the knowledge networks comprising human farming and gardening include a rich pattern that corresponds to the existence of mycelial webs in the soil, then they will begin to act significantly differently than if they do not contain those same mycelium-recognizing patterns. If our governmental and legislative systems do not contain structures that correspond to and acknowledge the human body's need for particular healthy food, then they will almost certainly

> If I am blind to the patterns of the climate, the ecosystem or my own organism, then I will not behave in ways that coordinate with their needs.

operate indifferently to that need. And if the invisible hand of the market cannot represent to itself the value of a living coral reef, then its calculations will proceed without regard to those reefs.

Systems cannot coordinate with what they do not register.

So a world hoping for is one in which human systems (psychological, economic, technological, informational, social, procedural) are much better able to responsively recognize the dynamic structural systems of nature. My belief is that our individual and collective capacity to relate with natural systems depends on our ability to be informed by the patterns of those systems in all areas of life. That means business, politics and art. It means diet, education and religion. There is no one domain in which we can fix all our problems, but we can try to discern complementary directions of change that might lead toward an improved planetary civilization if they are preferentially cultivated in multiple domains.

Consider the following cluster of perspectives from Western cultural history. Dante observed that, "*Art imitates Nature as well as it can*," while Oscar Wilde claimed that "*Life imitates art far more than art imitates life.*" And then Jackson Pollock went on to add, "*I am Nature.*" These three quotes illustrate complementary versions of the same basic insight. Dante suggests that successful artistic processes are meant to duplicate, in human technological and cultural spaces, the types of patternings that have proven to be beautiful, efficient and adaptive in natural systems. Wilde indicates that there is a two-way relationship whereby we affect the world in our attempts to reflect the world. And the abstract expressionist painter Pollock asserts that a person could authentically demonstrate the naturalness of their own being in ways that approximate the structural integrity and beauty of natural systems. It is clearly a complicated business to contemplate the relationship between human beings and Nature!

Nature vs Natural

At one level we are no different from Nature but in many ways we feel distinct and operate uniquely from the rest of the biosphere. The behavior of human minds, societies and technological systems sometimes seems to fit in nicely with the ecosystem and other times appears dramatically, even destructively, uncoordinated with other organisms and environments. I am tempted to describe this as a tension between *naturalness* and *unnaturalness* within the human conception of Nature. What do I mean by these terms? I will try to quickly draw some distinctions to help make it clear how I am thinking about these concepts.

In my phraseology, not all "Nature" is "natural."

Human beings created a practical (but imaginary) distinction between their psychological, cultural and technological experience and the idea of the total background of all the matter,

> *Systems cannot coordinate with what they do not register.*

biology and cosmos that provides the basis of human life and also generates the limitations to which that life is subject. Nature is a vast category. It is neither good nor bad. It equally includes beautiful fragrant roses and the lifeless, freezing void of interstellar space. Nature is both the softly beating heart of a gentle woodland fawn and the raging torrent of poisonous gases and fire billowing forth from an ancient volcano to devastate the biosphere for a million years. While the English language sometimes uses the word Nature to describe the indifferent totality of the nonhuman universe, it also frequently uses the word "natural" to imply a special positive value. For example, I would like to feel free to move and communicate myself more *naturally*. People travel great distances on quasi-religious pilgrimages to visit natural parks and to appreciate the wonders of the natural world. These phrasings suggest an attempt to communicate something more specific than the indifferent background of the world. It even seems to point at a category more particular than the totality of all biology. When a viral organism devastates and mutilates a formerly thriving beehive, then human beings are inclined to view that as somewhat unnatural. Through our neurophysiological and cultural training we recognize and privilege some arrangements over others at a very basic level. Despite the great cultural and individual diversity of human opinions, doctors in most cultures are more likely to recommend "forest bathing" (natural immersion) as a medical treatment rather than, say, "parking-lot bathing."

There is a subset of nature whose interlinked patterns, while remaining diverse and adaptive, correspond to conditions under which both human beings and ecosystems tend to thrive. These patternings might as well be honored with the word *naturalness* so that we can think more deeply about their relevance. It is important, in my view, to ponder concepts like these because they are ways of languaging the characteristics of a world worth hoping for and working toward.

The normative aspirational quality of "natural" is also hinted at in the Anglo-American term naturalization—namely the naturalization process by which an immigrant becomes a citizen. Although actual naturalization procedures are frequently flawed, corrupt or merely symbolic, nonetheless the word selection reflects an underlying image of a living being who becomes adaptively and productively (according to the local standard and sensibilities) embedded in the shared legal, economic and physical ecosystems of a nation. I am trying to emphasize a meaning of naturalness that suggests it is a positively-valued, interdependent, organizational quality that can differ by degree and which is non-identical to the totality of Nature.

This is a very interesting concept to play with because it seems to have simultaneous significance for health, aesthetics, ethics, scientific understanding and basic survival. Human systems tend to drift toward disorganization and dissatisfaction if they do not understand how to support regenerative ecosystems and if they do not appreciate the ethical responsibility and aesthetic beauty involved in relating with natural systems—and if they do not nourish themselves consciously and subconsciously in ways that contribute to a balance of interdependent thriving in their bodies, communities and relationships with other organisms.

So I am arguing for what I feel most passionate about. It is this: orientation toward the design space for a desirable, sustainable, interdisciplinary civilization at the planetary or interplanetary scale depends on aligning our various personal and social efforts around the clarification, appreciation and embodiment of naturalness. I could use a different word but this one is both personally evocative and widely understood in an intuitive sense. In other words, I am feeling toward an *ecomorphic eudaimoniacal eutopia*.

Um, what?

Historically literate readers are likely to be familiar with Aristotle's notion of eudaimonia—wherein all the good spirits, within and without, are flourishing very *well* together. It is the idea of full-spectrum, multidirectional thriving. One reason that utopians have often created dystopias is because their excessive top-down authority prioritizes some of our natural drives and needs as good while also taking it upon themselves to suppress, ignore or even murder other parts of our internal or external communities which they believe are divergent, upset-

> *While the English language sometimes uses the word Nature to describe the indifferent totality of the nonhuman universe, it also frequently uses the word "natural" to imply a special positive value.*

ting or trivial. Therefore when I use the word eudaimonia, I intend to imply all the major forms of complex, mutually-adapted, pluralism: interspecies well-being, intrapsychic well-being, professional neurodiversity, "all the chakras," and so on.

You can probably guess that eutopia is just a way of speaking about utopias so that we steer, as best we can, toward well-being rather than toward imposed visions of the perfect society. That's pretty obvious. So what about "ecomorphism?"

Becoming Ecomorphic

The presence of natural (eco) shapes (morphology) strikes me—when it is generalized across multiple domains of human activity—as an important tool for helping to evaluate whether our individual and social efforts are likely to converge toward enhanced naturalness. I would use the word ecomorphic to describe *the degree to which human systems are informed by complex natural systems*. When this happens across multiple kinds of human behaviors, then I believe there is an emergent trend toward naturalness. A trend that characterizes a hopeful future for sentient beings. That is definitely aspirational and abstract so let me try to give a few examples.

Most people move around in social environments each day. The actual movements of your body can be more or less reflective of relevant natural systems. Do your technological? Word choice? shoes fit and assist the structure of your natural feet? Imagine that you are always only walking on flat, hard surfaces or else sitting in simple, angular chairs and hunched over digital devices while being physiologically contracted around a constant stream of symbolic thoughts about unresolved social situations. That certainly cultivates very different moods than, say, hiking in the hills, allowing your mind to fill with the sensory patterns of the river, moving your anatomy with the responsive grace of a Tai Chi master. I can hazard a guess as to which kind of mood makes human beings more inclined to understand what a healthier, more natural civilization should be like. When psychological, social, behavioral and technological patterns are more informed by natural systems, then they evolve in a more benevolent direction.

Complex organic nutrients are recommended in our diet because these tend to move human bodies toward healthier and more beautiful outcomes than does the consumption of processed white flour and sugar. If developing children are regularly exposed to the sophisticated patterns of sound and color in immersive ecosystems, they seem to achieve greater visual and auditory acuity than children who are adapted in their formative years to the simple sounds and colors that tend to predominate in urban and commercial living spaces. If architectural spaces incorporate more trees, this contributes to better air quality, climate regulation, soil stability and aesthetic pleasure. These are only a few examples of a phenomenon that is widely felt and recognized by informed, sensitive and biologically healthy human beings. All I am adding here is the idea that a certain kind of responsive information patterning is involved in all these cases. When human knowledge, feelings, behaviors, artifacts and protocols demonstrate a higher degree of discernment, acknowledgment and responsiveness to natural patterns, then we trend toward more benign, regenerative and interdependent outcomes.

Put another way, the mapping of natural systems within human systems helps steer us toward a hopeful world. I am not emphasizing the human but rather trying to keep the human and the natural constantly in play together as concepts that must become much more compatible.

The widely-discussed problem of

Negative Megalith #5, by Michael Heizer. Dia Beacon, New York (Photo by Gary Newman)

the accumulating and destructive effects upon the world from large-scale, technologically-advanced, modern human civilization is not a problem about human beings, technology or society *per se*. I would argue that the problem is the inadequate re-presentation (the enactment of corresponding patterns) of activ-

> Humanity must know the world better in a great variety of ways.

ity behaviors, architectures, limits and needs within the embodied behavior of human systems. That is a solvable problem in the sense that we could recognize it and implement corresponding changes in all areas of life.

Today we talk about anthropogenic climate change. In these important discussions, commentators often get lazy and suppose that the problem is the fact of human influence itself when in reality the much more nuanced problem is the type or quality of the anthropogenic changes. Different qualities of change are, I claim, linked to the re-presentational richness implied in the way that natural systems are encoded within human systems.

Consider degrees of richness in the re-presentation of a maple tree. Start with a stick drawing and proceed to a photograph or naturalistic painting. It looks to the human eye as if more naturalness is showing up in these configurations. Then add some depth by 3D printing a plastic duplicate of the tree. Well, that looks good from the outside but, of course, the inside doesn't resemble the inside of a tree. So switch from plastic to complex, self-regenerative cellular biology with a variety of sophisticated electrochemical activity. Another layer of resemblance is achieved and the feeling quality continues to shift. What is the humanly-generating pattern still missing? It does not exist in isolation. Add a forest. Add the symbiotic webs that trees form with other organisms in the soil. Add the infra-acoustic sounds that it makes when you pluck a leaf too soon.

It is not difficult to understand that the increasing fidelity of the re-presentation to the complex natural reality determines a great deal about how well we can work with this maple tree. Here the question of ethics may arise. Suppose I knew everything about an organism but nonetheless did not appreciate or value it? Yet the complementary question arises too: suppose that I was deeply appreciative but, because I had an insufficient understanding of its actual structure, all my attempts to help actually generated harm? If I feed you what is poisonous for your structure, then it does not matter much that I *wanted* to nurture your health.

I think it is obvious that we must do both. Understanding must not be understood (sic) narrowly or superficially. The process of deepening, enriching and expanding the capacity of human systems to map natural dynamics involves all the forms of dynamic psychological, social and technological pattern-making. I am using a set of concepts such as mirroring, mapping, knowing, cognizing,

> If the future of life on Earth is not sustainable, regenerative, vivifying, attractive, interactive, flexible, mutual, creative, nutritious and profound, then it is not worth hoping for.

etc. that may sound outdated, left-brained, narrowly modern and linear-mechanistic but I am using them to imply a holistic, complex approach that is both ancient and futuristic. It is ancient in the sense that many archaic and indigenous cultures were able to locally embody behaviors that worked well with natural systems. However it is futuristic in the sense that our species needs to be able to detect, articulate and technologically implement natural design principles across a much wider variety of environments and scales than our ancestors evolved to accommodate. Humanity must know the world better in a great variety of ways.

The Many Moods of Mapping

To know a landscape more accurately means many things. It can imply a larger overview or a more nuanced zoom into the details. It may suggest being able to label the parts, but it may equally suggest the emotional and moral responses with which we depict our embodied relationship to the significances, vulnerabilities and affordances of that landscape. What does it look like through the infrared wavelength of light? What does it feel like to sit with it in silence? How does it change if I play the video back much faster or much more slowly?

All the ways in which the dynamic relational structures can be registered with greater resolution into technological, psychological and social facets of human experience are complementary versions of the same type of movement. It is a movement toward greater richness of representation. That does not imply a simplified mental photograph or set of statistics. The many mapping and mirroring processes are the ways in which complex human systems enter into deeper resonance with the dynamic morphology of complex natural systems. The more these "two" types of patterning can inform each other harmoniously, across disciplines and across various aspects of ourselves, the more we become participants in the cultivation of a naturalness-oriented civilization. *Ecomorphic eudaimonia*.

Buckminster Fuller obseved that when "a Man-contrived structure buckles unexpectedly, it does not fail. It only demonstrates that Man did not understand Nature's laws and behaviors." (Fuller, 1976) Right now our dominant global civilization is buckling. We have not designed it or evolved it in a manner that is adequate to the natural systems upon which it depends. It needs to be comprehensively restructured in a manner that corresponds more completely and richly to the needs, solutions and patterning styles of what we call Nature. This is possible. It has occurred in numerous ways over the course of human history and we are, in one sense, better positioned than ever to implement it since we have more capacity to peer into natural complexity than ever before, more capacity to produce human systems than ever before and more capacity to coordinate across cultures and disciplines. In the degree to which we see this possibility, we acquire a responsibility to clarify and serve the emergence of a highly ecomorphic civilization.

If the future of life on Earth is not sustainable, regenerative, vivifying, attractive, interactive, flexible, mutual, creative, nutritious and profound, then it is not worth hoping for. So we must hope for the type of civilization that is all of those things. Our commitment must be to build, allow and grow in ways that move toward whatever all those qualities have in common. I am calling that naturalness and I am suggesting that it is intimately connected with understanding that we must cultivate human systems of all kinds to be more faithfully informed by the *way* of ecosystems.

As with voluntary hopefulness, this is not a passive task. Naturalness is not simply given to human beings to either conserve or squander. It is a profoundly participatory process. Ecomorphic eudaimonia is an orienting principle that describes and encourages the cultivation of generalized thriving across both human and natural systems via the increase of reciprocal patterning between those two types of systems.

The only kind of world that I would suggest is worth "voluntarily hoping for" is one that secures the increase of experientially-verified feelings of naturalness in all domains.

III. Participatory, Ecologically-Oriented Spirituality

In his classic book, *The World as Will and Representation* (Schopenhauer, 1818), that famously cantankerous philosopher Arthur Schopenhauer discussed the supreme importance of what he called *aesthetic contemplation* saying that "the man who is tormented by passion, or want, or care, is suddenly revived, cheered, and restored by a single free glance into nature."

A free glance into nature? I find that phrase very beautiful.

Schopenhauer's argument is that upset within human psychology can be temporarily resolved by a deeply resonant perception of the beauty, richness and integrated complexity that natural systems have evolved to embody. Why is this important? It is significant because human consciousness has an important role to play in cultivating and inhabiting a so-called ecomorphic eudaimonia. There are issues around how attention, feelings, inner practices, attitudes, rituals, altered states and spirituality can help the emergence of a planetary-scale culture that protects, resembles, understands and amplifies the quality of naturalness.

What sort of people are needed for this task?

Pessimistic and misogynistic 19th century German scholars like Schopenhauer are worlds away from how I envision a vital indigenous shaman, but there is an important correspondence between them. They are both oriented toward a compelling and transcendental perception of natural systems. I am invoking them in order to contemplate the idea of human attention when it moves so deeply toward natural complexity that peak-like conditions arise that are of benefit to individuals and provide inspiration for social habits. In these states of participatory trance, human beings can experience a release from both personal stresses and local social assumptions. That capacity provides a leverage point from which to improvise new kinds of social customs as well as contributing vivid insights into the intrinsic worth of the way that nature operates and generates itself. These are enhanced experiences of the "mapping" that I described earlier in which natural forms pour more deeply into the human heart and imprint their patterning styles there with greater salience.

Of course it is true that altered states of consciousness, moral development and practices of inspirational communion are found in many great wisdom-traditions, but there are some special reasons to favor the archetype of the shaman at this moment in history. The kind of spirituality that supports ecomorphic eudaimonia has to exhibit several crucial features. It must be deeply ecological in order to appreciate the patterns and responsibilities that emerge from an experiential understanding of the interdependence of human beings and the rest of the biosphere. It must be embodied and health-oriented (e.g. "medicine woman") because it must cause minds and societies to serve the holistic intelligence of the living ecosystems of our bodies. It must facilitate more profound encounters with non-human intelligences. It must have a genius for flow-states because those are states in which we feel more naturalness and growth in ourselves—and also the compelling nature of flow-states will need to be tapped in order to encourage human participation in new social customs that move us toward a world worth hoping for. People have got to *feel* better

> What do "shamans" look like at the scale of the global village and in the age of internets, pandemics and space travel?

> Something in myself is crying out for a different kind of human civilization in which a deeper resonance exists between human patterns and natural patterns

and more empowered to learn about, and look after, environments than they do when ignoring or desecrating resources.

I could continue a long list of this sort, but I am sure you get the general idea which is that the classical image of the shaman approximates the kind people who need to proliferate for the production and sustainability of an ecomorphic eudaimonia. Obviously not everyone needs to specialize in being priests of naturalness, but a culture in which these skills are recognized and proliferate more widely does strike me as necessary. These are part of the citizenship experience of the eutopia toward which I have been gesturing.

A Call for Eco-Anthropic Mediators

David Abram, in *The Spell of the Sensuous* (Abrams, 1996), describes his experience of shamans as self-selected mediators who are tasked with managing the relationship between social and natural intelligences. These characters, often living on the outskirts of villages (the nature/society interface), operate as intermediaries between the needs and customs of human populations and the behavior of plants, animals, weather, etc. Through a fascinating and often improvised set of practices, this kind of shaman cultivates an extraordinary and multisensory appreciation for natural dynamics which can then inform the many domains of activity within the cultural space.

What do "shamans" look like at the scale of the global village and in the age of internets, pandemics and space travel? This is an open-ended question whose full exploration requires much more than simply my own pondering. Instead of telling what future shamans will look like in detail, permit me to say a few things about myself for we are coming close to the of this personal essay.

I am a poor example of a shaman for the planetary civilization. Although I try to daily immerse myself in (stay experientially updated about the details of) my local ecosystem, I do not always remember to touch the earth and smell the wind. I do not often enough peer into the nuances and exchanges among the insects until I reach that utterly astonishing point at which it feels there is a dialogue arising between us. I have not fought hard enough to make sure there are more trees in my city and more solar panels (re-presenting the energy assimilation tactics of the plants). Why do I live in a square building? The biosphere doesn't build with squares! Why have I not studied more diligently how to shepherd mycelial networks beneath the soil in my yard? I'm thirsty for engaging, civic festivals centered around immersion in and reverence for facets of nature. I want to listen better to the frogs and know more about how their DNA is structured. It seems to me that every human on Earth ought to be able to draw the continents, mountains and rivers of the whole planet from memory. I feel like I love the Earth, but how well do I even know what it looks like?

How did I through almost two decades of "education" and still not know the full anatomy of human bodies or the complex climate dynamics of this world? Why does the economy in my society still treat natural resources as externalities that it does not need to register?

I am making here a very personal confession about the emotional experiences underlying this whole essay. Something in myself is crying out for a different kind of human civilization in which a deeper resonance exists between human patterns and natural patterns. I am pointed toward that in my heart and so I am attempting to point toward it with my speech. For that world to emerge, I think we must each become more like shamans in our own ways. Ecomorphic eudaimonia has a chance *if* the trajectory of civilization improves toward participatory naturalness in multiple domains of activity, intelligence and instantiation. That means that human beings, and especially those who feel moved to work toward a civilization upgrade, must embody a deep appreciation, understanding, assimilation (and wise creation) of the qualities and patterns that are most beautiful, regenerative and interdependent in complex natural systems. There are many things we could call that process but I am choosing, for reasons touched on above, to place it under the heading of a new planetary shamanism. We all need to be a little more shamanic, in this sense, if we are going to shift our minds into voluntary responsibility for the ecologically-inspired human civilization that is, like, totally possible.

Terrence McKenna once said that "Nature is the center of the mandala." (McKenna, 1987) I agree. And that's something I would *opt* for with hope.

References

Abram, D. (1996) The Spell of the Sensuous. New York, NY: Penguin Random House.

Frankl, V. (2004) Man's Search for Meaning: The Classic Tribute to Hope from the Holocaust. London: Rider Publishing. (Original work published 1946).

Fuller. R. B. (1975). Synergetics: Explorations in the Geometry of Thinking. New York, NY: Macmillan.

Greenwood, J. (1994). Just [Recorded by Radiohead]. On The Bends. London: Parlophone.

Huberman, A. (2021). Andrew Huberman: Sleep, Dreams, Creativity, Fasting, and Neuroplasticity - Lex Fridman Podcast #164 [Video]. Youtube. https://www.youtube.com/watch?v=ClxRHJPz8aQ&t=9012s

McKenna, T. (1987). Nature is the Center of the Mandala. [Video] Youtube. https://www.youtube.com/watch?v=5DfW_1gj8Zk

Nietzsche, F. (2009). Beyond Good and Evil. [Online] (H. Zimmern, Trans.) Available at https://www.gutenberg.org/files/4363/4363-h/4363-h.htm [Accessed July 18 2020] (Original work published 1886).

Nietzsche, F. (2016). The Birth of Tragedy or Hellenism and Pessimism. [Online] (W. Haussmann, Trans.) Available at https://www.gutenberg.org/files/51356/51356-h/51356-h.htm [Accessed June 7 2020] (Original work published 1872).

Pascal, L. (2019). Eutopia. [Video] Youtube. https://www.youtube.com/playlist?list=PLKQlJulRFrup2HD3TRrPMms3AfjG6EK0j

Harris, E. (Director). (2000). Pollock [Film]. Sony Pictures Classics.

Rutt, J. (2020, Jan 13). A Journey to Game B. Medium. https://medium.com/@memetic007/a-journey-to-gameb-4fb13772bcf3

Schopenhauer, A. (1966) The World As Will and Representation. New York, NY: Dover Publications. (Original work published 1818).

Taleb, N. (2012) Antifragile. New York, NY: Random House Publishing Group.

Wilde, O. (2004). Intentions. Available at https://www.gutenberg.org/files/887/887-h/887-h.htm [Accessed August 11 2020] (Original work published 1891).

Contemplating Hope

Fariba Bogzaran

Blue Rose, 2020. 24 x 30, mixed media, by Fariba Bogzaran

Just imagine living without hope! If we are comfortable with that, then we will have a contented life.

Now consider the rest of the world. What is happening around us? Climate crisis, political unrest, inequity, current and possible future pandemics, and senseless wars. Every 24 hours, an estimated 180 or more species of plants, insects, birds, and mammals become extinct. How does it feel to know we, the human species, might be extinct next? How would these realities change our lives without hope?

Without hope we face the present moment—Here We Are!

Whether sleep or awake, we are inside a grand interconnected Dream.

We only have *Here* in this dream creation.

We have choices:

Observe it: We must accept.

Change it: We are not where we want to be.

Are we fully responsible for this

waking dream? Partially responsible? Or a victim of a nightmare?

Is hope a dualistic concept? A desire for an expected outcome? A wish how things would be rather than what they are? Is hope a passive version of prayer?

Hope, without intention or action, is an illusion.

In the history of the human species, our current global condition must reach out for hope plus action. I will use climate crisis and our connection to nature as an example.

In our evolution, human beings have reached a level of consciousness allowing the discovery of the inner universe of the mind. For the first time, the confluence of ancient wisdom with scientific methods and global communications demonstrate the possibility for positive collective awakening. Currently, we stand at the threshold of human evolution. We have the capacity to access the depths of our creative consciousness or regress to a lower state of mind.

Being one of the most dangerous species on earth, we are taking our planet to the edge of destruction. With minor shifts in earth conditions, we might find ourselves in a devastating situation and *hope will not be the answer and any action will be too late*. Once we reckon with our dualistic view of ourselves as separate from and above the natural world

Witness, 2020, 24 x 18, mixed media, by Fariba Bogzaran

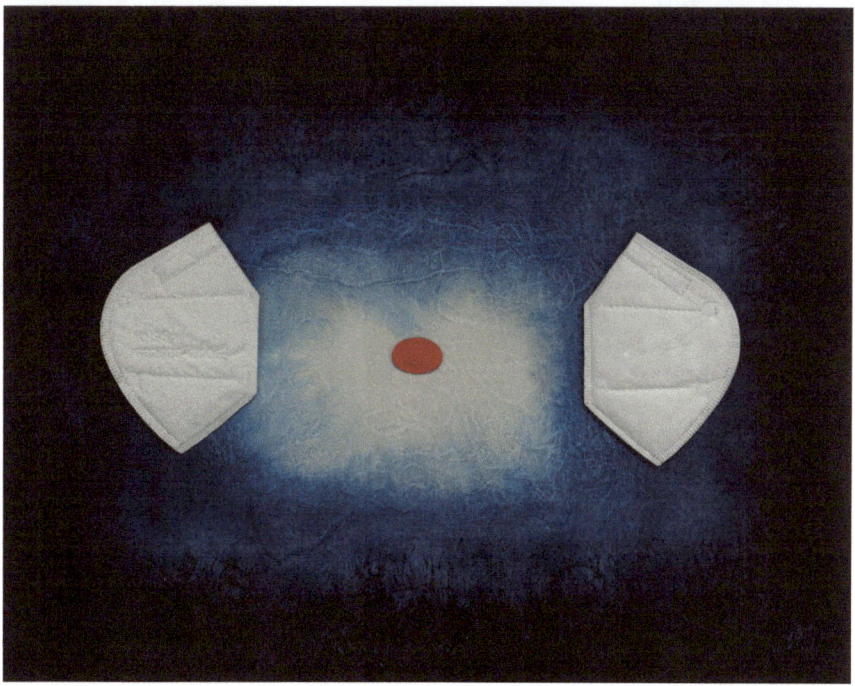

Distant Dialogues and Final Remedy, 2021, 18 x 22, mixed media, by Fariba Bogzaran

and instead become willing to think non-dually (that is, we are deeply connected and one with our natural environment), then there is a chance for transformation. Nature is deeply connected with itself and perhaps we are the only species currently disconnected from it. Earth will continue without us, but we can't survive without the right conditions on earth. Do we endure as species, or in a few decades, disappear like thousands of other species?

We are not completely at fault. The complex design of our brain compared to other species perhaps needs another million years to evolve so that there is no possibility of regression. Often, we forget that we have three brains: the high cortex, mid-mammalian, and

reptilian brains! A human being has the incredible potential to become an extraordinary artist, such as Bach, producing timeless creations that after centuries still elevate the spirit; an engineer creating complex rockets and sending astronauts to the moon; or a destructive being decimating itself and thousands of others! No other species on earth has the brain complexity or the capacity for such destruction.

The threshold between creation and destruction that has been observed throughout human existence requires reconciliation with the complexity of our brain and how to tame its unsettling tendencies. In meditation practices, we call this wild, untamed mind the "monkey brain," and the task becomes how to bring this mind to a state of equilibrium. This is perhaps one of the most revolutionary practices for humankind to embrace and deal with our still-developing brain. Of course, we also have an expansive human spirit and the capabilities of consciousness, such as dreaming the most

Blue Rose I, 2020, 20 x 20, mixed media, by Fariba Bogzaran

The Last Breath, 2020, 20 x20, mixed media, by Fariba Bogzaran

extraordinary dreams, and miraculous healings, telepathy, and precognition. And we observe, when the mind and heart are aligned in positive flow, the energy body is capable of deep capacities.

Another practice is creation, which is meditation in action. Creation moves our tendency away from destruction and brings a sense of connection to one's life and environment. It is much harder to create a fabulous work of art than destroy it. It takes inventiveness, courage, and persistence to build a marvelous architectural space, as compared to throwing a bomb and destroying it in a matter of seconds. Destruction is a cowardly act, but also it represents the reptilian brain in command of the higher cortex. The capacities for connectedness to each other and nature, deep compassion, and the elimination of prejudice and hatred are what remediate the relationship between creation and destruction. In my conversation with the Apollo 14 astronaut Edgar Mitchell,

Call to Avalokiteshvara, 2021, 40 x 30, mixed media, by Fariba Bogzaran

Birth Anew, 2020, 14 x 11, mixed media, by Fariba Bogzaran

The Sixth Extinction, 2020, 18 x 22, mixed media, by Fariba Bogzaran

he said as he was returning from their mission on the moon that was devoid of life, he was moved to tears with spiritual awe watching the beauty of our blue planet and the miracle of life on earth.

During the pandemic, like many others, I withdrew. In contemplation, I faced my choices. I needed to survive in an unpredictable time. I recalled the movie "Titanic" when the musicians started running around like others, but suddenly realized they would die anyway. They returned to their seats and continued playing their music. I decided to continue creating in my studio and create a rose garden with the intention of personal and collective healing. At the same time, my masks and gloves began to accumulate in my studio. Living in the heart of nature, the animals very quickly realized something ominous had happened. I had no human visitors. One by one, the wildlife surrounded my home, including a mountain lion. Resident bobcats, foxes, and raccoons became overtly friendly. The raven visited regularly in the afternoon for a call and response. I was living in a "zoo," but I was the one isolated in a cage.

The first piece I created came out of an image from Hypnagogia (the state just before falling asleep), containing a group of gloves knotted together forming a mandala. *Blue Rose*, I called it, as the daily reports of death mounted.

From the *Blue Rose* came the first piece, *Witness*, created from my first two masks and that piece became the inspiration for the rest. Nightly, the hypnagogic state became a way to connect with the world and experience the images of the next works. Next came the four masks in the form of the Celtic cross. In the process of creation, I felt and saw the Alchemical image of *Squaring the Circle*, hence the title of the work. The artwork became a portal for collective healing. As we heard thousands were dying daily from Covid, the next image of *Blue Rose I* appeared.

By entering the pain of those dying, along came the next piece called *The Last Breath*. I imaged myself being with thousands of those people who were alone and taking their last breath. As mass graves were created and the smoke of cremations filled cities, the deity of compassion with a thousand arms was invoked by *Call to Avalokiteshvara*.

These works were not made for art's sake; rather they became an occasion where I projected my intention for healing while being present to the departed. My studio wall became a memorial for the current situation, and for grieving with others, while the art itself became a portal to connect—an agent of change inside of my vision.

Do I have hope? *I am present to what is with the clear intention to travel in the invisible worlds to make a visible impact.* The artwork became the vehicle for transporting my intention to those suffering. The emergence of each work required incubation and dreaming time. While holding a glove or a mask, I think of all those who are departing senselessly, and those who are helping to heal. Out of this practice arose paintings I call *Portals of Light*.

What gives me the oxygen to breathe during such suffering? The love for our blue planet, the ocean, wildlife and the mystery of the roses!

Fariba Bogzaran, Ph.D., is a scientist/artist who founded the first graduate dream studies certificate program at JFK University in Berkeley, California (1996), where she was a professor for over twenty years. Bogzaran's interdisciplinary background is a confluence of in-depth studies and teachings in psychology, art, contemplative practices, shamanic and Taoist approaches.

All photography by Sina Dehghani

Portal # 5, Tablet of Inner Light: Symphonia #1, 2020, 20 x 28.5, mixed media, by Fariba Bogzaran

The Day the Horses Rode By

Reflections on the Redemptive Potential of Black Practices of Overcoming

Isoke Femi

One synonym for hope is optimism, which can be defined as a *"disposition or tendency to look on the more favorable side of events or conditions and to expect the most favorable outcome."* (Dictionary.com version 8.13.1.1)

Black culture gives rise to a kind of optimism that defies the story of black life since 1619. My research focused on the role of ritual expressiveness in Black cultural life. I proposed that this ritual expressiveness is rooted in African Diasporic cosmologies that carried over into the so-called New World, and provided a "way out of no way," giving rise to a unique, and often misunderstood optimism for African diasporic folks. Furthermore, these ways of being could and have provided healing beyond the Black communities in which they are grounded.

Isoke Femi is a psychological practitioner, minister of metaphysics, and black woman conjuror. She completed her advanced degree work at the Institute of Imaginal Studies, where her research was on the liberating potentialities of African-derived ritual, particularly the ritual pattern of call and response. Isoke has spent most of her professional life (since 1985) facilitating groups grappling with social oppression. Isoke maintains that liberation ultimately necessitates that humans recognize their divinity. For it is only the Divine Self, which is also our collective shared Self, that is able to alchemize the intense energies that emerge when groups attempt to reckon with a past characterized by domination and exploitation.

In this reflection piece, I want to illustrate these points by way of an incident that occurred in Montgomery, Alabama among an ethnically diverse group of travelers.

In my work, a guiding image has been the gospel song, *How I Got Ovah.*" This song, like so many others coming from the African Diaspora, has an uplifting and restorative quality. It ponders—by suggestion—the mystery of *getting over* in spite of slavery and subsequent anti-Black sentiment and treatment in the African diaspora. Implicit in the title is both the declaration that *getting over* occurred but also the question of how the author did it. In today's lexicon, the word most commonly used to refer to the phenomenon of "getting over" is resilience.

Perhaps my difficulty with the word stems from my sense that resilience is most often used to characterize an individual quality or capacity. I'm more interested in perhaps what might be called "cultural resilience."

Glide Memorial Church, 2016 (Wikipedia)

I imagine that Black people who share the spiritual heritage of the songwriter understand not only the question, but the answer to which it points. I suspect there are a number of explanations for how Black folks in the U.S. and other parts of the diaspora made it through, but in this piece I want to focus on the spiritual roots of this *getting over* of which Ms. Ward speaks in her gospel song.

> *"How I got ovah; how I got ovah; you know my soul looks back and wonders, how I got ovah."*
> —Clara Ward

Like so much Black music, this song evokes the experience of which it speaks, "gettin' ovah" or overcoming.

First, it is a declaration of already having accomplished the act of getting over. It states quite certainly that the getting over has occurred. In African American context, performance of the song, as well as the community's engagement with it, conjures the experience of getting over, and it is in this sense that I want to speak about hope—as the power to get ovah or overcome. From this perspective, I do not speak of a one-and-done, as in winning a race, or even as in overturning the structures of domination. To be sure, such a goal as dismantling oppressive structures is always in some way the aim of the subjugated.

But to limit overcoming to such a singular, even if lofty, ideal, is to miss something very important about a way of being. And so here I use the word "overcome" in reference to a way of being. It is a way of being that allows a people to remember. Overcoming, in this context, is conceived as a means by which a people learn to remember who, and what, they are in truth as opposed to who the *other* tells them they are. This overcoming must be performed repeatedly, until the art of remembering is held in the blood, the sinew, in the connective tissue of the collective.

Overcoming in this context refers to the repeated act of resisting soul loss, or loss of vitality and authenticity. In the case of African Americans in the U.S., soul loss would be the inevitable result of collective scapegoating over the course of several centuries had it not been for the overcoming practices of African-derived spirituality, finely tuned over the centuries. These practices have served as antidote to the suppression of the impact of trauma.

It could be said that Black folks in the diaspora intuited the meaning and value of the idea that, "impression without expression equals depression" (author unknown). Furthermore, we can well imagine that the cost of suppressing the response to nearly unrelenting projections of inferiority would most certainly result in depression if not despair. But despite the evidence of what Dr. Joyce Degruy termed "post traumatic slave syndrome,"(*Post Traumatic Slave Syndrome: America's Legacy of Enduring Injury and Healing.* Dr Joy DeGru, 2005.

> Overcoming can be a centuries-long journey into the heart of darkness while still holding on to the sense that something else is there with you, loving you and buoying you.

Uptone Press) which shows up as a host of public health issues among Black folks, despair is not common on the group level. In my view, this lack of despair has been in large part owing to the overcoming practices of African Americans.

Overcoming sometimes arises as a fleeting moment, such as when the captured sing a song of release, or ritually make divine contact, and that fear is momentarily rendered mute. Overcoming can be a centuries-long journey into the heart of darkness while still holding on to the sense that something else is there with you, loving you and buoying you. It can reveal itself as a holding force that knows what you are; knows what you are made of. When one gains awareness of this holding as a meeting with a transpersonal force, a crucible forms whereby spiritual capacities might be honed, if that be one's spiritual will.

Under the influence of these applied *getting over* practices—of music, spoken word, embodied grace and authenticity—heart as well as soul qualities are preserved and refined. The collective becomes the repository of powers that only show up when these practices are brought to bear.

Overcoming—the act of expressing authenticity—allows the presence and expression of love under loveless conditions; laughter when ain't nothin' funny; hip swaying and dipping in assertion of sovereignty, even when doing so might bring on the wrath of the jailers as well as one's own folk. Overcoming can mean revealing one's prophetic voice despite countless forms of silencing.

The benefits of honing overcoming capacities may extend beyond the preservation of soul qualities. It may also help to preserve the heart, which Baby Suggs Holy declares, in Tony Morrison's *Beloved*, to be the prize. Overcoming can thus result in finding in one's heart, to everyone's wonder and bewilderment, love even for one's captor. This connection to heart energies can allow the invisible web of belonging to reveal itself in response to all attempts to erase belonging.

And most of all, overcoming is discovering time and again that what a people is defies the laws made by humans, and that what one truly is makes possible not only survival, but thriving. Overcoming in the way that I am using it here is nothing shy of miraculous.

Black people in the United States learned, of necessity, practices of overcoming. Those capacities—the capacity for tapping into subtle realms of invisible power as well as the capacity for

> Overcoming—the act of expressing authenticity—allows the presence and expression of love under loveless conditions; laughter when ain't nothin' funny.

expression and release tell a story about why Black folks are still here. Those practices were honed in the hush harbors where folk gathered to bear witness and testify to the anguish of captivity.

Those practices were refined under the blazing southern sun where the folk labored without cease, without recompense, and without any right of protest. Those skills and capacities went mostly unnoticed, though they have shed a holy light onto the planet for centuries.

Around the globe, the creative genius of the enslaved and their descendants—through their music, spoken word, embodied grace and authenticity—has been keenly felt, and often imitated. In the following story, describing an unusual occurrence, a racially, culturally and socioeconomically mixed group of folks find themselves in a situation where the need for practices of overcoming arises. It is a story that demonstrates the intercultural potentialities of these modes of experiencing.

GLIDE Memorial

Briefly consider the context of the story: GLIDE Memorial is a foundation and a church, located in the heart of the Tenderloin (TL) district of San Francisco. The TL is home to some of the city's poorest and most marginalized people. What can easily be hidden from view in more affluent neighborhoods is far more visible here. Poverty, unsanitary conditions, lack of grocery stores, open drug sales and use, and untreated mental health distress present themselves in open view.

This vibrant and ever-struggling neighborhood borders Union Square where opulent hotels and upscale retail markets beckon the affluent of San Francisco and beyond.

GLIDE earned national and international acclaim as a result of the bold and tireless work of its founders, Rev. Dr. Cecil Williams and San Francisco poet laureate Janice Mirikitani. Reverend Williams was assigned to GLIDE Church in 1964. At the time he was, by appearance, a suit and tie minister with a short cropped haircut. However, within a very short time, he was moving towards the fulfillment of a lifelong dream of preaching and ministering to a radically diverse congregation, with all that diversity brought with it. White shirt gave way to African dashiki, and the conservative haircut to a billowy Afro.

Before the term "liberation theology" was widely known, Williams instituted at least one of its principles: "for the people". But Williams also brought the ideas of radical acceptance and unconditional love—two ideals that led to a distinct branding of the liberation theology movement. Eventually all barriers to inclusion, including the hymnals and the crucifix, were removed from the sanctuary. Like the Black culture from which Williams springs—a culture of inclusivity—Williams declared, "The church is not the building, but the people." GLIDE's doors opened (and remain open) for high and low alike.

Shortly after Williams arrived, Janice Mirikitani joined to support the work. Mirikitani's genius for operationalizing the dream of a just and loving community, and her commitment to the women and children of the Tenderloin, combined with Williams' courage to speak truth to power, advocate for the people, and put his body on the line for justice. Williams and Mirikitani were able to transform lives, support liberation movements, influence policy makers, and feed the people.

These commitments and the actions spurred by them, have insured GLIDE's

> He dreamed of a holy pilgrimage to the place where the horrors of the institution of slavery and its offshoots could be faced head-on.

role in San Francisco and beyond as a moral authority offering guidance and leadership on some of the most important and controversial issues of our time.

Alabama Pilgrimage

So it is no surprise that the senior leadership of GLIDE championed an experience that has become known as the *Alabama Pilgrimage*. With the help of donors across various sectors, the pilgrimage has, for three years running, enabled over 300 folks to make the trip to Montgomery, Alabama, where key historical sites of slavery and liberation stand. We go to "explore the wreck and not the story of the wreck" …"to see the damage that was done and the treasures that prevail." (*Diving into the Wreck*, by Adrienne Rich)

The inspiration for GLIDE's Alabama Pilgrimage came to Rabbi Michael Lezak (GLIDE's Social Justice Rabbi) as he pondered Bryan Stevenson's, *Just Mercy: A Story of Justice and Redemption* (2015).

Stevenson lays bare the truth about mass incarceration of Black people as a modern day morphing of the system of slavery. In his book, Stevenson invites us to face the truth of what the narrative of racial superiority has wrought. After exposing the through-line from slavery to mass incarceration, he issues a four-point challenge: 1) Get proximate to the problem and its effects; 2) Create new narratives; 3) Do uncomfortable things; and 4) Stay tethered to hope.

Lezak takes this challenge to heart. While Lezak's passion for justice has been rekindled by Stevenson's work to slow the hemorrhaging of Black men by state-sponsored cruelty and even murder, his thirst for justice reaches back to when he was a student of Manning Marable, who first introduced him to culture heroes like Malcolm X.

Organizing and leading a GLIDE-sponsored pilgrimage to Montgomery Legacy Museum; and the National Memorial for Peace and Justice, both co-founded by Stevenson, brought Lezak closer to realizing his longing to be a justice-serving rabbi.

He dreamed of a holy pilgrimage to the place where the horrors of the institution of slavery and its offshoots could be faced head-on. He wanted folks to be brought to their knees. These two sites became for most the key moments of the Alabama Pilgrimage.

The conceptualization for this facilitated trip was motivated by deep spiritual, social, psychological, and justice commitments. The participant group would be highly diverse and possess varying levels of understanding and capacity for bearing witness to what lay ahead.

We would need to track and work with the fragile racial dynamics, ever present in U.S. cultural life. We would need to address the educational differences among us. Some of the people on the trip—even some of African American ancestry—did not know of the history of lynching in this country. In fact, the participants included staff and congregants from across GLIDE's community (a multi-faith and non-religious community); members of Rabbi Noa Kushner's Jewish congregation, The Kitchen, as well as agencies and organizations from San Francisco including a group of healthcare leaders from the University of California San Francisco School of Medicine.

A number of Black folks in the group were children and grandchildren of those who migrated from the South to the North over the course of three or four decades, seeking relief from anti-Black terrorism. Perhaps understandably, their families never spoke of the hard things they'd witnessed or suffered through.

Given our motivations, each year we have prepared ourselves and each other for the pilgrimage in pre-Alabama classes held in the inspirationally-named Freedom Hall at GLIDE. The purpose of these classes is to build beloved community before embarking on the pilgrimage, to get proximate with each other, and to learn. We learned from Rabbi Lezak important Hebrew concepts such as *t'shuvah* (to turn; to make amends), *cria* (to tear), *Mizraim* (a name for Egypt, or the squeezed place) and *chesed* (loving kindness).

We agreed that this pilgrimage would rest on a covenantal foundation, meaning that we would hold it to be holy and far from business as usual. We were invited to cleave to one another but, at the same time, white folks were asked to be mindful of the habitual ways that they are taught to lean in on people of color for comfort and reassurance when racial wounds are activated.

My training in group work is rooted in several domains: Re-evaluation Counseling, where I first learned the beauty of emotional or affective release as an indispensable aspect of healing from the wounds of oppression; Imaginal psychology, which contributes to the psychology of group life, the role of ritual and poesís in making room for what cannot be easily digested through the filter of normative identity; and Black culture and identity, where authenticity and embodied existence were gifted to me by my people and their people before them.

I see my function to be that of caring for the affective experiences of the folks on the pilgrimage and attending to soul's evocations. With the motto, "impression without expression equals depression" as a guide, I have insured, to the best of my ability, the creation of space for the expression of experience.

With this lengthy but necessary context complete, I offer you my version of what happened on one warm spring day in Montgomery, Alabama just a few years ago.

Montgomery, Alabama

On March 14, 2019, at the final gathering of our pilgrimage, over 100 brave souls gathered in the large community room above the Dexter Avenue King Memorial Baptist Church, where Martin Luther King Jr. was pastor from 1954 to 1960. This was the home of the famous bus boycott that non-violently put a crack in the ironclad racial apartheid of the region.

We came here to close out the pilgrimage. Rabbi Lezak called the group together for this final goodbye. Working his personal and Jewish magic, he reminded us of why we had come here and declared again our covenantal relationship to each other, to this place, and to the people whose lives were taken to feed the sick needs of white supremacy. He offered that after three hard days we had claimed to be a new justice Torah. I was up next to lead the group in an integrative experience encompassing all that had transpired on the pilgrimage.

I had thought long and hard the previous night about how to help the group integrate the days' experiences of visiting the Memorial and Museum—both of which only begin to capture the brutality of slavery's legacy and the country's persistent post slavery efforts to block Black progress. Each day ended with people processing the emotions and insights engendered by what we'd experienced.

Some of the group expressed numbness; others heartbreak. Many wore the familiar look of tightly held rage. And still others simply sagged from the weight of it all. But now we had to bring some kind of closure to the event, and it was on me to lead that.

I invited people to pair up and make eye contact, and to silently convey their deep connection and gratitude for being on this journey together. Within minutes, eye contact gave way to hugs, many of them tearful. Miguel Bustos, Senior Director of GLIDE's Center for Social Justice, offered the Prayer of St. Francis, which further softened the field.

Suddenly, folks who faced the huge plate glass window with a view of the main road gasped, and focused—nearly in unison, as if some invisible thread connected them to the spectacle on the street below. Within seconds, everyone's attention was on that scene. Folks pressed against each other to see what was happening: A small procession, maybe a block long, of white folks, unlike any parade we Californians had ever witnessed. People in the parade, as well as the six or eight horses in front wore garb reminiscent of the Klan, white robes. These polite "paraders," claimed the space of the street with confidence and apparent dignity. (Later, a white man from our group found them and engaged in a matter of fact conversation with some of their members who identified the group as "True Americans.")

Just like that, as our vulnerable and raw group looked down onto the street, the loving and tender unifying energy, which only moments before had suffused the room, was gone. The feeling of love was vanquished by the ghosts of a past that would not yield, that refused to surrender to the call of a new and different dream.

Chaos suddenly snatched the moment and the space. No one knew what to do. Several men expressed their urgent intent to go down there and confront the paraders. Yet we all knew our brothers didn't really want to do that. This impulse was some remnant of a past in which males took the role of protector—facing danger head-on, fighting fire with fire. I could feel it too, this urge to stand up to terror and declare our freedom from this aspect of our collective history.

As I worked hard to hold the group, I could also feel its fear, like ice water in the veins, fear that lives at the base of the skull, ever on the alert to fight, flee or freeze in the face of threat. It seems to shut down the neocortex altogether. Immersed in this fear, all thoughts come from autopilot.

My heart sank. Why was this happening? Why was this procession outside our window now? Why now? We were so close to ending, and what a beautiful ending it had promised to be.

What to do next? The facilitator in me reached for what to do. I willed myself to "be still and know." Breathe! I told myself. I thought about the core human capacity memorized and practiced in my amazing graduate school education—"reflexive participation."

This moment with my people in Montgomery presented a perfect opportunity to "surrender through creative action to the necessities, meanings and possibilities inherent in the present moment" (Aftab Omer, personal communication. 12/96).

I knew the chartered bus that would take people to the airport stood silent half a block away, just 2 hours before departure time. I was losing the group. Would this be the final memory of the pilgrimage? Would we have to board the bus in this state of fragmentation?

I stood to the side listening to the urgent buzz of unsettled voices, feeling the heat of the room close in. What was the *necessity* of this moment? To bring the group back to coherence; to give space for how folks were affected; and to take back the space.

Two stories floated to the surface of my mind, one anecdotal, the other captured through art. The first was from an interview I had heard with Bernice Johnson Reagon, founding member of Student Non-violent Coordinating Committee (SNCC) Freedom Singers.

Ms. Reagon told of an all too common occurrence during the freedom movement era of the 1960's. Black folks used the churches not only as houses of worship but also as a network of safe harbors for strategizing, checking in, tending to folks, and galvanizing the spirit of the movement. Not infrequently white police would saunter uninvited into the sanctuaries of the churches. Sometimes they would spread out around the sanctuary, often taking down names of those they recognized. Reagon recounts how the energy would change in these spaces— terror sucking out the air.

After a little while, someone from the pews would begin to hum or voice a song that was familiar to all. Slowly at first, and then with more force, "song would take back the room," recalled Reagon.

In the second story, "Baby Suggs Holy," the "unrobed, unlettered" ex-enslaved preacher woman, calls the folk to a clearing where spirituality can spread out in the ways my people used to prefer.

After having them dance, laugh and cry together, ending in a group catharsis, she tells them that "the only grace they would know would be the grace they could imagine." She invites them to love themselves despite the lack of love in this place. She ends this invitation with these words:

". . .and the beat and beating heart, love that too. More than eyes or feet. More than lungs that have yet to draw free air. More than your life-holding womb and your life giving private parts, hear me now, love your heart. For this is the prize." (*Beloved*, Toni Morrison. 1987)

The reverie and reflection of these two stories happened in a flash.

Ah ha! I knew. This moment called for ritualizing. Folks needed to be able to express how they were affected by the evocative spectacle on the street below. They needed to express their experience, without having the experience take us down.

To put it plainly, we needed to create our own hush harbor right here and now. And somehow we needed to move from a state of disempowerment to one of self-compassion, dignity and, hopefully, joy. Something wanted to rip us apart. It is that some something that kept people of all races from standing up to the invisible hand of oppression. It counts on division, separation. So we needed to re-establish connection.

In my research I had learned that by beginning with the first impulse to express, the pump is primed. The first step was to get the group to return to the circle. The first thing that I needed in that moment, arose from within me. I could feel the power of its effect upon the group and me as I spoke the first words. I could trust that the next words and gestures, prayers and actions would follow, building one upon the other.

The preach that came from me went along these lines: "We're taught to pay attention to the negative; to shake our fist at evil. But only Light dispels darkness. We can choose right here and now to withdraw our attention from the negative to dispel it. What we've seen here has sent a jolt of cortisol through our systems, and right now our task is to master the cortisol burst. Let us begin by calming the nervous system."

I spoke these words with the calm certitude with which they'd been offered

> The feeling of love was vanquished by the ghosts of a past that would not yield, that refused to surrender to the call of a new and different dream.

to my mind, and which I hoped the group would accept as their own. The people at the window began to peel themselves away and slowly return to the circle. The trance state brought on by the fight/flight/freeze reaction we'd all entered loosened its grip enough so that something more meaningful and potent could come through.

> We're taught to pay attention to the negative; to shake our fist at evil. But only Light dispels darkness.

I then invited the group to sit in silence for a moment and notice what had come up for them. After some time in silence I asked people to allow a gesture to come into their minds that could convey how they felt and what they may have wanted to do in reaction to the parade.

"What gesture describes your state of mind? At the count of 3 I will ask you to show us your gesture—all at once. Then hold that position for as long as you can so that we can all see each other's gestures."

This practice serves several functions, but suffice it to say that all too often we ask people to just stop feeling or experiencing what they are feeling or experiencing. But our practices, rooted in care of the soul, aim to restore experience, not suppress it. This is one way we show respect for the soul.

Next, I asked for just a few people to bring words to their gestures, in order that what was there could be spoken into the circle. Naturally folks expressed a number of thoughts, feelings and urges. Most of these we just held with respect. Some warranted response from me as the facilitator.

Ce'Mara's prayer

A key moment of response on my part arose when Ce'Mara, a GLIDE staff person and young mother in her 30s exclaimed with unapologetic passion and moral authority, "I feel like we need to blanket this entire region with prayer. For the suffering that happened here, for the suffering that is still happening here. I want to bless this place. We get to go back home to San Francisco, but what will happen with our brothers and sisters we leave behind?"

In the spirit of call and response, I asked Ce'Mara, "Would you be so kind as to start the prayer?"

Ce'Mara closed her eyes and extended her arms as a prayer began to take shape in her heart, mind and on her lips. We are an improvisational people, so the prayer rolled off her tongue as if she'd written it somewhere. It transformed the space immediately given her authenticity and spiritual power.

When Ce'Mara finished her prayer, another Black person, followed by yet another lifted their voices in prayer. After a few Black folks prayed, several others offered their prayers.

At some point, another GLIDE staff person, Lamont, reminded us of a song he had composed and offered earlier in the pilgrimage, "We can change the world". We joined him in singing the song, allowing "song to take back the space." And with each succeeding prayer or offering, the energy in the room transmuted into something more holy, even more powerful than when we'd begun.

Once the collective prayer was completed, our beloved Vernon Bush, director of the GLIDE Ensemble (chorus), led the group in a call and response chant that completed the restoration of experience.

I am somebody; I am someone
My voice gives power to everyone
My body's able to hear the call
I'm ready to give my all and all

Many magical things happened in that last hour. Ghosts of the past had haunted that room on that lovely spring day in Montgomery. Perhaps the ghosts came to give us yet another taste of what Black folks raised in this area knew all too well—a reminder of the Old South's reign of terror.

But just as the enslaved folk managed to make "somethin' outta nothin'", to create and make holy what others defiled, so also did we perform a little miracle in that room that day. We ritualized, preached and ministered to each other. Wisdom sprang up, channeled by multiple members of the group, and shouts of Amen, both figurative and literal, met one holy gesture after another.

Ce'Mara's prayer was a curative offering on behalf of all. No mere protest; rather, it was a healing offering, one that called the group back to its own sovereignty. We may never be able to apprehend the impact of the generosity conveyed by her intent to "blanket the region with prayer."

She did not single out the healing of Black folks; the offer was for everyone. And it did not stop there. Her call to pray for the blood-soaked land implied a universal sharing of the heart. My preach, Lamont's and Vernon's songs, as well as the fervent desire for true freedom that we all shared, were all prayers of sorts.

Among us, the spirit of African religion rose up to meet the thief who'd come to take our blessing. We in that room were connected to the wisdom of the African diaspora where there is no dogma attached to the religion. We, like many before us, had to dig deep into our souls to find its roots. Perhaps the African DNA is slow to surrender to captivity, slow to give up its soul.

> She did not single out the healing of Black folks; the offer was for everyone. And it did not stop there.

The African roots of religion privilege physicality and expressivity. These roots inspire the sort of improvising that gave birth to the Negro Spirituals that are so loved around the world. That moment in that room at that church tap the roots grounded in West African soil as well as the blood, sweat, tears, moans, and wails of enslaved Africans here in America.

As they have done for hundreds of years and will do for unknown hundreds more, African and African-American ancestors helped us shape those religious inclinations into something new and universally compelling.

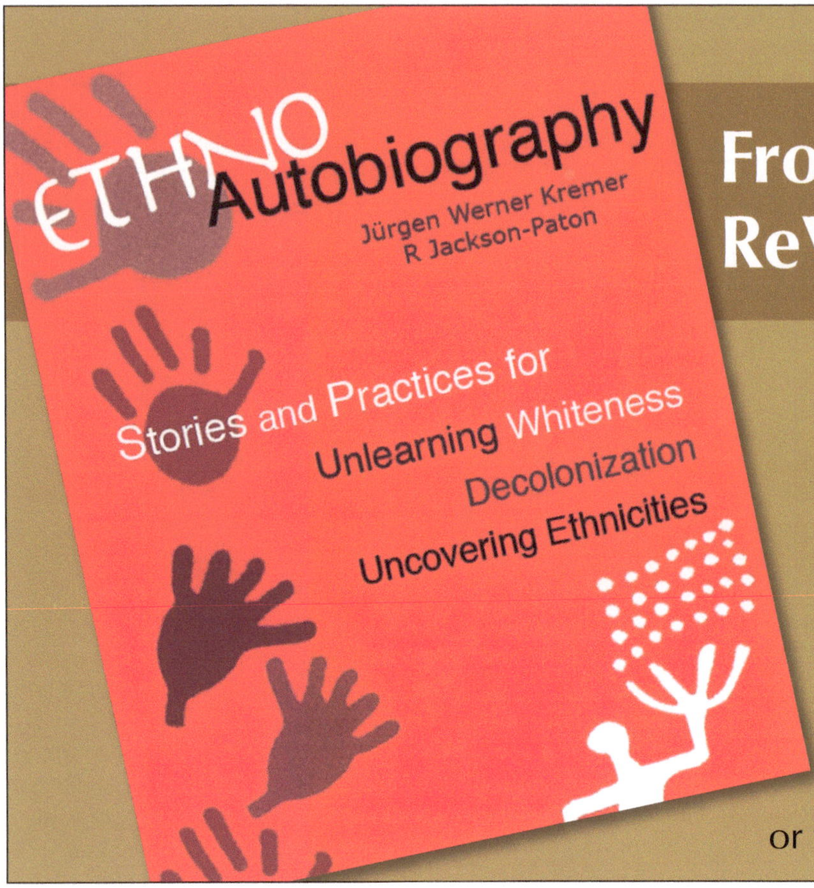

From ReVision Publishing

Ethnoautobiography
Jürgen Werner Kremer
R Jackson-Paton

Stories and Practices for Unlearning Whiteness, Decolonization, Uncovering Ethnicities

504 pages

Only $39.95
Includes shipping

Order from:
ReVision Publishing
PO Box 1855
Sebastopol, CA 95473
or visit www.ReVisionPublishing.org

Subscribe to ReVision - A Journal of Consciousness & Transformation

For new subscriptions or renewals, please visit:
ReVisionPublishing.org/subscribe

ReVision Publishing • PO Box 1855 • Sebastopol, CA 95473

www.ingramcontent.com/pod-product-compliance
Lightning Source LLC
Chambersburg PA
CBHW041419190426
43193CB00038B/21